How
MELANCHTHON
Helped Luther Discover the Gospel

How
MELANCHTHON
Helped Luther Discover the Gospel

THE DOCTRINE OF JUSTIFICATION IN THE REFORMATION

Lowell C. Green

How Melanchthon Helped Luther Discover the Gospel:
The Doctrine of Justification in the Reformation

Published by:
1517 Publishing
PO Box 54032
Irvine, CA 92619-4032

All Scripture quotations, unless otherwise indicated, are from the King James Version.

Scripture quotations marked (RVS) are from Revised Standard Version of the Bible, copyright © 1946, 1952, and 1971 National Council of the Churches of Christ in the United States of America. Used by permission. All rights reserved worldwide.

Publisher's Cataloging-In-Publication Data
(Prepared by The Donohue Group, Inc.)

Names: Green, Lowell C. (Lowell Clark), author. | Keith, Scott Leonard, writer of supplementary textual content.
Title: How Melanchthon helped Luther discover the gospel : the doctrine of justification in the Reformation / Lowell C. Green ; foreword by Scott L. Keith.
Description: [New edition]. | Irvine, CA : 1517 Publishing, [2021] | Originally published: Fallbrook, Calif., U.S.A. : Verdict Publications, ©1980. | Includes bibliographical references and index.
Identifiers: ISBN 9781948969543 (hardcover) | ISBN 9781948969550 (paperback) | ISBN 9781948969567 (ebook)
Subjects: LCSH: Justification (Christian theology)—History of doctrines. | Luther, Martin, 1483–1546. | Melanchthon, Philip, 1497–1560.
Classification: LCC BT764.2 .G7 2021 (print) | LCC BT764.2 (ebook) | DDC 234.7—dc23

Printed in the United States of America

Cover art by Brenton Clarke Little

In Memory Of

Werner Elert
and his wife
Annemarie nee Froboss

In Honor Of

Samuel F. Salzmann
and his wife
Hedwig nee Reu

Contents

Abbreviations

ADB—*Allgemeine Deutsche Biographie*, 1875–1910.

AE—*Luther's Works*, American Edition, 1955ff.

Aland—Kurt Aland, *Hilfsbuch zum Luther Studium*, 1956ff.

Allen—*Opus epistolarum Des. Erasmi Roterodami*, ed. P. S. Allen et al., 1906–1947.

Apol—*Apology of the Augsburg Confession*, cited by article and section nos.

ARG/ARH—*Archiv für Reformationsgeschichte / Archive for Reformation History*.

AS—Erasmus von Rotterdam, *Ausgewählte Schriften*, 1967ff.

BC—*The Book of Concord: The Confessions of the Evangelical Lutheran Church*, ed. Theodore G. Tappert.

BekS.—*Die Bekenntnisschriften der evangelisch=lutherischen Kirche*, Göttingen, 1930ff.

Beut.—Otto Beuttenmüller, *Vorläufiges Verzeichnis der Melanchthon-Drucke des 16. Jahrhunderts*, with entry no.

Br—*D. Martin Luthers Briefwechsel*, Weimar Edition, 1930ff., cited by volume no. and letter no. or page no.

ChH—*Church History*.

Cler.—*Desiderii Erasmi Roterodami opera omnia*, ed. J. Clericus, 1703–1706.

CR—*Corpus Reformatorum*, 1834ff.

CSEL—*Corpus scriptorum ecclesiasticorum Latinorum*, 1866ff.

CTM—*Concordia Theological Monthly*.

DZLE—*Dokumente zu Luthers Entwicklung*, ed. Otto Scheel, 1929.

ELC—*The Encyclopedia of the Lutheran Church*, 3 vols.,
    ed. Julius Bodensieck.

Ep—Epitome, *Formula of Concord*, cited by article and section nos.

Hammer—Wilhelm Hammer, *Die Melanchthonforschung im Wandel
    der Jahrhunderte*, 1967ff., cited by volume and entry nos.

Hartfelder—Karl Hartfelder, *Philipp Melanchthon als Praeceptor
    Germaniae*, 1889.

HTR—*Harvard Theological Review*.

KK—Köstlin and Kawerau, *Martin Luther: Sein Leben und seine
    Schriften*, 1903.

KuD—*Kerygma und Dogma*.

LCC—Library of Christian Classics, 1953ff.

Lohse—*Der Durchbruch der reformatorischen Erkenntnis bei Luther*,
    1968. Anthology ed. Bernhard Lohse.

LQ—*The Lutheran Quarterly*.

LuJB—*Luther=Jahrbuch. Jahrbuch der Luther=Gesellschaft*.

MBW—*Melanchthons Briefwechsel*, ed. Heinz Scheible, 1977ff.

MSW—Charles Leander Hill, tr., *Melanchthon: Selected Writings*,
    ed. Elmer E. Flack and Lowell J. Satre, 1962.

RE—*Realenzyklopädie für protestantische Theologie und Kirche*, 3rd
    ed., 1896–1913.

RGG—*Die Religion in Geschichte und Gegenwart*, 3rd ed., 1957–1965.

RN—*Revisionsnachtrag* to WA.

SA—*Melanchthons Werke*, Studienausgabe, ed. Robert Stupperich,
    1951ff.

SCJ—*Sixteenth Century Essays and Studies / Sixteenth Century Journal.*

SD—Solid Declaration, *Formula of Concord*, cited by article and section nos.

Suppl—*Supplementa Melanchthoniana*, 1910ff.

SVRG—*Schriften des Vereins für Reformationsgeschichte*, 1883ff.

ThLZ—*Theologische Literaturzeit.*

TR—*D. Martin Luthers Tischreden. 1531–1546.* Weimar Edition, 1912–1921.

Unbek F—*Unbekannte Fragmente aus Luthers zweiter Psalmenvorlesung 1518*, ed. Erich Vogelsang, 1940.

WA—Weimarer Ausgabe: *D. Martin Luthers Werke: kritische Gesamtausgabe*, 1883ff., cited by volume no. (occasionally by section no. and also by page no. and line no.).

WA Bibel—*Die deutsche Bibel*, Weimar Edition.

ZKG—*Zeitschrift für Kirchengeschichte.*

ZsTh—*Zeitschrift für systematische Theologie.*

ZThK—*Zeitschrift für Theologie und Kirche.*

Preface

This investigation of humanists and reformers in search of an evangelical doctrine of justification goes back a quarter of a century. Much of the research involves studies conducted by the writer during his graduate work at the University of Erlangen under Werner Elert, Paul Althaus, Wilhelm Maurer, and others.

The author's earlier work was completed in the doctoral dissertation, "Die Entwicklung der evangelischen Rechtfertigungslehre bei Melanchthon bis 1521 im Vergleich mit der Luthers" (1955), which was accepted with the predicate of *magna cum laude*. The writer is deeply grateful to Werner Elert, his chief doctoral advisor. This proved to be the last dissertation written under Elert, for he died during its final stages. The undersigned is greatly indebted to the late Paul Althaus, who graciously assumed the work of advisor during the last three months of the writer's doctoral program and the *Rigorosum* examinations in February 1955. Wilhelm Maurer served as coadvisor under both Elert and Althaus and provided much helpful criticism and warm encouragement. The Erlangen faculty had suggested that the inaugural dissertation be published in English rather than German in order that it might reach the writer's native readership. It has taken twenty-five years to reach this point. The present book, which incorporates many additional studies, bears only occasional reminiscences to his dissertation.

Nevertheless, several of the principal ideas were in the 1955 work—the attempt to avoid the anti-Melanchthonian stance of many previous scholars, the conviction that Luther's arrival at his Reformational doctrine of justification did not occur prior to the school year 1518–1519, the use of the earliest Melanchthoniana, in many cases scarcely known to Reformation scholars, and the discovery that the relationship between Luther and Melanchthon was not exclusively that of teacher and pupil but that Luther also learned from Melanchthon. In his 1955 dissertation the author had shown that Melanchthon preceded Luther in such concepts as faith, grace, and forensic justification. This youthful work was one of the first serious studies on Melanchthon in several decades. It offered a number of bold hypotheses and provoked controversies and discussions which have not yet subsided. However, the writer will avoid unneedful polemics where possible and refer to his previous publications in order to keep this volume within manageable bounds. Nevertheless, some of his previous critics will find many points where he has tacitly accepted their corrections with gratitude.

Acknowledgments are due the following libraries for the use of rare materials or for their generous assistance in other ways. The *Universitätsbibliothek* of the Friedrich and Alexander University of Erlangen-Nürnberg, which includes the Kolde Collection, the *Ratsbibliothek* of Nürnberg with its unique Strobel Collection of Melanchthoniana, and the library of the Christeneum in Hamburg-Altona, which lent the writer its *Codex MS Nr. 16, Aa 3/4*, were all most helpful. The Perkins and Divinity School libraries at Duke University, the Regenstein library at the University of Chicago, the libraries at St. Louis University and Concordia Seminary, St. Louis, and the Reu Memorial Library of Wartburg Theological Seminary, Dubuque, Iowa, all made indispensable contributions to the research incorporated in this volume.

The author expresses his thanks also to the library of Appalachian State University, and especially to his wife, Violet, reference librarian, whose technical assistance, encouragement, and tender loving care have been beyond measure. This library purchased substantial parts of the costly Weimar edition and other valuable materials for his use, and the University Research Committee made a number of substantial grants through the years for purchasing books, providing photocopy, and funding the typing of the manuscript. Roy Carroll, chairman of the Department of History at Appalachian State University, and Hugh Lawrence Bond, professor of history, read the manuscript and offered many valuable suggestions.

The writer is deeply indebted to Verdict Publications for its willingness to undertake the costly venture of publishing this book, and especially to Robert D. Brinsmead and Norman Jarnes for their encouragement and assistance in editing and producing the volume.

Finally, the writer feels constrained to express his gratitude to a number of individuals who have encouraged him along the way of his professional development: Samuel F. Salzmann, emeritus professor at Wartburg Seminary, who prodded him into undertaking graduate studies; Paul Leo, late professor at Wartburg Seminary, who advised him to study in Germany and helped pave the way to Erlangen; Julius H. Bodensieck, who inspired and encouraged him during his studies in America and Germany; and Ernest W. Wallace of Texas Tech University, whose guidance in research techniques prepared him for scholarly research at a European university. The book is dedicated to the two men who were most responsible for its conception and appearance: Professor Salzmann, the chief influence during the writer's early theological studies, and Professor Elert, his doctoral advisor, whose wise guidance and warm encouragement have left their imprint upon every page.

Lowell C. Green
Day of St. Paul, 1979

Foreword

Scott L. Keith

Background

I met Dr. Lowell C. Green in 1997 while attending courses for an MA in reformation theology at Concordia University in Irvine (CUI). At the time, I was still finishing my BA from CUI, but managed to get a special dispensation to take this one course. (In truth, the next semester I was lucky enough to take another MA course from Dr. James Kittleson on Luther.) The course was entitled "The Life and Theology of Philip Melanchthon." At the time, Melanchthon was an even more unknown character than he is now. Most of what was easily available to confessional Lutherans on the topic was confined to what could be gleaned from F. Bente's, *Historical Introduction to the Book of Concord*. This work covers a goodly deal of Melanchthon history and theology, but poorly. But as a side benefit to the MA course offering, the CUI bookstore began to carry Dr. Green's little work, *How Melanchthon Helped Luther Discover the Gospel*.

I had already had a somewhat developed interest in Melanchthon. I had read all the biographies available in the CUI library, as well as the three translations of his *Loci* that were available in English at the time: the 1521, 1543, and the 1555. I had also begun translating another edition of the *Loci*, the 1535, into English. So, when Dr. Green, the only LCMS Melanchthon theologian I knew of, showed up on campus, I was thrilled.

His lectures were always at night and always about three hours long with only intermittent breaks. He was a small man in stature, but a theological giant to me. He was, and is to this day, one of the smartest men I have ever met. He lectured in what I came to find out is the German style. That is, he would prepare a manuscript of a lecture, and read what he had prepared. Somewhat formulaic by modern American standards, though he always left ample time for questions. He was very much the sage on the stage rather than the guide on the side. He was there to fill your head with what his head contained. It was amazing.

Out of class he was somewhat formal, but kind. He and his wife hosted a traditional German Advent party for all of the students at one point. Every student was assigned to bring something, and they provided the main course. There was traditional German food, hot mulled wine, as well as coffee and pastries. We discussed theology and sang carols. It was quite amazing. From Dr. Green, as well as from many other teachers and mentors through the years, I learned that being a theologian was as much about making life-long relationships as it is about anything else.

In class and out of class he taught me about who Melanchthon really was. He was not a traitor to Martin Luther or Lutheranism. He was not even necessarily a mystery or an enigma. He was a scholar and a Biblical theologian of the first rate. I learned that Melanchthon's educational trajectory led him to different methodologies than did Luther's. At the end of the day, Melanchthon was trained in Christian Humanism, and Luther was an Augustinian Monk and Priest. These varied backgrounds often led to a different manner and use of language. More on this later.

Why Melanchthon

It was in Dr. Green's lectures and this volume, that I first learned that as early as 1519, Melanchthon developed the Reformation doctrine of forensic justification by faith, as gleaned from St. Paul's Epistle to the Romans, and on that doctrine, he stood firm throughout his life. Furthermore, Dr. Green asserted that, for Melanchthon, the rediscovery of the gospel—that is, the message concerning the believing sinner's acceptance by grace alone for Christ's sake alone—was the central concern of the Reformation.

Meeting Dr. Green that fateful semester led to my belief, that understanding Melanchthon's role in the doctrinal development of

the Lutheran Church is necessary in order to codify a greater understanding of the roots of what is a distinctly Lutheran systematic and
confessional structure. Additionally, when Melanchthon is relegated
as unimportant, due to his perceived later doctrinal errors, his contributions to not only Lutheranism, but also the Church as a whole,
are too easily overlooked.

Dr. Green provided a clarification of his positions and a clear
understanding of his influence on the Reformation and Lutheranism,
as a whole. This clarification assists the scholars and the Church
by facilitating a clearer dialogue through which the true benefits
of Melanchthon's influence can be studied, interpreted and appre-
ciated. Historic Lutheranism is often accused of antinomianism.
Through his formulation of justification as forensic declaration, the
will and the relationship of good works to salvation, Melanchthon
was systematizing not only justification by faith, but also the necessity of love and good works in response to the free gift. The good
news was clearest in the writing of the Apostle Paul as explained in
the Reformation doctrine of salvation by grace alone through faith
alone. This teaching, according to Melanchthon, and Dr. Green, is
incomplete without the addition of a changed will compelled to be
sent out in love to share the gospel, spread the "good news" and
be the ambassador of Christ to family and neighbor. When only given
half of the message, the historic Lutheran doctrine is left incomplete.
Lutheranism needs a better understanding of this, and its own, often
overlooked and underappreciated father in the faith. Dr. Green provided the church with one of the clearest explanations of these reali-
ties in *How Luther Helped Melanchthon Discover the Gospel*.

The Book is divided into three main parts Part I: *The Problem of the
"Young Luther,"* Part II: *How Melanchthon Helped Luther Develop His
Views*, Part III: *The Reformation Doctrine of Justification*.

In Part I, Green spends three chapters establishing the fact that
Luther the reformer and Lutheranism the confession of faith was
not built in one night. Luther and his theological propositions were
gradually shaped by study, mediation, and conversation concerning
Scripture. Luther's eyes were illuminated one disputation and commentary at a time to not just the presence of categories like Law and

Gospel, but to the essential and necessary distinction between them. Green successfully counters the narrative that Luther's most radical assertions are found in his passionate debates against Scholastic theologians. Instead, he identifies the time between 1512 and 1518 time as a transitional road paving the way for what would become the Reformational vocabulary of grace, justification, and law and gospel. Documents like the Heidelberg Disputation and Luther's early Galatian's commentary demonstrate that Luther was very much operating with Augustinian and Scholastic definitions for these pivotal words. This to the effect that while Luther could formulate argue that grace is not attained by the Law but rather the Cross, grace was still operating as a substance rather than what would later be asserted that grace is an attitude on the part of God. Green points out that as modern readers of these works, we are often blinded by hindsight. That knowledge of the confessions, and the later Luther cause us to read words like law and grace with the full force of the Reformation behind them. This blinding hindsight does not cause grave doctrinal errors but can cause us to overlook or loose curiosity in the history and development of the doctrines and definitions to which we boldly cling and confess. Amongst this oft overlooked history and development sits the contributions of Philip Melanchthon.

Part II introduces Melanchthon as an important player in the movement known as Biblical Humanism. The Humanists were known for their tireless pursuit of original sources summed up by the phrase *ad fontes* that is, back to the fount or sources. This pursuit to hear both contemporary and ancient authors alike in their own words found its greatest purpose when driving towards the unfiltered Christian Scriptures of the Old and New Testament. This meant going beyond the Latin translation of these texts in the Vulgate and into the older Greek and Hebrew texts. This unveiled the presence of inaccurate or prepositionally loaded translations within the text of the vulgate itself. As an heir of the humanist tradition Melanchthon brought an intimate and expert knowledge of these definitional issues with him when he was called to teach at Wittenberg University in 1518.

Melanchthon's command of grammar, dialectic, and rhetoric shone through as he lectured through the book of Romans under the auspices of teaching students Greek. These lectures eventually

gave way into the writing of the Reformation's first systematic text
the 1521 Loci Communes Theologici. In these lectures and in the
Loci itself, Melanchthon cemented the use of terms like the imputation of righteousness and re-framed grace in its proper definition as
an attitude rather than a substance. These definitional moves alongside Luther's increasingly evangelical assertions built the foundation
for the Reformation's recovery of a Biblical doctrine of justification.

Green closes the book in Part III by furthering the exploration
and explanation of how Luther and Melanchthon worked together to
institute and maintain offices of teaching and preaching unilaterally
anchored in the doctrine of justification. Green asserts that not only
was justification central as the article upon which the church stands
or falls but also that it was unifying. From justification, stemmed
agreement on issues like good works, sanctification, and even the
simultaneity of the Christian life expressed by *simul iustus et peccator*. The unification ultimately stemming from a new precision found
in the grammar of imputation. That is to say that the imputation of
Christ's righteousness provided a key to salvation by grace through
faith on account of Christ alone by providing the necessary framework for "alone" to operate. Imputation when fully outlined gives
Christ the credit for salvation, and also all goodness derived and
worked through believers in the Christian life.

Though Green's purpose is to demonstrate the ways in which
Luther and Melanchthon worked together, he is also no stranger to
the ways and moments when these men worked and spoke differently. In particular, Green highlights that Melanchthon was more
willing to make an inward path for opponents before they accepted
every precept of Evangelical doctrine. Untimely, Green demonstrates
that these differences were overcome by Luther and Melanchthon's
unified preaching and teaching of imputed righteousness and justification. As the book concludes, Green utilizes dogmatic and confessional texts like Luther's catechisms and Melanchthon's writing of
the Apology of the Augsburg Confession, as well as various letters
and correspondence to show the clear synthesis of their thought. All
of this works together to both make a strong case for a positive disposition toward Melanchthon and his role in the reformation while
simultaneously contributing to the contextual history of Luther's
though and work.

Introduction

Hardly any subject of historical investigation has received more attention than Martin Luther and the Protestant Reformation. Karl Schottenloher's *Bibliographie zur deutschen Geschichte im Zeitalter der Glaubensspaltung 1517–1585* (1933ff.) is largely restricted to the German Reformation and yet comprises seven stately volumes in quarto format. Despite growing secularization today, interest in this subject continues to increase. Courses in the Reformation are among the most popular in college history departments as well as in the offerings of theological seminaries. Once thought to be the restricted domain of Protestants, this field has been immeasurably enriched in recent years by the research of Roman Catholic scholars. Reformation studies are now accepted as an integral part of ecumenical pursuits not only because this movement of the sixteenth century ended with a divided Christendom in the West, but also because Protestant and Catholic thinkers alike are learning to solve some of the subsequent dilemmas by retracing the steps of history.

The sheer bulk of research and publication on the Protestant reformers has created formidable problems. It is impossible for even the specialist to become acquainted with more than a fraction of the 65,000 items in Schottenloher's listings, which are by no means exhaustive. Moreover, important aspects of the period remain unsolved. How then is the generalist in history, theology, or the new ecumenics going to make his way through this awesome mountain of materials? This book has been written with both the generalist and the specialist in mind. While it seeks to make its subject matter so clear that the intelligent layman or college student can follow its course without undue anguish, it also hopes to provide the specialist with new discoveries and interpretations which will help to resolve some of the unsolved problems.

Many people hold the notion that whatever problems of the Reformation remain, at least our knowledge of the cardinal doctrine of justification is secure. One commonly hears the opinion that, "As everyone knows, Luther characteristically taught that justification takes place by the twofold action in which the believer receives forgiveness of sins and the imputation of Christ's righteousness." Unfortunately, this statement is not correct. It is perhaps more characteristic of Melanchthon, but even for him it is badly in need of qualification. While Luther might not have rejected this formulation out of hand, his own formulations sounded very different. We shall see the basis for these assertions as we proceed with our investigation.

We cannot clarify what the Protestant reformers taught in regard to justification nor how they became separated from the Roman Catholic Church until we revise our historical picture of the early events of their movement. It has often been assumed that Luther's *Ninety-Five Theses on the Power of Indulgences* in October 1517 were a revolt resulting from his new Protestant view of justification. But there are two errors here. The *Ninety-Five Theses* were not a revolt, nor did they even oppose the received doctrine of forgiveness of sins. Furthermore, Luther had not yet come to his Reformational understanding of justification. Accordingly, one of the central theses of this book is the proposition that the Indulgence Controversy was the cause rather than the result of Luther's evangelical discovery of justification. Despite commonly-held views to the contrary, his teachings between 1509 and 1518 were in basic accord with good Catholic doctrine of that time. Three factors which helped mold him into the Protestant reformer were the opposition of the Roman Church after October 31, 1517, his earlier Biblical studies, which now came to fruition, and the influence of the Biblical humanists.

Martin Luther himself is such a commanding figure in history that it has been very difficult for scholars to give adequate attention to the men and women among whom he moved. Investigation reveals that Erasmus and Melanchthon had a greater share in discovering and formulating the Protestant doctrine of justification than has hitherto been recognized. All three men held distinctive positions. But Erasmus was a kind of catalytic agent assisting Melanchthon in developing his teaching on justification, while Melanchthon in turn was an important catalyst in the formulation of Luther's doctrine.

More than a hundred years ago August Tholuck lamented: "Were an indulgence peddler to come among us today, he would find business abominably poor, for no one now has a disquieted or tortured conscience."[1] Paul Tillich despaired of ever making justification "relevant" to contemporary man. Why has justification until recently seemed like a needless and old-fashioned concept from the remote past? Perhaps one reason has been that man has felt he could handle his guilt alone. This was easy enough as long as one's insight into sin was placidly superficial and as long as the God of Scriptures was reduced to a pleasant old gentleman devoid of divine wrath. But the wars since 1939 have demolished such notions. The atrocities of Buchenwald and My-lai, of Dresden and Hiroshima have uncovered an inhumanity and depravity in mankind that had hardly been taken seriously for hundreds of years. The time is ripe. Once more man realizes that he is guilty of demonic deeds and that God, if He has any principles whatsoever, must arise to vindicate these victims. This forces the guilty sinner to capitulate before his Maker and Judge and to plead for mercy. All but the shallowest worldling of the twentieth century should have a new empathy with Luther's agony in the monastery cell, with his horror in the presence of the Just Judge (*coram Deo*!), with his soul-piercing cry: "How can I find a gracious God?" By implication, the religious leader today has the renewed obligation to lead his fellow man through such an experience of law and gospel, as the reformers called it. Unfortunately, the "social gospel" has recently diverted the attention of large denominations, like the Lutheran Church, from the *articulus stantis et cadentis ecclesiae* (the article on which the church stands or falls). No matter how important social activity might be and is, whenever the church loses the article of justification, she loses her right to exist at all.

Some scholars have tried to study Luther as though the movement stopped with him and did not include the development of the Lutheran Church or the writing of the Lutheran Confessions. The large number of Luther scholars includes many who are not Lutherans and many Lutherans who are hostile to the Lutheran Confessions. This in itself could be a valuable factor in adding breadth to the field. Actually, as I shall demonstrate in the opening chapter, this has not been the case. Rather, a deadlock has occurred. The purveyors of the Young-Luther approach have made their case. An adequate reply from their opponents has long been overdue. It might be said that the Young-Luther approach presents a reformer who is basically "Catholic" in his teaching, whereas the approach of those who think that the Lutheran Confessions are the legitimate continuation of the Mature Luther presents a reformer who is basically "Lutheran." As a matter of fact, the two parties can be said to consist of a group which rejects the view of justification in the Lutheran Confessions and a group which affirms them. If I correctly understand such writers as Heiko Oberman and Leif Grane, they are saying that their position is "objective" because they isolate Luther from the Lutheran Confessions, whereas my position is "subjective" because I find a basic concord among Luther, the Confessions, and the Sacred Scriptures. This is fallacious. Instead, it should be recognized that both sides are proceeding from certain prior assumptions and that the validity of the results depends at least in part on the conscious awareness that one shares a certain bias and on the careful examination of those assumptions. But if Oberman and Grane feel that only the opposing position has begun with prior assumptions, they are overlooking their own biases and cannot possibly conduct an impartial investigation. And if it is felt that the scholars who accept the theological positions of the *Book of Concord* are "subjective" while those who reject them are "objective," there is danger of sacrificing all scientific methodology. This book is written with the certainty that the forensic justification described in the *Concordia* is basically true to the insights of Paul, that the Young Luther failed to understand justification fully, that in his later years Luther came to a fully evangelical doctrine, and that the Mature Luther explicitly rejected the views of the Young Luther. We shall see that the views of the Young-Luther supporters are no longer tenable and that an examination of the original sources supports this position. We shall thereby remove the artificial barriers separating Luther from the Confessions of the church which bears his name. We shall find him an advocate of forensic justification.

In the following pages we shall first seek to demolish several faulty constructions of Luther's life and thought in order to ascertain what he was really like and what he actually taught in his early period (before 1518). Then we shall turn to his colleague. We shall first observe similar pre-Reformational views in Melanchthon. But then we shall see him moving from an "analytic" to a "synthetic" understanding of justification. And we shall see how he helped Luther discover an evangelical doctrine of the nature of faith, the meaning of grace, and the gift of imputed righteousness.

There is a dearth of good, current writing on Luther in English. Such literature on Melanchthon is almost nonexistent. Comparatively few scholars have become interested in Melanchthon, and the quality of the work conducted by some of these has generally been below the standards of Luther research. An almost blind hatred toward Luther's co-worker on the part of Lutherans of various parties has seriously hindered historical and theological investigation. Melanchthon committed some serious mistakes in judgment, and these are to be rejected. But the good far outweighed the bad. This will become increasingly clear as we investigate how Melanchthon helped Luther discover the Gospel. For Melanchthon made important contributions to the full discovery of forensic justification. The fact that the Lutheran Church has a basically negative attitude toward its second theologian reveals how deeply it lacks an authentic self-consciousness and how extensively it has failed to carry out its assigned place in history. At least this is true if its purpose is to bear testimony to the article of justification,—the *articulus stantis et cadentis ecclesiae*. May this present study provide a small contribution toward fulfilling that sacred obligation.

Note

[1] August Tholuck, *Gewissens-, Glaubens- und Gelegenheitspredigten* (Berlin, 1860), p. 20. Cited in Werner Elert, *Morphologie des Luthertums*, Vol. I (München: Ch. H. Beck, 1952), pp. 44f. Eng. ed.: *The Structure of Lutheranism*, tr. Walter A. Hansen (St. Louis: Concordia, 1962), p. 49.

The Problem of the "Young Luther"

Part I

ERFURT

Historiographical Prolegomena

The Present Crisis in Luther Studies and a Fresh Approach

Since the advent of the "Luther Renaissance" at the beginning of this century, studies on the life and work of the reformer have enjoyed high prestige and generous financial backing. In the wake of the brilliant studies by Karl Holl (1866–1926), his pupils and others carried on the work so that one writer could recently claim that Martin Luther has been investigated more thoroughly than any other figure in history except Jesus Christ. One of the characteristics of the Luther Renaissance has been the rediscovery of the early works of the reformer and an exaggerated emphasis upon the Young Luther that has not entirely subsided. Some recent scholars have reached conclusions on Luther's development which simply cannot correspond with established notions. The resultant dissension and unwillingness to seek a reasonable consensus has reached crisis proportions in the guild of Luther researchers. Much of this dissension has concentrated on the doctrine of justification, the nature of Luther's spiritual struggles and breakthrough into his understanding of justification, and the time when that discovery took place.

Before 1900 a general consensus had regarded Luther's doctrine of justification as essentially the same as that of Philipp Melanchthon and the Lutheran Confessions. This consensus had largely rested upon the evidence from Luther's later works, especially from the *Large Commentary on Galatians* (1531–1535). However, it has been shown that this *Commentary* did not come directly from Luther's pen but through the mediation of men who, some have said, were pupils of Melanchthon.[1] Instead of carefully investigating the question whether the *Commentary* might nevertheless provide valuable insights, many unfortunately lost interest in the mature reformer and became preoccupied with the rebelling monk. Holl played the Young Luther against the Mature Luther and simultaneously conducted polemics against Melanchthon and Confessional Lutheranism in a series of thought-provoking and influential essays.[2] It should be borne in mind that Holl himself came from a mild Lutheranism that was strongly influenced by Swabian pietism. In addition, his thinking included significant admixtures from the philosophy of Kant, German idealism, and the theology of Ritschl. Holl introduced the terms "synthetic" and "analytic" justification, based on the work of Kant and Ritschl. Rejecting the "synthetic" (forensic or imputative) doctrine of the past, he defended an "analytic" view (justification as inner renewal), which he had little difficulty in supporting from the early works of Luther.[3] Pupils of Holl such as Erich Vogelsang accepted the early view of justification as fully Reformational and fixed the date of Luther's discovery of the Gospel at about 1513.

Quite apart from the question of its validity, this new view of justification created divisions which were to have lasting effects. A wall was created between Confessional Lutheranism and many scholars that was to be harmful for all concerned. This brought a certain distance between the church and Luther studies which was not beneficial to either side during the troubles of the Hitler era. Some outstanding scholars, like Emanuel Hirsch, for example, became involved in Nazi ideology and were unable to provide from Luther's writings the needful antidotes for the issues of that time. In fact, Luther's views were distorted and used to support Hitler's program. Luther studies were divorced from the church and from everyday Christian living. And his teachings on justification and sanctification were relegated to the arena of scholarly controversy. These problems again surfaced in the abortive discussions on justification at the assembly of the Lutheran World Federation in 1963 at Helsinki, where it became clear that Lutheran scholars from around the world did not agree with themselves, with the Lutheran Confessions, or with Luther.[4] The divisive influence of the theological views of Karl Holl and Gustaf Aulen[5] were probably leading causes for this disarray. Furthermore, the new portrait of Luther, strongly tinged by liberalism, romanticism, and pietism, hindered an understanding between the Protestants and the Roman Catholics. It presented the reformer as a rebellious hero who, in posting the *Ninety-Five Theses*, struck hammer blows which resounded around the world, shattered the tyranny of the medieval papacy, and irrevocably destroyed the unity of the church. This construction totally obscured Luther's irenic intentions in 1517–1519 as well as his ecumenical interest and his concern for the *magnus consensus* of the church Catholic.[6]

At a time when the international as well as interconfessional aspects of Luther research are being stressed, it is perhaps significant to note that the first massive attacks on the Young-Luther movement came from scholars in the New World. This can be said despite the fact that several Europeans have objected to the findings of the Holl School[7] and despite the fact that many American writers have largely followed its results. In 1951 the Finno-American, Uuras Saarnivaara, published his findings under the title, *Luther Discovers the Gospel*, based on his earlier dissertation at the University of Chicago.[8] He presented a useful analysis of the secondary literature in various languages,[9] contrasted the position of the Young Luther with his mature theology, and called for dating the "tower experience" at the end of 1518.[10] Although I could not agree with Saarnivaara at every point, I came to substantially similar conclusions in my doctoral dissertation of 1955 at the University of Erlangen.[11] From my studies of the early Melanchthon and his doctrine of forensic justification, I had unavoidably come to see the differences in justification between Melanchthon and Luther in their earlier and later periods, as well as the changes which Luther underwent after the Indulgence Controversy. I had learned that this controversy had spurred him to rethink his position on penance and justification. A third American, Ferdinand Edward Cranz, employed a still different method. His work, which was oriented toward Luther's views on justice and the social order, was published in 1959 under the title, *An Essay on the Development of Luther's Thought on Justice, Law, and Society*.[12] Cranz found an important change taking place in Luther's thinking in 1518. As a monk, Luther had previously held to Neoplatonic categories in which the visible world was downgraded in favor of the invisible world of the spirit. This had been linked with legalistic concepts of

Law and Gospel in which the Gospel was seen as "spiritual law" in contrast to the "literal law." Moses was the giver of the old law, and Christ of the new law.[13] Luther overcame this group of early concepts when he reached new clarity on law, justice, and the existence of the two realms of society.[14] Cranz dated the finding of the evangelical understanding of *iustitia Dei* at 1518–1519[15] and found the Reformational doctrine of justification fully developed by 1522.[16]

European Reformation scholars have scarcely noticed the work of the Americans mentioned above, but a parallel movement has occurred in Europe, with the preponderant position of the Holl School and the early dating of Luther's breakthrough subjected to serious criticism. The European debate began when Ernst Bizer published his monograph in 1958, *Fides ex auditu*, in which he identified Luther's evangelical breakthrough as the discovery that the Word is the means of grace by which God bestows righteousness upon the sinner, and dated that discovery at 1518.[17] A pupil of Bizer, Oswald Bayer, developed this idea further in his monograph, *Promissio*, in which he concentrated upon the concept of the promise and found Luther's new insights developed with special clarity in the 1520 treatise, *On the Babylonian Captivity of the Church*.[18] Bizer's controversial position had a wholesome effect upon Luther studies in Europe because it helped demolish obsolete notions which had gone unchallenged and provided fresh air in what had become a stuffy and complacent establishment of Luther scholars. However, many who felt that Bizer was right in his call for a redefinition of the evangelical discovery and in a later dating for its occurrence were not completely satisfied with his identifying it as the disclosure that the Word was the decisive means of grace. It was pointed out that this presented a Luther heavily influenced by Karl Barth. Regardless how scholars reacted to the details of Bizer's presentation, many were impressed and spurred to important new investigations.

It is significant that while recent studies calling for a 1518 dating of Luther's evangelical breakthrough have usually been independent of each other and have followed very different procedures, they have supported each other. Martin Seils has made a valuable study of Luther's understanding of the manner in which God and man work together. In such a study the terms "active" and "passive" are crucial. The results of such a study can well be expected to clarify their usage.

Seils does not disappoint us, and his findings are especially helpful in interpreting the *Preface* of 1545. He finds that in the early Luther a *Theologia crucis* had prevailed in which justification had depended to a certain extent upon humility—a form of cooperation of the faithful with God. Man played an active role in his own justification. But beginning in 1518, there was an unmistakable change. Luther then stressed that man is entirely passive in his own justification and that God alone is active.[19] It seems that Seils holds the key to these words in which Luther described his evangelical breakthrough:

> I had indeed been captivated with a deep ardor for understanding the words of Paul in the Epistle to the Romans [1, 17] . . . "The righteousness of God is revealed in it." . . . There I began to understand that this righteousness of God is that by which the righteous man lives as by a gift from God, namely by faith. And this is the meaning: the righteousness of God is revealed through the Gospel, that is, the passive righteousness (*iustitiam passivam*) with which the merciful God justifies us by faith. . . .[20]

In his evangelical breakthrough, accordingly, Luther had relinquished his earlier belief that man somehow cooperates with God in producing righteousness as the basis for his justification. Instead, he had come to the insight that saving righteousness is exclusively the work of God and is therefore passive from the standpoint of the believer. This finding of Seils seems to accord very well with Cranz's results. Indeed, Cranz's results seem to amplify Seils' findings in an impressive manner. Cranz found an important breakthrough in Luther's thinking about 1518 in which Luther for the first time distinguished the temporal and spiritual realms, as well as the theological concepts of Law and Gospel, and learned to identify justification as exclusively the divine work, with sanctification set apart as the human response to justification.[21] Both scholars independently found that Luther's spiritual problem was first solved when he learned to distinguish between the work of God and the work of man.

The work published by Kurt Aland was completely different. It was the result of a joint seminar with Ernst Kinder. This was the first investigation of the time and nature of Luther's discovery which included an intensive study of the correspondence, a relatively neglected source in past discussions. It also concluded that Luther's decisive breakthrough took place in 1518.[22] The Heidelberg systematician, Albrecht Peters, has also weighed the evidence and accepted 1518 as the time when the Reformational insight into justification first appeared.[23] In 1977 the noted historian, Martin Brecht, formerly of Tübingen and presently at Münster, published a perceptive article in which he made a powerful case for the later dating. Noting that the distinction of Law and Gospel was a basic part of Luther's fully Reformational theology, he found Law and Gospel confused in the *Dictata super Psalterium* (1513ff.) and in the letter to Spenlein.[24] In fact, clarity was lacking until 1518, when the reformer's presentation on justification began to assume its final shape.[25] It is interesting and gratifying to see the accelerating tendency of prominent scholars toward such a position.[26] Whereas in the 1950's and 1960's it was difficult to find a journal editor or book publisher who would accept material presenting this position, today there is a new openness to give it consideration.

Two enormous problems today confront those who call for the year 1518 as the time of Luther's evangelical breakthrough. (1) The content of Luther's works prior to 1518 does not accord with that of his mature period, so that advocates of the later dating of the breakthrough call those early writings pre-Reformational. This evokes the charge from the former group that the advocates of the later dating are following their own preconceived notions. It shall be our endeavor to meet this charge by permitting the later Luther to speak for himself—a procedure which will provide sufficient evidence to refute that accusation. (2) Luther's autobiographical statement in the 1545 *Preface* to his collected Latin works[27] explicitly states that he did not understand the Gospel before the school year 1518–1519 and that it was in 1519 that he first came to his Reformational insights. The defenders of the earlier dating have, of course, sought to dismiss this important primary evidence. Some have said that Luther's advanced age of sixty-two years made his testimony invalid, or that he was notoriously poor in remembering dates (an untrue allegation), or that Luther really meant to speak of 1513 and the beginning of his first lectures on the Psalter rather than 1519 and his second series of lectures on the Psalms. However, the primary sources are piercingly clear and unambiguous, for Luther himself declares:

> Again in that same year [scil., 1519] I returned to interpreting the
> Psalter anew. I had confidence in the fact that I was more skillful,
> after I had taught St. Paul's Epistles to the Romans and Galatians, and
> the Epistle to the Hebrews.[28] I was torn by a deep desire to under-
> stand Paul in the Epistle to the Romans. But what stood in the way . . .
> was a single word in Chap. 1[17]: The righteousness of God . . .[29]

One of the most impressive defenders of the older position is
Heiko Oberman. In an essay which, like Pilate's inscription, was
issued in three languages, he writes crisply:

> In the past this Preface has been molded in so many directions and
> Luther scholars have deduced from its few pages so many differ-
> ent Luther-figures that a usage of these passages in our time has
> almost become *the* characteristic of unscientific Luther research.
> Therefore a few introductory observations:
>
>> In my opinion it has proved to be impossible to use this Preface
>> to date with any degree of precision the so-called "Turmerlebnis." The
>> preceding *theological* decision of the scholar involved, as to which
>> point in the thought of Luther is to be regarded as "the centre" and
>> what therefore is to be proclaimed as the break with the scholastic
>> tradition, has always been the decisive factor in the *historical* fixation
>> of the year and date of the "Turmerlebnis."[30]

Before the scientific historian is moved to renounce the *Preface* of
1545, however, Oberman's statement needs to be examined critically. Who are these individuals in the past who have so distorted
Luther's words that perhaps the *Preface* ought now to be disregarded? One's first inclination might be to think of the older writers
who supported the early dating of the evangelical discovery—men
like Emanuel Hirsch, Ernst Stracke, or Heinrich Bornkamm,[31] who,
attempting to maintain a "preceding theological decision," i.e., that
the theology of the *Lectures on Romans* was Reformational, had to
alter the plain meaning of the *Preface*. However, it appears instead
that Oberman is referring to his opponents in the debate—to those
who have accepted Luther's own testimony that he first learned
to know the Gospel in 1518–1519. Oberman's introduction, with
the words, "what therefore is to be proclaimed as the break with the
scholastic tradition," is the unwarranted insertion of a "preceding

theological decision" on his part that leads him to advocate his own "historical fixation of the year," which differs from that of the primary source. Therefore, since Luther's words are in danger of being "molded in so many directions," it would be better to rule them out of the discussions and replace them with the corrections of such writers as Oberman.

The thoughtful reader might be prompted to ask the question, "Is the warning not to consult Luther's own account in the *Preface* of 1545 perhaps based on the discovery that the document is not historically reliable?" Interestingly, the writers who have tried to rule the *Preface* out of court have not challenged its authenticity but have only objected to its revelation. The historical introduction in the Weimar edition[32] fails to mention the location of the holograph, which is therefore presumably lost, but no one has questioned that the *Preface* as Luther saw it published in 1545 was authentic. To be sure, Paul Kalkoff insisted that the *Preface* was to be taken with a grain of salt, and Ernst Stracke went through it with a fine-toothed comb and purported to have found minor discrepancies.[33] But such petty points cannot overthrow the importance of this unique self-disclosure of Luther. It therefore remains as the most authoritative single source on his development. Oberman warns that the document has been misused so often that it would be better not to use it again. Nevertheless, the rule still stands: *Abusus non tollit usum*. And we shall note later that the *Preface* is accompanied with so many parallels from Luther and contemporary witnesses that it is unassailably corroborated. It is not the *Preface* that needs support but the studies of those who presume to exclude so fundamental a historical source in favor of their own "historical fixations" or their "preceding theological decisions." We shall heed Oberman's caution against allowing our own "preceding theological decision" to determine "the historical fixation" of the time as well as the character of Luther's discovery.[34] Instead, we shall let Luther himself determine what was Reformational and permit him to tell us when he first reached that stage.

Leif Grane is more adroit than Oberman in his interesting new book, *Modus loquendi theologicus*.[35] Like many before him, Grane wants to establish the *Lectures on Romans* as the norm for Luther's theology and thinks that those who prefer a later work as norm are somehow reading their own views into Luther.[36] He seems to feel that all who start with the Mature Luther are proceeding subjectively, while only those who, like Grane, begin with the Young Luther are proceeding objectively. As a matter of fact, the most "objective" historian operates with certain beliefs and values which constitute a bias, and the greatest danger is to think that only one's opponent has a bias and thus overlook one's own bias. It might be said that every scholar is either for or against the Lutheran Confessions. Although this is not readily apparent, what is really involved is the question whether the "true reformer" is Luther as reflected in his later writings and in the Lutheran Confessions or whether that position should be rejected in favor of the early works. Oberman, Grane, and other Young-Luther advocates take a position which is essentially anti-Confessional, whereas my position is almost inevitable to one who has committed himself to the teachings of the Lutheran Confessions. My view is that only a forensic justification permits the distinction of Law and Gospel. And the Mature Luther asks his readers to accept this distinction as norm for his teaching to determine whether it is pre-Reformational or fully evangelical. We shall proceed on this basis.

Scholars such as Holl, Oberman, and Grane, who want to thrust aside the clear testimony of Luther's autobiographical statement in the *Preface* of 1545, not only put themselves in the embarrassing position of rejecting their major primary source to establish their own theories, but they also conflict with a massive barrage of other primary evidence. Conversely, Martin Brecht has demonstrated that the discovery of "passive righteousness," which Luther in 1545 connected with the second series of lectures on the Psalter,[37] was actually offered almost word-for-word and given early expression in the *Operationes in Psalmos* (c. January 1519).[38] Since one of the reasons for the present crisis in Luther studies rests on the fact that the materials relevant to its solution are very extensive and therefore unknown to many scholars, I have gathered in Table 1 a number of parallels to some of the disputed assertions of Luther in his *Preface* of 1545. These parallels abundantly show that those assertions were not isolated instances but were so well supported that it will no longer be possible to dismiss them as in the past.

TABLE 1

A Comparison of Luther's Self-Disclosure in the
Preface *of 1545 with Parallels from Other Sources*

Statements in *Preface* of 1545	Parallels from Other Sources
The date of his evangelical discovery was in 1519 (WA 54: 182, 4.9; 184, 12; 185, 12; 186, 21.30). Previously, he had given lectures on the Psalter (136, 21), on Romans, Galatians, and Hebrews (185, 12). He had taught the Scriptures for seven years prior to his discovery (183, 25).	*Commentary on Galatians* (1519) was the beginning of his Reformational theology (TR II, No. 1963). In 1539: for twenty years he had taught that faith alone justifies (WA 50:596, 19). For thirty-five years (1483–1518) he had been a son of Hagar, not Sarah (WA 47:682, 22).
In the matter of the Jubilee Indulgence he had taken a moderate course, basically upholding the medieval positions on penance and justification (WA 54: 180, 5; 185, 1).	He defended the pope's position on indulgences in Theses 61, 71, 73, 81, 90, 91 (WA 1:236–38). He did not understand the indulgence in 1517 (WA 51:539, 5). Melanchthon underscored Luther's moderation in 1517 (CR VI:162, 21).
He had been unable to explain Romans 1:16f. (WA 54:185, 14; 186, 4).	Note the absence of a satisfactory interpretation of the quotation from Habakkuk 2:4 at Romans 1:16f. (WA 56:10–11, 171–73; WA 57/I:14, 133–34; WA 57/II:23, 80; WA 57/III:226).
Consequently, its concept of *iustitia Dei* had troubled him greatly (WA 54:185, 17; 186, 3; 186, 14).	*Iustitia Dei* a thunderbolt (TR II, No. 1681; TR III, No. 3232; TR IV, No. 4007). *Iustitia* as judgment (TR V, Nos. 5247, 5553, 5693; cf. WA 40/II:331f., 444f.; WA 44:485, 32).
Finally he received help in the discovery that *iustitia Dei* in Romans 1:16f. meant the saving, not the punitive righteousness of God (WA 54:180, 5).	TR V, Nos. 1681, 3232, 4007, 5247, 5553, 5693; WA 40/II: 331f., 444f. See esp. TR, No. 5518, in form given by Besold (WA 48:617). Genesis lectures (WA 44:485, 34). Early presentation of the new insight, c. January, 1519, in WA 5:144.

Statements in *Preface* of 1545	Parallels from Other Sources
Because his writings prior to 1520 made many concessions to papalism, readers are advised to use them with great care (WA 54:179, 22.34). N.b.: the *Preface* accompanied Volume I of his collected Latin writings (1516–1520).	Testimony of 1519—he had been wrongly taught by the scholastics (WA 2:414, 22). His *Commentary on Galatians* of 1519 of no use by 1531 (TR II, No. 1963).

Toward a Viable Hermeneutic of Luther Interpretation

Brilliant papers have advanced scholarship in the past despite the fact that their authors may have used certain faulty procedures. The purpose of the following discussion is not to ridicule or discredit writers who use other methods. Rather, it is to reflect upon various kinds of hermeneutical approaches in order that these may be brought into the open.

1. **The Young Luther (1509–1518) as Norm: The Early Lectures on Psalms or Romans.** We have previously seen the importance of the Luther Renaissance of the 1910's and 1920's and have taken note of the superb although misleading work of Karl Holl and his brilliant followers. Quite naturally, the Holl School followed its distinctive hermeneutic even if this was not formally stated. Some marks of this tendency were pietism, German idealism, and Ritschlian liberalism together with a certain resentment toward Confessional Lutheranism. Holl in particular found in Luther a religion of conscience and morality against which he projected a theology of the Young Luther drawn in large measure from the *Lectures on Romans* and other writings which are actually pre-Reformational in content.[39] This hermeneutical trend adopted the theological presupposition that Luther's normal view of justification was "analytic" or effective,[40] opposed forensic or imputative elements as corruptions or even forgeries from the hated Melanchthonian

direction, and consequently rejected the autobiographical *Preface* of 1545 as an error of old age. Its adherents felt that the reformer in any period must be interpreted in the light of his early works and that the Young Luther must be the basis for determining the statements of the Mature Luther. We cannot accept this hermeneutic, because Luther in later life rejected his early works as the norm for Reformational teaching. It will require careful lower and higher criticism to make sure that we are citing Luther and not Melanchthon or his followers, but this is the price that must be paid for scientific responsibility.

2. **The Young Luther as Norm: The *Theologia Crucis*.** Throughout his life Luther emphasized a theology of the cross, maintaining that the message of Christ crucified was the heart of the Christian faith. This emphasis should be distinguished from his *Theologia crucis*, a particularly scintillating set of ideas which Luther presented from about 1514 until about 1518 or even later, with the well-known theses of the *Heidelberg Disputation* (1518) representing a kind of culmination. The most prominent advocate of this stage in Luther's development has been Walther von Loewenich. In a brilliant monograph, he has attempted to normalize these early ideas of Luther by relating the later theology to the *Theologia crucis*.[41] We shall have occasion to see, however, that Luther's theology in the spring of 1518 was in transition and that the views reflected there conflict with his mature understanding of Law and Gospel. Although the thought of the *Heidelberg Disputation* marks an important advance over that of the *Lectures on Romans*, it is not fully Reformational and therefore cannot be used as the norm for interpreting the later Luther. We must seek elsewhere for a viable hermeneutical norm.

3. **The Transitional Period (1519–1527).** Luther cannot properly be called the Protestant reformer before July

1519, when he first rejected the supreme authority of popes and councils and began to acknowledge the Holy Scriptures as the final authority. His writings from 1519 until 1524 were marked by preliminary solutions.
He moved to his final position during 1525–1527. During the early transitional period came excommunication, the ban, and the final break with the Roman Church. The positions taken in the reform treatises of 1520 were gradually to recede from his thought. For example, the doctrine of transubstantiation, still held in 1520, would disappear, and the emphasis upon the royal priesthood and the prominence of the laity would give place to a more authoritarian view of the ministry. In another context, Bengt Hägglund has noted that the polemic against Latomus of 1522 still bears echoes of the sanative understanding of justification,[42] and Martin Seils has correctly observed that the exposition of the *Magnificat* from the same year contains reverberations of the view of humility which was characteristic of the early *Theologia crucis*.[43] Luther reminds us again and again that he did not come to his insights all at one time but that his theology developed slowly.[44] What were the factors which led Luther to change or at least clarify many of his leading concepts after 1521? In the conflicts with the enthusiasts he clarified his views on the church and its ministry, under fire from the sacramentarians he developed his mature doctrine of the means of grace, and in controversy with Erasmus he reflected with fresh vigor his thoughts on the monergism of grace and the spiritual capabilities of man. At this point we cannot explore the question whether Luther later modified his views expressed in *De servo arbitrio*, but it is clear that the *Great Confession on the Sacrament* (1528) was the first major treatise in which the Mature Luther gave a conscious presentation of his thought in terms which he would never again revise.

4. The Mature Luther (1528–1546). Veit Dietrich, the
Nürnberg reformer who had once lived in the Luther
home as a male servant, wrote in 1544 that Luther
came to his ripest insights in his later works: "Through
him, as a special vessel, God's Word went forth from
day to day; and the longer [he proclaimed it], the more
brightly and the more widely it shone forth. Thereby
many have come unto the knowledge of God and
shall be saved."[45] As Dietrich indicated, it was in this
last period that Luther reached his definitive formulations from which have grown the teachings of the
evangelical churches. This is the period of the catechisms and the *Smalkald Articles* by Luther, and the
Augsburg Confession, Apology, and *Treatise on the Pope*
by Melanchthon—all of which became ecclesiastical
symbols. The existence of such Confessional writings was important not merely because later genera-
tions acknowledged them as norms, but also because
Luther acknowledged them as norms of his own fully
Reformational theology. The leading thought in these
symbols, as well as from the other works of the older
Luther, is that the mature reformer regarded the proper
distinction of Law and Gospel not only as the principle
for a valid theology and churchly proclamation, but
also as the hermeneutical principle by which his early
works should be judged.[46] This is surprising to those
who would have expected him to declare Christology or
even justification to be that principle, but it should be
remembered that in the thought of the Mature Luther
the relationship of Law and Gospel included justification and Christology. It was this that made his theology fully systematic and coherent although he had not
formulated a system of dogmatics—a project which
he left to Melanchthon to accomplish. Two problems,
however, make the study of the older Luther difficult.
This period of decisive importance has been seriously
neglected by the scholars of the twentieth century

and therefore calls for much pioneer labor. And the hermeneutics of Luther interpretation is complicated at this juncture by the transmission of the texts, which is increasingly marked after 1528 by the influence of Melanchthon and his pupils. The aging reformer did not have time to prepare much of his work for publication, so his pupils, who were also disciples of Melanchthon, assumed the task of preserving and publishing works which would otherwise have been lost to posterity. One must not denounce them for this, but the circumstances demand additional concerns on the part of the modern researcher. Besides, other materials, such as the *Table Talk*, many sermons, lectures, and disputations, were written down without any supervision by Luther. One of the concerns of this monograph shall be to handle these matters critically and responsibly.

Finally, a word of caution must be given against the practice of reading Reformational ideas into statements of the Young Luther. The stance of sober criticism suggests that a thought is held to be pre-Reformational until such time as it is explicitly Reformational. This may be qualified with the observation that the Reformational concept may have been implicitly present before it was clearly asserted or that, through the loss of some of Luther's works, such a statement could have been made before its first occurrence as we possess it.

The Problem of Luther's "Conversion" and the "Tower Experience"

Many great religious leaders in history have reported a conversion experience. This is true of Paul, Augustine, Francis of Assisi, John Calvin, Ignatius Loyola, August Hermann Francke, and John Wesley as well as Luther. Eminent Luther scholars in this century have spent much time probing the mystery of Luther's "conversion." Strongly imbued with ideas of pietism, the Enlightenment, and romanticism, they have sought to reconstruct Luther's religious experiences in accordance with their own tendencies. Pietism suggested that his conversion should be a once-for-all experience, the Enlightenment saw it as a liberation from churchly authority, and romanticism sought the emergence of the individualist or hero. The careful scholar today is prone to protest such a reading of recent ideas into history. We doubt that Luther had a conversion in the manner of the Great Awakening, we see him reflecting the late medieval respect for traditional authority, we know that he was not an individualist in the modern sense, and we shy away from the concept of the hero in history.

One of the obstacles to solving the problem of the Young Luther has been semantic practices. Scholars ought to ponder the questions: Can we speak of a "conversion" in Luther? If so, in what might it have consisted? How might it be similar to or different from the conversions of pietism or of the Great Awakening in America? It appears that the word "conversion" is so heavily weighted with baggage from the seventeenth or nineteenth centuries that it should be applied to Luther only with the greatest caution. But whether the word is used or not, its underlying assumptions have colored previous Luther research. Closely related is the question of the "tower experience." Where and when did this experience occur, and in what did it consist? This is a difficult question from the standpoint of scientific history, for there are no original sources in the strict sense. Taken by itself, the much-discussed "tower experience" is hardly accessible to historical scrutiny. The notions of a "conversion" and a "tower experience" are poorly attested. But Luther's own account of his evangelical discovery enjoys the best documentation.[47]

Does either of these notions coincide with the reformer's self-revelation? It would appear that Luther did not experience any single "conversion" in the commonly-accepted sense of the word but that he did have a number of religious experiences from time to time. In fact, all his life he spoke of the omnipresence of spiritual struggles in his life and in the lives of other believers. He himself mentioned several incidents in the 1530's when Bugenhagen had talked with him;[48] and Melanchthon, who first met him in 1518, spoke of having often witnessed Luther's struggles.[49]

Much of the dissension among Luther scholars has come from the endeavor of some to dismiss certain kinds of evidence which did not agree with their hypotheses. For example, Melanchthon's important testimony in his *Preface* of 1546 to the second volume of the collected Latin writings of Luther,[50] to the effect that Luther received solace from an elderly monk during the period 1505–1508, was rejected simply because it seemed to conflict with ideas about the "tower experience." Such writers usually sought to strengthen their questionable procedures by repeating trite accusations that Melanchthon was an unreliable or poor historian. We know, of course, that Melanchthon was a competent historian who had devoted considerable effort in researching Luther's biography. Rather than rejecting the testimony of one who knew Luther so well, we should try to find a better location for this information and not link it with the "tower experience." Melanchthon's biography is far more preferable as documentation than the anonymous accounts in the *Table Talk*. Reformation scholars must be slower to reject historical sources in favor of their own hypotheses, especially when the material which contradicts their findings is as important as Luther's autobiographical *Preface* of 1545 or Melanchthon's biographical *Preface* of 1546.

If we should attempt to take all the primary evidence seriously, we might present the following spiritual struggles of Luther:

TABLE 2

Luther's Spiritual Struggles

Approximate Date(s)	Nature of Conflict
1505–1508 n.d.	According to Melanchthon: Whether forgiveness availed him. According to Luther: Whether his contrition was valid to obtain forgiveness.
1513–1514	Righteousness of God: punitive or soteriological? Hatred of God and His Law, which condemned. Struggles over predestination (e.g., WA 56:385–86). Am I included in God's saving will?
1516–1517	Whether his penance was authentic and valid.
1518–1519	Whether his active righteousness was worked by God, and whether it was sufficient. Problem of Law and Gospel.
1519–1521	Deviation from Catholic norm. "Am I leading others to damnation?"
1527	Sad; despairing of grace.
n.d.	Doctrinal disputes.

Source of Citation	Historical Reference
Old monk at Erfurt who preached and counselled: God commands you to say, "I believe in the forgiveness of sins."	CR VI:159, 2.
	KK I:67f.
Old teacher who said: God commands you to hope.	WA 40/II:411, 15; TR I:47, 21.
Came to position of Augustine: that not the sinner but God Himself creates the good works upon which justification rests. *Opera fidei*, not *legis*, are called for (=Holl's "analytical" justification in. Luther).	WA 3:464ff., somewhat as understood by Vogelsang; TR V, No. 5247.
	WA 56:254–55; WA 57/II:68–9, etc.
	TR II, No. 1820.
Relief from Staupitz regarding predestination: see it in the wounds of Christ.	TR V:293, 28.
Counsel of Staupitz: the commandments lose their bitterness when seen in the wounds of Christ.	WA 1:525–26.
Confirmed by studies of Biblical humanists.	
That not active righteousness, though worked by God, but the passive righteousness of Christ avails.	WA 54:185–86.
	WA 48:617, 10.
Law and Gospel must be distinguished.	TR V, No. 5247.
	TR V, No. 5518; cf. CR VI:160, 45; 161, 31.
Analogy of faith. "I am following God's Word"; my teachings are in the *magnus consensus*.	WA 8:413–14.
	TR I, No. 300.
	Cf. WA 30/II:268ff.; WA 50:509ff.; WA 51:469ff.
Bugenhagen—comfort and humor.	TR I:47, 25.
Romans 11:32 and prayer.	CR VI:158, 33.

When we have this material before us, we begin to see how scholars in the past have distorted the historical evidence in order to force it into their pet theories. To impute to Luther a single spiritual struggle after the model of a pietistic or romantic conversion is doing violence to the evidence. Instead, we must let the sources speak for themselves. They reveal that Luther experienced *Anfechtungen*, struggles or even torments, all his life. Which of the experiences sketched above should be identified as the "tower experience"? Which should be equated with the breakthrough described in the autobiographical *Preface* of 1545? Was the "tower experience" the same as the breakthrough Luther described in 1545? Such questions are interesting but not crucial. The crucial thing is to lay aside preconceived notions and consult the primary evidence. This shall be the endeavor of our investigation.

The problem of Luther's "conversion" is burdened by its association with the half-legendary "tower experience." According to a widely-held tradition, Luther's evangelical discovery of God's saving righteousness took place in a dramatic experience in the tower of the Black Monastery at Wittenberg. The term "tower experience" was brought into the modern debate by Hartmann Grisar, a Jesuit polemicist of the old school who attempted to discredit Luther's evangelical discovery. Grisar stood in a long line of scholars reaching back to Johann Cochlaeus, the reformer's contemporary and bitter foe, and extending into the present through Paul J. Reiter and Erik H. Erikson as well as John Osborne, where it reflects an appropriate counterpart to the exaggerated hero worship of earlier Protestant writers.[51] The controversy over the tower experience has been greatly handicapped by two circumstances. Strictly speaking, the historical sources are too limited to form a scientific conclusion from them, and since the tower was subsequently torn down, little is known about that structure itself. The historicity of the tower experience is therefore uncertain.

What can we reconstruct from this elusive tower experience? It appears that in his earlier years Luther's study was located in a room within the former tower. It is thought that Luther was struggling to understand the words of Romans 1:17: "For therein is the righteousness of God revealed from faith to faith: as it is written, The just shall live by faith." The story itself is based upon several accounts from the *Table Talk* which unfortunately contradict one another. In a saying ascribed to Luther in a fragment from 1532, he was struggling over the words "just" and "merciful" since it seemed to him that the claim of God's pure righteousness conflicted with the sinner's need for mercy. God was just; therefore He must punish. But suddenly a new insight dawned upon Luther when it occurred to him that the "righteousness of God" is instead the divine attribute by which He saves the believing sinner. In that flash Luther's problem was solved, for light had been shed upon a mystery which had plagued him for years. At last his doctrine of justification was ready.[52]

This statement from the *Table Talk* concludes with a sentence which has caused much confusion and controversy. Part of the difficulty in interpreting it is due to its bilingual nature. Luther had conversed in German, but the amanuensis had utilized several shorthand abbreviations in Latin. The result was this mixed sentence: "Dise kunst hatt mir der *S S* auf diss *Cl* eingegeben." ("This art was given me by inspiration of the Holy Spirit on/at this *Cl*.") The first abbreviation is easily resolved: *S S* means *Spiritus Sanctus* or Holy Spirit. But what follows? The resolution of *Cl* provoked a bitter controversy over rival interpretations. Grisar injected what some people call the anal interpretation. He insisted that *Cl* meant *cloaca* or toilet. According to Grisar, Luther wanted to say that his spiritual breakthrough took place in the toilet of the monks.[53] The inference that the fundamental doctrine of Protestantism was received in a moment of relief on the toilet distressed many scholars, who saw in this interpretation the sinister design of a Jesuit priest to discredit their beliefs. They came back with grim and determined refutations.

It was pointed out that the resolution of *Cl* with *cloaca* was grammatically impossible since that noun is feminine whereas *diss* is evidently neuter accusative. Seeking for more appropriate nouns in the neuter case, Wilhelm Preger suggested *C[apite]l* (chapter house), and others proposed *Cl[austrum]* (a closed-off room), reflecting the custom of providing a heated study in the otherwise unheated monastery of the Middle Ages. There were strengths and weaknesses in such solutions. An argument against these proposals, however, was that two of the five principal versions of this *Table Talk* used the word *cloaca* instead of the abbreviation.[54] It appeared that the Protestant scholars who offered such resolutions of the difficult abbreviations were really making the defense of the besieged rather than engaging in an impartial investigation. In fact, this posture of defense seems to have hindered them from imaginative action, for how else can one explain the strange silence which followed the publication by Ernst Kroker of his simple and natural solution?

Kroker, who as editor of the *Table Talk* in the Weimar edition was especially well informed on the matter, expressed his surprise that Roman Catholic and Protestant scholars alike had interpreted the words, "on this cloaca," as referring to the toilet of the monks in the Black Monastery. He calmly pointed out that the word "this" would have been out of place had Luther intended to say that his illumination occurred in the toilet. In that case he would not have said, "on *this* cloaca," but rather, "on *the* cloaca." If we were to take these words literally, odd conclusions would result. The use of the demonstrative adjective ("on *this* cloaca") at that moment would either infer that Luther was sitting not at the table but on the commode, or else that he wanted to stress that the enlightenment came to him while sitting upon his own toilet rather than that of someone else. It is therefore absurd to say that Luther came to his evangelical discovery under such circumstances. Kroker notes that one of the five principal versions states that the illumination by the Holy Spirit took place in Luther's study in the tower. These seemingly conflicting accounts can be readily explained if one takes the reference to the cloaca figuratively. Since he spoke in German, Luther, of course, had not used the word *cloaca*. But we should not be surprised if we find that he used a vulgar word. Kroker proposed the following as Luther's original statement: "Diese Kunst hat mir der Heilige Geist auf diesem Scheißhaus gegeben." ("This art was given me by inspiration of the Holy Spirit in this shit-house.") In this remark Luther was indulging in his typically pithy vocabulary by calling the whole world, as fallen from its Creator, a dung-heap and locating his study in the tower room within that context. Kroker, of course, is able to cite parallel vulgarisms in Luther.[55] Kroker's solution also meets the *desideratum* previously demanded by the neuter gender. However, it is questionable whether the demonstrative *diss* is really a neuter accusative or only an abbreviation for either *dieser* (feminine) or *diesem* (neuter), and Kroker does not bother to discuss this point.

In retrospect, it seems strange that scholars a generation ago became so agitated over the assertions of Grisar or over Luther's conversation which Grisar was interpreting. What difference did it really make? Besides, the whole story of the tower experience was so scantily documented that its existence is scarcely within the pale of that which is historically verifiable. One can only agree with the recent conclusion of Heinrich Bornkamm that it would be better to discuss Luther's evangelical discovery apart from that story. But this discovery is best studied in the autobiographical sketch of 1545,[56] which is far superior for scientific research. Nevertheless, we should not forget that even this superior account deals with only one of many religious experiences of the reformer and does not even mention a "tower experience." In examining the Young Luther, we must be particularly prepared to observe various steps in his search for justification. There were many of these preliminary discoveries. Eager scholars have often correctly pointed out an important episode in his development but have made the mistake of trying to identify this as his "conversion." We shall attempt to avoid this pitfall while we remain mindful of the fact that for Luther every day of his life was the struggle between the wrath and love of God as revealed in the Law and the Gospel.

Notes

[1] It is of course true that only a few fragments of the 1535 *Commentary on Galatians* were written by Luther directly. The critical edition in WA 40 gives the stenographic notes of Georg Rörer in the upper part of the page and his own expansion of those notes in the text which he prepared for publication on the lower part of the page. But Martin Greschat has seriously exaggerated the problems in his *Melanchthon neben Luther. Studien zur Gestalt der Rechtfertigungslehre zwischen 1528 und 1537* (Witten: Luther-Verlag, 1965), pp. 11–16. Rörer was not a pupil of Melanchthon, as Greschat thinks, but had completed his master's degree before coming to Wittenberg. Greschat's allegation, "Rörer's copies did not intend to give a literal reproduction of Luther's lectures" (p. 16), is totally contradicted by ample internal and external evidence. It is generally recognized among Luther scholars that Rörer's intention and result was an extremely complete and accurate transcription of the respective lecture, sermon, or conversation. Of course, the scientific scholar must still recognize that these copies were written by Rörer and not Luther, and accordingly exercise suitable precautions.

[2] Of special importance was Holl's essay of 1906 (1922), "Die Rechtfertigungslehre im Licht der Geschichte des Protestantismus," *Gesammelte Aufsätze zur Kirchengeschichte*, Vol. III (Tübingen: J. C. B. Mohr, 1928), pp. 525–57, his understanding of Luther's doctrine as "analytisch," p. 532, and his jaundiced and inaccurate description of Melanchthon, pp. 535–37.

[3] In his epoch-making book, *The Critique of Pure Reason*, Immanuel Kant divided all rational judgments into those of an analytic and those of a synthetic

nature. An analytic judgment was one based upon a premise that was *a priori* and within the subject, while a synthetic judgment was one based upon a premise without the subject. See Kant, *Kritik der reinen Vernunft*, ed. Raymund Schmidt, 1930 (Hamburg: Felix Meiner, 1956), pp. 45–54, 207–86, etc. This was a leading concept in German idealism. Albrecht Ritschl applied the Kantian terminology to justification, asserting that all views were either analytic or synthetic, himself opting for a synthetic justification. Ritschl, *Die christliche Lehre von der Rechtfertigung und Versöhnung*, Vol. III, 4th ed. (Bonn: Adolph Marchus, 1895), pp. 34ff., 77ff., et passim. Holl brought this problematical terminology into the twentieth-century debates. Besides the references in the preceding note, see *Gesammelte Aufsätze*, Vol. I, pp. 117f., 125, et passim. Friedrich Brunstäd, a valuable scholar in the Lutheran Confessions who knew philosophy thoroughly as well as theology, defended this usage in his *Theologie der lutherischen Bekenntnisschriften* (Gütersloh: C. Bertelsmann, 1951), pp. 75–8. Brunstäd also defends the term "effective," saying that it is applicable when applied to a synthetic view of justification but inadmissible when connected with an analytic view.

[4] At the 1963 assembly of the Lutheran World Federation in Helsinki, an embarrassing impasse was reached when representatives were unable to reach any consensus upon the fundamental Lutheran doctrine of justification. The controversy was made more difficult due to the addition of exegetical problems of modern critical theology. For literature, see the book prepared for the assembly by Warren Quanbeck, *Christ, Yesterday, Today, Forever: A Study Document on Justification* (New York: National Lutheran Council, 1963), 39 pp., and the report published later by the Lutheran World Federation Commission and Department of Theology, *Justification Today: Studies and Reports*, published as Supplement to *Lutheran World*, Vol. XII, No. 1 (1966), 75 pp.

[5] Aulén, an influential Swedish scholar, challenged the supremacy of the atonement as taught by Anselm and advocated instead a "dramatic" view in which Christ was the victor over sin, death, and especially the devil. See Gustaf Aulén, *Christus Victor: An Historical Study of the Three Main Types of Atonement*, tr. A. G. Hebert, 1931 (New York: Macmillan, 1951), p. 163. Aulén claimed that Luther did not use the terms "satisfaction" or "merits of Christ" in the traditional way (p. 9), and he virtually dismissed forensic justification as legalistic (pp. 107, 150). In Aulén's dogmatics book, *The Faith of the Christian Church*, tr. Eric Wahlstrom and Everett Arden (Philadelphia: Muhlenberg, 1948), there is no section on justification at all but only on forgiveness. The warning is given that the word "justification" is misleading (pp. 291f.). An admonition is given against what is essentially the Holl position (pp. 299–300), in which sanctification is the cause of justification (p. 300), and Luther is said to make "justification include sanctification" (p. 300).

[6] The anti-Catholic portrayal of Luther was stimulated by the German *Kulturkampf* of the 1870's. For an attempt to counteract such distortions, see my article, "Erasmus, Luther and Melanchthon on the *Magnus Consensus*: The

Problem of the Old and the New in the Reformation and Today," LQ 27 (1975): 364–81. The *Augsburg Confession* and Luther's 1539 treatise, *Von den Konziliis und Kirchen* (WA 50:509ff.), were ecumenical in tone.

[7] A number of independent thinkers rejected the findings of the dominant Holl school. See especially the writings of Wilhelm Walther, Carl Stange, Werner Elert, and Paul Althaus.

[8] Uuras Saarnivaara, *Luther Discovers the Gospel New Light upon Luther's Way from Medieval Catholicism to Evangelical Faith* (*St. Louis: Concordia, 1951*).

[9] Ibid., pp. 40–49.

[10] Ibid., pp. 103–19.

[11] Lowell C. Green, "Die Entwicklung der evangelischen Rechtfertigungslehre bei Melanchthon bis 1521 im Vergleich mit der Luthers" (unpublished Dr. Theol. diss., Theological Faculty, Friedrich and Alexander University of Erlangen, 1955).

[12] F[erdinand] Edward Cranz, *An Essay on the Development of Luther's Thought on Justice, Law, and Society*, No. XIX in Harvard Theological Studies (Cambridge: Harvard University Press, 1959).

[13] Ibid., pp. 12–17.

[14] Ibid., pp. xvi–xvii; chap. IV.

[15] Ibid., p. xiv.

[16] Ibid., p. 42.

[17] Ernst Bizer, *Fides ex auditu: Eine Untersuchung über die Entdeckung der Gerechtigkeit Gottes durch Martin Luther* (Neukirchen: Verlag der Buchhandlung des Erziehungsvereins, 1958); a revised edition appeared in 1966.

[18] Oswald Bayer, *Promissio: Geschichte der reformatorischen Wende in Luthers Theologie* (Göttingen: Vandenhoeck & Ruprecht, 1971). See also his "Die reformatorische Wende in Luthers Theologie," ZThK 66 (1969): 115–50.

[19] Martin Seils, *Der Gedanke vom Zusammenwirken Gottes und des Menschen in Luthers Theologie*, No. 50 in Beiträge zur Förderung christlicher Theologie (Gütersloh: Gerd Mohn, 1962), esp. pp. 25–61.

[20] WA 54:185–86.

[21] Cranz, pp. xiv, xvi–xvii, 46, 58–71, et passim.

[22] Kurt Aland, *Der Weg zur Reformation: Zeitpunkt und Charakter des reformatorischen Erlebnisses Martin Luthers*, No. 123 in Theologische Existenz Heute (München: Chr. Kaiser Verlag, 1965); excerpted in Lohse, pp. 384–412.

[23] Albrecht Peters, *Glaube und Werk: Luthers Rechtfertigungslehre im Lichte der heiligen Schrift*, No. 8 in Arbeiten zur Geschichte und Theologie des Luthertums (Berlin and Hamburg: Lutherisches Verlagshaus, 1962); see esp. pp. 34–40. Cf. his article, "Luthers Turmerlebnis," *Neue Zeitschrift für Systematische Theologie* 3 (1961): 203–36; reprinted in Lohse, pp. 243–88, esp. pp. 254f.

[24] Br I:35–6.

[25] Martin Brecht, "Iustitia Christi: Die Entdeckung Martin Luthers," ZThK 74 (1977): 179–223.

[26] Among the American and European scholars who have either endorsed the 1518–1519 dating of Luther's evangelical breakthrough or else have expressed dissatisfaction with the early dating might be mentioned Axel Gyllenkrok, Matthias Kroeger, Lennart Pinomaa, Franz Lau, and especially the following: Ian D. Kingston Siggins, *Martin Luther's Doctrine of Christ*, No. 14 in Yale Publications in Religion (New Haven: Yale University Press, 1970), esp. pp. 3–8. Carter Lindberg, "Prierias and his Significance for Luther's Development," SCJ 3 (October 1972): 45–64. Otto W. Heick, "The Just Shall Live by Faith," CTM 43 (1972): 579–90. See also my own presentation in *The Mature Luther*, Vol. 3 in Martin Luther Lectures (Decorah: Luther College Press, 1959), pp. 113–32. A good summary is given in John Dillenberger, *Martin Luther: Selections from His Writings* (Garden City: Doubleday, 1961), pp. xvii–xx.

[27] WA 54:179–87.

[28] The *Lectures on Hebrews* were completed by April 1518 (WA 57/III:xix).

[29] WA 54:185, 12ff.

[30] Emphasis Oberman's (p. 7). Heiko A. Oberman, "'Iustitia Christi' and 'Iustitia Dei': Luther and the Scholastic Doctrines of Justification," *Harvard Theological Review* 59 (1966): 1–26. Dutch version: "'Fides Christo Formata.' Luther en de scholastieke theologie," in *Ex Auditu Verbi*, Festschrift for G. C. Berkouwer (Kampen, 1965), pp. 157–75. German version: "'Iustitia Christi' und 'Iustitia Dei': Luther und die scholastischen Lehren von der Rechtfertigung," Lohse, pp. 413–44. Oberman's assertion that the *Iustitia Dei* is the *Iustitia Christi* does not solve the problem at all. It presents no real advance over medieval ideas.

[31] Emanuel Hirsch, "Initium theologiae Lutheri," *Festgabe für D. Dr. Julius Kaftan* (Tübingen: J. C. B. Mohr, 1920), pp. 150–69; reprinted in Lohse, pp. 64–95. Ernst Stracke, *Luthers großes Selbstzeugnis 1545 über seine Entwicklung zum Reformator. Historisch-kritisch untersucht*, No. 140 in SVRG (Leipzig: M. Heinsius Nachf., 1926); excerpted in Lohse, pp. 107–14; an example of how not to study the sources. Heinrich Bornkamm, "Zur Frage der Iustitia Dei beim Jungen Luther," ARG 52 (1961): 15–29; ARG 53 (1962): 1–59; reprinted in Lohse, pp. 289–383; the best defense against Bizer by a Holl pupü.

[32] WA 54:176–78.

[33] Ibid., p. 177.

[34] We avoid the problematical term "Turmerlebnis."

[35] Leif Grane, *Modus loquendi theologicus: Luthers Kampf um die Erneurung der Theologie (1515–1518)*, No. 12 in Acta theologica Danica (Leiden: Brill, 1975). In a very graceful manner Grane cites the case for the later dating of Luther's discovery, sees it as a circular argument in which one determines what is "Reformational," and then documents this preconception (pp. 11–13) and suggests moderation and humility (pp. 13–15). Grane's book promises to make a substantial contribution to the debate. Unfortunately, I did not receive a copy of it until my manuscript was virtually completed, and I am therefore unable to evaluate it thoroughly.

[36] Ibid., pp. 17–19.

[37] WA 54:185.

[38] WA 5:144; Martin Brecht, op. cit., p. 221.

[39] See esp. Karl Holl, "Was verstand Luther unter Religion?" *Gesammelte Aufsätze zur Kirchengeschichte*, Vol. I (Tübingen: J. C. B. Mohr, 1948), pp. 1–110 and esp. pp. 35–107. This important manifesto of nineteenth-century liberalism in Luther interpretation is available in a new paperback, *What Did Luther Understand by Religion?* (Philadelphia: Fortress, 1977).

[40] "Effective" here is a translation of the German adjective *effektiv*, which is, however, a stronger word than the English cognate. The English word can mean as little as efficient or impressive, whereas the German word connotes the actual accomplishing of a task undertaken. *Effektive Rechtfertigung* ("effective justification") therefore means that the individual is not merely declared righteous but that he is simultaneously changed into one who performs good works. This concept, which is widely used by German theologians, actually makes sanctification a part of justification. Whereas such thoughts abound in the Young Luther, the mature reformer insisted that although justifying faith would always produce good works, such works were in no way a part of justification itself.

[41] Walther von Loewenich, *Luthers Theologia crucis* (München: Chr. Kaiser, 1929, 4th ed., 1954); tr. by Herbert J. A. Bouman, *Luther's Theology of the Cross* (Minneapolis: Augsburg, 1976). My position on this book is further clarified in my review in LQ 29 (1977): 196–99.

[42] Bengt Hägglund, "Die Rechtfertigungslehre in der frühen Reformationstheologie," *Theologische Beiträge*, Vol. VIII (1977), pp. 108–18. His position differs from mine in that he regards Luther's position of 1522 as fully Reformational whereas I see it as transitional. He develops the section of the *Rationis Latomianae confutatio* (1522) where Luther speaks of a twofold gift, the *gratia* and the *donum* (WA 8:103–7). Hägglund writes: "As Theobald Beer correctly perceived, we are here dealing in Reformational doctrine with a double justification: First the total forgiveness of sins through the mercy of God and then the new righteousness worked by the gifts of the Spirit, the daily battle against sin" (p. 116). In reply, I would say that although Hägglund is not completely wrong, the later Luther carefully separated the gift of the new life of sanctification from the initial gift of grace in justification. Luther's letter to the clergy of Lübeck from January 12, 1530, would appear to offer a better interpretation or else corrective for WA 8:106–7: ". . . primo loco autem caput doctrinae nostrae tractetis et plantetis, quod est de iustificatione nostri, aliena scilicet iustitia nempe Christi per fidem nobis donata, quae pervenit per gratiam iis, qui per legem prius territi et peccatorum conscientia afflicti suspirant redemptionem" (WA Br V:221, 15). The objection could of course be raised that we do not possess this letter in the holograph, but, in rejoinder, parallels could be produced.

[43] Seils, op. cit., p. 58.

[44] TR I:146, 12–16; TR II:281, 11–13; TR V:210, 6–16; WA 54:185–86.

[45] WA 52:5.

[46] The older Luther repeatedly said that his evangelical discovery consisted in learning how to distinguish properly between Law and Gospel. This conception today therefore seems to offer that hermeneutical principle which includes many other insights and provides the best procedure for interpreting the works of the Young as well as the Mature Luther. TR, No. 5518, presents an important statement of Luther which has come down in two of the best redactions—those of Heydenreich and Mathesius. The important parallels from Besold have been overlooked by many scholars, and therefore the resultant text is given here: "Ich war lange jrre, wuste nicht, wie ich drinne war. Ich roch wol etwas, ich wuste aber nicht, was es war, bis so lang das ich vber den *locum Rom. 1.* kam: *Iustus ex fide vivet.* Der halff mir. Da sahe ich, von welcher *iustitia* Paulus redet: Do stundt zuvor im text *iustitia*, da reimet ich das *abstractum* vnd *concretum* zusamen vnd wurde meiner sache gewis, lernte inter *iustitiam legis* vnd *euangelii* discernirn. Zuvor mangelte mir nichts, denn das ich kein *discrimen inter legem et euangelium* machte, hielt es alles vor eines *et dicebam Christum a Mose non differre nisi tempore et perfectione.* Aber do ich das *discrimen* fandt, *quod aliud esset lex, aliud euangelium,* do riß ich hindurch" (TR V:210; WA 48:617). For a parallel on "rhyming" the abstract and the concrete (the "concrete" is my sin and the "abstract" is God's grace), see a sermon from 1531: "Drumb ist das die kunst: *si consciencia laboraverit, discat non multum cum lege, sed cum gracia agere et dicat: Ego sum peccator, sed* ich reyme die gnade darczw. *Sed* ist die grosst kunst von eynander scheyden ßunde und gesecz und zwsammen reymen Ssunde und gnade" (WA 34/II:145, 29–146). This is from the Nürnberg text; the Rörer parallel renders "zwsammen reymen Ssunde und gnade" as "zusamen tragen *peccatum et gratiam*" (WA 34/II:145, 18–146).

[47] WA 54:179–87.

[48] TR I:47, 25; 62–3.

[49] CR 6:158; SA VI:323, 35.

[50] CR 6:155–70.

[51] Hartmann Grisar, *Luther,* Vol. I: *Luthers Werden. Grundlegung der Spaltung bis 1530* (Freiburg: Herder, 1911), pp. 171–79, 304–26. Vol. III: *Am Ende der Bahn—Rückblicke* (Freiburg: Herder, 1912), pp. 978–88. Excerpts in Lohse, *Durchbruch,* pp. 19–63. In spite of Grisar's bias against Luther, this large work retains its value. The picture of Luther as a psychotic was developed by the Danish psychiatrist, Paul J. Reiter, *Luthers Umwelt, Charakter und Psychose,* 2 vols. (Copenhagen: Leven & Munksgaard, 1937–41), by Erik H. Erikson, *Young Man Luther: A Study in Psychoanalysis and History* (New York: Norton, 1962), and in the Broadway drama by John Osborne, *Luther: A Play* (New York: New American Library, 1963).

[52] TR II, No. 1681.

[53] Grisar, Vol. I, pp. 316ff. (=Lohse, pp. 49ff.); Vol. III, pp. 978–88. Grisar distorted his source when he had Luther saying: "ich befand mich wie in einer Latrine und im Reiche des Teufels," taken out of this: "Eratque iustitia illa mea nihil aliud quam latrina et suavissimum regnum diaboli" (WA 40/I:137, 24–5; Lohse, p. 52). What Luther actually said was that his own righteousness (good works) seemed to him like a latrine and the most pleasant reign of the devil. Grisar's shorter biography was less scholarly and contained more invective than the larger work. See Hartmann Grisar, *Martin Luther: His Life and Work*, tr. from 2nd Ger. ed. by Frank J. Eble (St. Louis: Herder, 1930; reprint: New York, AMS, 1971). The psychological background (pp. 86–8) and the discovery in the tower (pp. 105–10) were written without sympathy for his subject.

[54] The various texts are conveniently brought together and analyzed in Ernst Kroker, "Luthers Tischreden als geschichtliche Quelle," LuJB 1 (1919): 114–16. The entire article (pp. 81–131) is indispensable for the study of the tower experience.

[55] Ibid., pp. 116–20. We are warned against judging Luther's vulgarisms in isolation from the general crudeness of his times by Heinrich Boehmer, *Luther in Light of Recent Research* (New York: Christian Herald, 1916), pp. 193–99. Some examples provide important parallels to the cloaca statement. Against his opponent, Alveld, in *De captivitate Babylonica:* "Praetereo caetera, ne te enecem sentina huius graveolentissimae cloacae," "I will pass over other things for fear I might asphyxiate you with the sewage of this stinking cloaca" (WA 6:500, 19). In a conversation of 1531 Luther remarked on the bravery of Joshua's soldiers and said: "Wenn ich da wer gewest, het ich fur furcht in die hosen geschissen," "Had I been there, I'd have shit in my pants" (TR I, No. 335). In a conversation of 1531 or 1532 Luther said that when the devil tempted him, he taunted Satan: "Leck mich in gem A[rsche]," "Lick me in the ass" (TR I:64, 16). Both of these comments are common in all-male company today. However, when Luther provided verses for the fecal woodcuts of Cranach mocking the papacy (WA 54:346–73 and appendix), he exceeded today's locker-room graffiti. Nevertheless, he not only described the pope but also himself in terms of "shit." See the strange conversation of 1542–1543: "Ich bin der reiffe dreck, so ist die welt das weite arschloch; drumb sein wir wol zu scheiden," "I am a ripe stool [i.e., in old age] and the world is the wide anus; therefore we soon will separate" (TR V, No. 5537). Cf.: "Deinde adorabunt nostra stercora" (TR II, No. 2616b). In Cruciger's Summer Postil of 1544 Luther is quoted as having said in a sermon: ". . . die Welt [ist] nicht anders denn ein großer Sewstal . . . ," ". . . the world is only a huge pigsty . . ." (WA 22:185, 5; WA 17/I:406, 29). Luther's crude language shocks our modern niceties, but it was part of the style of his age. Many parallels exist from as late a writer as Shakespeare.

[56] WA 54:179–87.

2

The "Catholic" Luther (1509–1518)

The Persistence of Medieval Concepts in the Young Luther

There has been an increasing awareness that the humanists and reformers of the sixteenth century cannot be adequately assessed except against the background from which they emerged. This means that men like Luther and Melanchthon must be studied in the context of their medieval predecessors as well as that of their contemporaries.[1] The neglect of such knowledge made it possible for capable scholars to confuse Luther's pre-Reformational works with his mature thought. In recent years there has been a growing trend to supply the needed studies of late medieval theology in its relation to the reformers.[2] Only when this task is at least partially completed will we be able to determine what was old and what was new in the thinkers of the sixteenth century.

Around 1513 Luther probably had a preliminary breakthrough in which he discovered that the righteousness of God is not merely punitive but also redemptive. But contrary to Karl Holl, Emanuel Hirsch, Erich Vogelsang, and others, this was not the definitive discovery of the evangelical concept. Rather, it was the recovery of insights taught by Augustine and held by many who followed him. Luther's exposition of Romans 1:17 in the *Lectures on Romans* (1515–1516) was surprisingly meager and lacking in the later evangelical doctrine. However, it did manifest the new insight that God's righteousness might not only judge but also save sinners.

The righteousness of God is indeed the cause of salvation. And here again the "righteousness of God" should not be taken for that by which he is righteous in himself, but as that by which we are justified by himself, which is done by means of faith in the Gospel. This is from Blessed Augustine, On the Spirit and the Letter, C. XI [18]: "Therefore it is called the righteousness of God because he makes them just by imparting it. For example, health is of the Lord, by which he makes them healthy."[3]

Here justification is definitely what Holl calls "analytic" in Luther as in Augustine. There is no trace of the "passive righteousness" of 1545.

As he gave it in his self-disclosure of 1545, Luther's own description of the discovery of 1518–1519 was completely different. Noting his difficulty with the "righteousness of God" prior to that discovery, he wrote:

I even hated that term, "Righteousness of God," which I had been taught, in the usage and custom of all the doctors, to understand philosophically concerning formal or active righteousness (as they call it), by which God is righteous, and punishes unrighteous sinners.[4]

Finally, after a long and arduous struggle, Luther came to the insight that justification does not depend upon righteousness within the individual, even though it might be effected by God Himself, but on the alien righteousness of Christ.

At last, by the mercy of God, after I had pored over this night and day, I came upon the context of the words, "In it the righteousness of God is revealed, as it is written, 'He who through faith is righteous shall live.'" There I began to understand the righteousness of God as that by which the righteous one lives by means of a gift of God, which is truly by faith. And this is the meaning: through the Gospel is revealed the righteousness of God, namely, the passive righteousness, by which merciful God justifies us through faith, as it is written: "He who through faith is righteous shall live." At that moment I felt that I had been born again, and that I had entered paradise itself through opened gates.[5]

From the standpoint of scientific history this primary testimony of Luther is the most important source available for tracing Luther's decisive discovery of the Gospel. It is true, of course, that there are some historical problems in interpreting the statement, but this does not excuse those who attempt to discard it. If we analyze the statement, there are two important items we should note. First, Luther here describes an experience of 1518–1519 in the later vocabulary of the 1530's. Second, he asserts that it consisted in the discovery that justification rests upon "passive righteousness"—that is, the substitutionary righteousness of Christ received as a free gift by faith—rather than upon an active righteousness that is worked within. To use the somewhat problematical terminology of Holl, Luther here states that through his evangelical discovery of 1518–1519 he moved from an "analytic" to a "synthetic" justification or, in other terminology, from an effective to a forensic concept. Prior to 1518 Luther's understanding had been largely medieval. But then a total break with medieval conceptions of justification as inner renewal took place.

Heinrich Bornkamm, in his youth a pupil of Holl, wrote a reply to Bizer's challenge in which he tried to be fair to his opponent while giving a scholarly consensus regarding Luther and the *iustitia Dei*:

> Regarding the sense of the discovery there is little serious difference, since Luther himself explained this clearly enough in his report [the Preface of 1545], in a number of table talks and in other testimonies.—*Iustitia Dei* designated not the condemning righteousness, not the divine attribute, but the righteousness which is given as the gift of God through faith, not the *iustitia activa* but the *iustitia passiva*, as he expressed it in 1545 with a term which can be documented after 1525.[6]

Although Bornkamm has recognized the dangers implicit in combining several experiences of Luther into one tower experience, he has here confused Luther's discovery of about 1513 (that the "righteousness of God" is not exclusively condemnatory but can also be redemptive) with that of 1518–1519 (that the "righteousness of God" is not intrinsic but extrinsic—that is, the substitutionary righteousness of Christ).[7] Long before, Heinrich Denifle had correctly noted that the former concept, recovered by Luther about 1513, had been held by a number of previous teachers in the Middle Ages. In his lectures on Romans and Galatians Luther certainly taught that the good works on which salvation is based are the gift of God, not the contribution of men. Thus, Holl's perception of the Young Luther's doctrine of justification as "analytic" was not far amiss. Luther taught in the *Lectures on Romans* that not *opera legis* (works of the Law) but *opera fidei* (works of faith), worked by the infused grace of God by the Holy Ghost, effect the *iustitia Dei* or justification.[8] But if salvation rested upon a righteousness within the believer, one could never be certain of his salvation. One could never be sure whether his faith was adequate or whether his works (even if worked by God) were in fact sufficient. He must inevitably confuse acceptance with spiritual attainment.[9] Luther's perplexity remained in the *Lectures on Romans*, even after the time Bornkamm thought the breakthrough had taken place.[10] This was clearly manifest when Luther wrote:

> We are absolutely not ever able to know whether we are justified or whether we believe. Therefore, just so we estimate that our works are works of the Law and we sinners humbly desire to be justified by his mercy.[11]

Luther was saying that one could never know whether the measure of good works needed to achieve a favorable verdict (for an "analytic" justification) was adequate. Apparently, one's justification could not be determined until one was perfected in the hereafter. One could therefore have no full assurance or certainty of his salvation. After the breakthrough of 1518–1519 Luther emphatically rejected this view and vigorously affirmed the certitude of faith. This change in Luther, after which he proclaimed that the believing sinner is certain of his justification and eternal salvation, was strongly opposed by his Roman Catholic opponents and has remained a problem in the ecumenical discussions today. Subsequent controversies underscore the importance of this change in Luther.

Meanwhile, at the time of the *Lectures on Romans* or the publication of the *Ninety-Five Theses*, Luther evidenced many aspects of "Catholic" religion. He continued to regard the authority of the Roman Church above that of the Bible, held daily masses for the living and the dead, conveyed indulgences on the people, taught the existence of purgatory, espoused the medieval teaching of transubstantiation, venerated the Blessed Virgin Mary, and invoked the saints.[12] Even as late as 1520 Luther defended occasional masses for the dead.[13] Into that year he continued keeping the seven canonical hours and reading his breviary until through pressure of other duties he fell so far behind that he was unable to catch up again.[14] If other accounts are correct, he did not abandon the reading of private masses until 1522.[15] Years later he confessed: "What was I doing and how did I live in the monastery, when for fifteen years I daily crucified Christ and pursued all manner of idolatry!"[16] Luther was ordained to the priesthood in 1507. Therefore, if he offered the sacrifice of the mass for fifteen years, it was not until 1522 that he completely discontinued this practice which so grossly conflicted with Reformational teaching. This underscores our contention that the later years of Luther must establish the norm for the fully Reformational teaching.

Those who advocate dating the evangelical breakthrough in 1513 concur that that breakthrough furnished Luther with the Reformational understanding of Romans 1:17: "For therein is the righteousness of God revealed from faith to faith: as it is written, The just shall live by faith [Hab. 2:4]." As Kurt Aland has noted, if Luther came to his remarkable discovery as early as 1513, it is very strange that he did not reveal or share those new insights until the Indulgence Controversy broke out.[17] But as a matter of fact, the new understanding of Romans 1:17 did not appear in Luther before 1518. The quotation from Habakkuk 2:4 is cited in the New Testament not only in Romans 1:17 but also in Galatians 3:11 and Hebrews 10:38. Yet in his expositions of these Epistles between 1515 and 1518, Luther seemed unable to explain those words. In the various comments on Romans the words were treated without the evangelical insight,[18] which is also true of the gloss to Galatians 3:11.[19] In the scholia to Galatians 3:11 and Hebrews 10:38 Luther skipped the *Locus classicus* of Reformational doctrine without even mentioning this crucial verse.[20] But in the glosses to Hebrews 10:38 he seems to have made some progress toward the later evangelical position.[21] The Latin text of the word, "Now the just shall live by faith," is written in widely-spaced lines, leaving space for the interlinear gloss: "He who fulfills the commandments of God not by works but by faith."[22] This comment is not sufficiently explicit to determine that it is any advance over the distinction between *opera legis* and *opera fidei*, an early forerunner of the Reformational distinction of Law and Gospel, and therefore cannot be pressed.[23] But the annotation written in the margin seems to represent a significant advance over anything Luther had said before early 1518—the time when he would have discussed Hebrews 10:38.[24] This comment is as follows:

> These are words of consolation, of necessity for those who suffer, lest they lose their faith. For faith, that is the life of the Christian, is the operation of God more than of us, that is, our most genuine suffering.[25]

In other words, in the Christian life, which Luther sees here under the context of his *Theologia crucis*, one does not lose heart in suffering, because God has promised that those who are just shall be able to endure by faith. Even this significant statement does not appear to solve the problem of the righteousness of God over against the sinner's plight. Instead, it seems to support Luther's later remark that, after completing the *Lectures on Hebrews*, he was still torn by an ardent desire to understand the *iustitia Dei*.[26] Moreover, this gloss has come to us only in the recension of the unreliable Aurifaber.[27] There is no proof that it stemmed from the time of the lectures (early 1518). Aurifaber's written source is unknown, and the textual problem is compounded by our knowledge that not only did Aurifaber add foreign material to his texts to make them more useful, but that Amsdorf, who lectured on Hebrews in 1521, had himself made corrections of the text of Luther's *Lectures on Hebrews*.[28] From the standpoint of strict historical criticism we must therefore say that we have no treatment from Luther of the classical passage on justification (Hab. 2:4; Rom. 1:17) in his lectures on Romans 1:17, Galatians 3:11, or Hebrews 10:38.

Another indication that Luther's writings prior to 1520 contained much "Catholic" material which the mature reformer could not accept is given in his autobiographical *Preface* of 1545. Luther had long resisted the project of publishing an edition of his collected works but had finally relented. The new edition appeared in separate sections for his German and his Latin works, with the first volume of the German works issued in 1539 and the Latin works beginning in 1545. Luther saw only the first volume of each section go to press. The earliest work in the 1539 volume went back to only 1522. But the 1545 volume reached back from the year 1516 until 1520 and included a period the Mature Luther regarded as pre-Reformational.[29] He therefore felt impelled to warn the readers in his *Preface* lest they be misled by these "Catholic" writings.

> ... I beg the pious reader ... that he read those things with judgment, yes, with deep pity. And may he be mindful that I was at one time, when I got involved in that matter, a monk and senseless papist, like a drunk man, literally buried in the teachings of the pope ... So you will find in those my earlier writings many and great things which I humbly conceded to the pope, things which in my later writings and later times I hold to be the worst blasphemy and abomination and which I relentlessly attack. ... Therefore, when in the year 1517 indulgences were peddled (I would like to have said 'proclaimed') in these parts for most shameful gain, I was then a preacher, a young doctor of theology as it is said. I began to advise the people and to counsel them not to give ear to the harangue of the peddlers. ...[30] ... Treated contemptuously, I published the *Indulgence Theses*, the *Sermon on Indulgences and Grace*, and the *Explanations of the Ninety-Five Theses*. In these I came out for the honor of the pope, writing that indulgences should certainly not be condemned, but that good works of charity should be preferred to them.[31] ... I had then already [by July 1519] read and taught the Holy Scriptures most diligently privately and publicly for seven years, so that I knew them nearly all by heart. By then I had also drunk thirstily of the elementary knowledge of Christ and faith, namely, that we are made righteous and saved, not by works, but by faith in Christ ... I had already defended publicly the proposition that the pope is not the head of the church by divine right, but I had not yet drawn the conclusion that the pope must necessarily be of the devil. ...[32]

These words are most destructive to Holl's interpretation of Luther. This fact led Holl to impugn their reliability in his assertion that they were from the failing memory of an aging Luther. However, there is no indication of senility in the *Preface* of 1545, and the facts and dates discussed there by Luther appear to be reliable and to accord with other primary evidence.[33] Let us turn to some of the parallel statements by the Mature Luther, which will show us that the testimony in the *Preface* was not an isolated occurrence but was consistent with his thinking after 1527.

The so-called *Large Commentary on Galatians* presents the following remark of Luther from July 1531:

> Formerly when I was a new theologian and doctor, Paul seemed to me to be very foolish when he glorified his own vocation throughout his Epistles. I did not understand his reason. I was indeed ignorant that the ministry of the Word is so great a thing. I understood nothing concerning the doctrines of faith and true knowledge. . . .[34]

This disclaimer applies to the years immediately following 1512. A month earlier in 1531, however, Luther had remarked that his theology was only incipient in 1519: "I had not realized that my first Commentary on Galatians was so weak. Oh, it is of no more use for this generation! It was only my very first light against confidence in works."[35] Luther did not deny that the earlier *Commentary on Galatians* had contained some good theological insights, but he called it an inferior work with only the first light after his evangelical breakthrough (*tantum prima lucta mea*) following the night of trusting in works. Here is a direct parallel to the remark in the *Preface* of 1545 that by 1519 he had "hungrily devoured the first fruits of the knowledge and faith of Christ" (*primitias cognitionis et fidei Christi*). And if he had found only the first light in a breakthrough shortly before revising his *Lectures on Galatians* (1519), it follows that prior works were essentially "Catholic" or pre-Reformational in Luther's opinion by 1531.

One of the signs that Luther recognized an important change in his thinking after 1518 is seen in the number of works which he substantially revised and republished after that time. He replaced the *Lectures on the Psalms* of 1513–1516 with the *Operationes in Psalmos* of 1519–1521,[36] his *Treatise on Threefold Righteousness* of 1518 with the *Treatise on Twofold Righteousness* of 1519,[37] and his *Seven Penitential Psalms* of 1517[38] with a thorough revision eight years later.[39] This all corroborates the *Preface* of 1545, where he indicated a sweeping change in 1518–1519.

Holl paid the price for his disrespect of so important a source as the *Preface* of 1545. There Luther had clearly said that his evangelical discovery was the insight that the saving righteousness in justification is passive—that is, the righteousness of Christ imputed to the believing sinner. He had then added that he had found something similar in Augustine's great work, *De Spiritu et Litera*, a welcome confirmation of his discovery, but that Augustine had not clearly explained the concept of imputation.[40] Holl attributed this statement to the addled thinking of an aged man, branded justification by imputation as "synthetic," delusive, and Melanchthonian,[41] and in its place set up an "analytic" doctrine drawn from the teachings on justification in the Young Luther (mainly between 1513 and 1518). Holl misled himself and other brilliant scholars into thinking that the discovery of the tower experience, which they dated about 1513, was that the righteousness of God (*iustitia Dei*) described in Romans 1:17 was not the punitive but the saving righteousness of God. Although Luther may have first learned that in 1513, it was not the Reformational discovery but the adoption of "Catholic" views going back to Augustine and earlier. Holl transformed Luther's evangelical discovery into the mere recovery of what "Catholic" theologians had known from the beginning, as Roman Catholic critics such as Denifle had abundantly proved.[42] Luther scholars were thereby sidetracked into fruitless interconfessional polemics and diverted from the true nature of Luther's monumental breakthrough. As Luther himself made abundantly clear, it was his discovery of the difference between an active and a passive righteousness that changed his whole life, not his rediscovery of the difference between punitive and saving righteousness. Assuming that an important rediscovery took place about 1513, we might say that for the next five years he developed his views of justification in full accord with the "Catholic" teaching from the past. This view of the Young Luther presented two principal ideas. First, works of faith (*opera fidei*) worked by God provided the making righteous (*iustum facere*) upon which the favorable judgment of justification was based, not works of the Law worked by man (*opera legis*). Second, in justification the sinner completely humbled himself (*humiliatio*) by "justifying" God's just sentence as Judge (*iustificatio passiva*), and therefore God in return justified the sinner (*iustificatio activa*). These concepts were accompanied by a medieval understanding of faith, grace, and righteousness, and were organized within the concept of Luther's famous *Theologia crucis*. In any case, when Holl rejected the Mature Luther and based his view of "analytic" justification on the works of the Young Luther, he was confusing "Catholic" doctrine with the teachings of the Reformation. We shall find abundant proof for our position in the succeeding pages of this volume.

The Problem of Neoplatonism in the Young Luther

The Mature Luther avoided a sharp dichotomy between the body and the spirit. In his understanding of the sacrament, as well as in his attitude toward creation, he had a positive attitude toward the material world. He knew of no revelation of God apart from the Incarnation—the infant Christ-Child snuggled on his mother's breast. Neoplatonism, to the contrary, takes a negative attitude toward creation and exalts spiritual above material things. It is no secret that scholars have found traces of the teachings of Pseudo-Dionysius the Areopagite as well as other Neoplatonists in the Young Luther. There are three possible ways in which this phenomenon can be dealt with. We may simply deny that Luther ever held Neoplatonic teachings on the ground that they conflict with Reformational teachings. Or we can defend these teachings and extend them to the Mature Luther while disarming them of their obvious intent. Or else we can treat them developmentally as stages in his early career which he later overcame. The first two options have the obvious disadvantage of avoiding rather than confronting the evidence. Accordingly, we shall reject them in order to follow the developmental approach.

Perhaps the finest study that has been published on Luther's early Neoplatonism is the small book by August Wilhelm Hunzinger, *Luther's Neuplatonismus in der Psalmenvorlesung von 1513–1516* (1906).[43] Despite the fact that Hunzinger's findings have been uncongenial to Luther researchers and have been relegated to the background, one must agree with the judgment of Wilhelm Link and Heiko Oberman that the book needs to be removed from its obscurity and studied today.[44] However, when this is done it yields results at variance with the position of these two writers. It is important to note Hunzinger's background. The place of his birth and theological training (Mecklenburg and Rostock University under Wilhelm Walther), his teaching positions (Leipzig and Erlangen), the scene of his pastoral ministry and early death (Hamburg)—all underscore his orientation as a marked Lutheran by persuasion. He regarded forensic justification as a central concern for the Mature Luther and therefore found that the first lectures on the Psalms were frankly pre-Reformational and Neoplatonic. Hunzinger showed that the early *Dictata super Psalterium* were completely dominated by an Augustinian form of Neoplatonism[45] which Luther had to overcome and leave behind him before he became the reformer.[46] In a finding which surprisingly anticipated the recent conclusions of Cranz,[47] Hunzinger related the Neoplatonic asceticism of the Young Luther to the monastic asceticism which the reformer also overcame a few years later when he came to his fully Reformational insights.[48] In those early years Luther followed the Neoplatonic distinctions between visible and invisible, corporeal and spiritual, sensible and intelligible, exterior and interior, superior and inferior, present and future, terrestrial and celestial in a philosophical system which can in no way be harmonized with his later thinking.[49]

Luther's evangelical breakthrough of 1518–1519 would involve the overcoming of the intellectualistic faith-concept of Neoplatonism,[50] coinciding with the explicit rejection of Pseudo-Dionysius the Areopagite.[51] But during the first lectures on the Psalter (1513–1515) Luther had taken a completely different attitude in the scholium to Psalm 18:11 (17:12, Vulg.): "He made darkness his secret place . . ."

> 'The hiding-place of God is darkness': Firstly, because he dwells in faith by way of mystery and darkness. Secondly, because 'He dwells in inaccessible light,' and thus no mind is able to reach him, unless he lay aside his own light and be aided by a higher light. Accordingly, the Blessed Dionysius teaches that one steps into anagogical darkness and ascends by means of negations. Because God in this way is abscondite and incomprehensible. Thirdly, the mystery of the incarnation is able to be understood. Because he lies hidden in humanity, which is his darkness, in which he is not able to be seen or even heard. . . .[52]

Here Luther is not merely following the language of the Areopagite but is distorting Scripture in the light of Neoplatonism.[53] In his works after 1518, Luther almost never spoke of the Incarnation as in any way obscuring God but as showing the full revelation of the Father's love. Luther planned to publish his lectures on the Psalter and began revising them in 1519. But by then he had come to his evangelical discovery, and the notions of the *Dictata super Psalterium* were left behind him. It is instructive to compare his interpretation of Psalm 18:11 in the *Dictata* with that in the new *Operationes in Psalmos* (1519–1521). Luther did not repeat a single sentence or retain a single concept in the revision but rewrote it completely.[54]

In view of this, we shall not be surprised to discover that the Reformational concept of faith, so indispensable to the doctrine of justification by faith, was lacking in these works before 1518. By 1519, when Luther revised his *Dictata super Psalterium*, faith had become *fiducia—trust* in God. Under his earlier Neoplatonism the concept of faith had been more an intellectual exercise than trust in divine love. Luther's exposition of Psalm 31:7 (30:7, Vulg.) is a case in point: "'But I will hope in the Lord,' i.e. in spiritualities, with which the Lord of truth exists, because these are truths and verities. . . .'"[55] Hunzinger is certainly right when he observes that in these words hope in God is the same as hope in spiritualities, although, as the Lord of truth, He is simultaneously distinguished from truths and verities.

> Therefore God has a double position, as Lord of truth, over against the spiritualities, which are truths and verities. On the one hand he is their highest and personal point, in which the spiritualities come together, so that to hope in the spiritualities is the same as to hope in the Lord. On the other hand, these spiritualities are relatively independent and intelligible entities (verities=Ideas, Forms, Reasons) which are distinguished from God and compose the invisible creative world surrounding God and with which he has fellowship and stands in a covenant. Beyond doubt Platonic speculation, even if unconscious, lies here at the basis . . . according to which the archetypes (Ideas, Verities) of the eternal truths (Ideas), which come to expression in the intelligible world, are contained within God.[56]

Thus, in Luther's *Dictata* "faith" is in peril of being confused with the epistemology of Neoplatonic philosophy. Faith becomes the perception of the invisible, the intelligible, the spiritual. Out of such an object of faith, Hunzinger wrote, ". . . the concept of faith was derived. Therefore everything specifically Christian is lacking in this concept of faith. The nature of faith is placed in its mere relationship with that which is simply invisible."[57] It appears that his judgment of the early Luther was not too harsh. There was no way from such a concept to the doctrine of justification by faith alone. The later rejection of Luther's *sola fide* by his Roman Catholic contemporaries with their Neoplatonic concepts is therefore not surprising.

Careful historians are aware of a transitional or middle period in Luther's development, starting with the evangelical breakthrough of 1518–1519 and extending for a few years or until the mature period, which begins about 1527. Luther produced a number of important works during these years, including revisions of his sermon on righteousness, his exposition of the Penitential Psalms, and his lectures on the Psalms and Galatians. These works showed the new understanding of the righteousness of God. At the same time, they often contained vestiges of his pre-Reformational teachings. For example, in his *Treatise on Christian Liberty* (1520) Luther made the following statement with a relic of his earlier Neoplatonism:

> . . . Every Christian is of two natures, spiritual and bodily. According to the soul he is called a spiritual, new, and inward man; according to his flesh and blood, he is called a bodily, old, and outward man. Because of this difference they are spoken of in the Scriptures, where they stand in stark contradiction to one another, concerning liberty and servitude.[58]

Luther carried this dichotomy between body and soul further when he said that things done for the body could not help the soul and that what happened to the body would not harm the soul.[59] Perhaps these words had a bearing on Zwingli's later teaching that a physical substance such as bread could not convey a spiritual gift such as the body of Christ. In any case, Luther's statement from 1520 was an evidence of the transition he was undergoing. This sharp dichotomy between body and soul was a temporary relic which does not fit his thinking from 1519 to 1526 as a whole.

A more important phenomenon was the persistence of some Neoplatonic concepts into Luther's later years in his teaching on justification, the sacraments, and sanctification. His close co-worker, the humanist Melanchthon, held that philosophy should stand at the service of the Reformational movement as the handmaid of the Gospel. Through logic and rhetoric, philosophy should help in defining and proclaiming the evangelical message. Philosophy should never be allowed to determine the content of that message but should only serve its outward form. Whether it was possible for Melanchthon to implement such a program is a complicated problem we cannot deal with at the moment. Our question is whether Luther, like Melanchthon, tried to limit the influence of philosophy to the outer form of his teaching or whether he allowed it to alter the content of his doctrine as well. In separate studies Wilhelm Maurer has extensively researched the effects of Neoplatonism in both Melanchthon[60] and Luther. He has concluded that Luther's use after 1518 of mystic imagery or of words such as *raptus* or *exstasis* was a matter of medieval vestiges in form which did not affect the content of his teaching.[61] The primary evidence supports Maurer.

> Luther's application of bridal mysticism is an interesting example of Neoplatonic influence. It did not, however, alter the content of his doctrine of justification. Of course, he could have taken this directly from the Scriptures since the concept itself is Biblical. Using the relationship of bride and groom as an example of that between Christ and the believer, however, entered Luther's early works from previous writers such as Augustine and Bernard of Clairvaux. This symbolical language was not discarded but adapted to the new insights gained in his evangelical breakthrough in what Luther called the *fröhlicher Wechsel*—the joyful exchange between Christ and the believer.[62] In the *Treatise on Christian Liberty* he wrote:

Faith . . . unites the soul with Christ like a bride with her bridegroom. As St. Paul says [Eph. 5:30], out of this marriage it follows that Christ and the soul become one body; that which belongs to both, good or bad, becomes the property of both. That which Christ has belongs to the believing soul, and what the soul has belongs to Christ. Christ has all good things and salvation; these belong to the soul. The soul has all sort of vice and sin; these become the property of Christ. Here begins the joyful exchange and giving of the ring. . . . Is this not a joyful deal where the rich, noble, and faithful bridegroom Christ leads the poor, despised, unpleasant little harlot into marriage, frees her from all evil, and adorns her with all goods? Thus it is not possible that her sins should damn her, for they all lie upon Christ and have been destroyed by him. Thus she has so rich a righteousness in her bridegroom that she can overcome all sin, even if it already lies upon her.[63]

For several years this Christological concept in mystical language played an important role in Luther's thinking. It is found in his preaching, in his exegetical lectures such as the *Operationes in Psalmos*, and in his *Rationis Latomianae confutatio* (1521) before it gradually recedes again. The fact that it later reappeared in the doctrine of the *Unio mystica* under Lutheran Orthodoxy shows its permanent significance. The fact that it was removed from the article on justification in the seventeenth century and given a place of its own under the "Order of Salvation" reveals the problems it was felt to cause. In his polemic against Latomus, Luther had developed ideas which went back to Athanasius in the fourth century, and before him to Irenaeus' doctrine of the *anakephalaiosis*. The joyful exchange was founded in the Incarnation. God's Son became flesh (*incarnatus*) so that men might be God's sons (*deificatus*). Thereby Christ was made sin (*impeccatificatus*) in order that man might be forgiven by divine grace (*gratificatus*).[64] In later Lutheran dogmatics these ideas would be assigned to Christology. Closely related to these ideas was Luther's discussion of the inner renewal of the believer in his treatise against Latomus. In a penetrating analysis of the terms *donum* (gift) and *gratia* (grace) in this treatise, Bengt Hägglund has suggested that justification for Luther meant both that the sinner was *declared* righteous (wrath replaced by *gratia*) and also *made* righteous (sinful corruption replaced by the *donum*). Hägglund sees the accent placed upon a sanative righteousness—an actual healing from sin. He writes:

> The striking thing is that Luther here describes the inner change, the incipient healing from corruption which he also terms *iustitia*, not merely as a fruit of faith, but also connects it with faith in such a way that it is a presupposition of grace. Faith as the gift of God, *donum dei*, is at the same time both righteousness and a reason for God's not reckoning the sin which remains as sin, a reason that the wrath of God is removed.[65]

This conclusion of Hägglund may surprise many readers. However, his analysis of Luther in 1521 seems to be supported by the sources he refers to. For instance, Luther reached back to the allegorical interpretation of the Good Samaritan as he had employed it in the early *Lectures on Romans*.[66] He wrote:

> Here the parable concerning the half-dead man who was cured by the Samaritan applies as a whole and in the first place. He was not healed all at once, but at once he began to be cured. When the Levite and the priest as ministers of the Law saw him they did not help him. The Law, as I said, serves to reveal sin, but Christ heals through faith and leads back to the grace of God.[67]

As we have noted elsewhere, in the polemic against Latomus of 1522 we are dealing with Luther in transition. In his *Lectures on Romans* Luther had earlier placed sanative healing in the center of his doctrine of justification. But this was no longer his intention in 1522. Now justification was separate from and preceded the sanative healing. Like good works, this was the fruit of faith. In later years Luther would not normally describe the new life of the regenerate as sanative healing. Rather, he would use a concept which later theologians called "sanctification." The distinction between justification and sanctification was present in the Mature Luther even though such terminology was not characteristic of his writings.

Another Look at the *Ninety-Five Theses*: Cause, Not Effect, of Luther's New Understanding of Justification

The customary interpretation, which attributes an evangelical understanding of justification to Luther from 1513 onward, necessarily calls for the reflection of that doctrine and its consequences in Luther's pronouncements on the indulgence in 1517 and 1518. Strangely enough, Luther's view of sin, penance, and justification at the time of the Indulgence Controversy does not seem to have significantly differed from that of the Roman Church. I have treated this phenomenon at greater length elsewhere.[68]

We have already noted that the older Luther repeatedly said he had made shameful concessions to the papal doctrine of the indulgence at the time he wrote the *Ninety-Five Theses*. The text of the *Theses* confirms this assertion. Even Luther's commentary on the *Theses* in his much-neglected *Resolutiones disputationum de indulgentiarum virtute*, from the spring of 1518, reflects his pre-Reformational thinking.[69] Although the *Indulgence Theses* are often mentioned, they have seldom been studied intensively.

The Latin phrase, *poenitentiam agere*, is a key to interpreting the *Ninety-Five Theses*. It can mean either "repent" or "do penance." Protestant scholars commonly give it a Reformational twist by translating it as "repent."[70] However, the whole context of the *Theses*, in which Luther is arguing for the superiority of deeds of penance over the purchase of indulgences,[71] suggests that *poenitentiam agere* here means "do penance." The *Theses* presuppose the medieval notion of purgatory, earth, and heaven. The question of which aspects of penance are done on earth and which are done in purgatory is an important theme of the *Indulgence Theses*.[72] The insistence that the humble believer prefers the agony of doing penance to the easy way of buying indulgences,[73] and the way of suffering to the security proclaimed by false preachers,[74] links the *Theses* with Luther's *Theologia crucis* of that period. In any case, the medieval doctrine of penance, which still marked his theology at this time, cannot be harmonized with the later evangelical doctrine of justification. In consonance with the "Catholic" position, Luther still taught that two things take place in the sacrament of penance. The guilt of sin (*culpa*) is removed by forgiveness or non-imputation, while the penalty of sin (*poena*) is removed by the believer in acts of penance. Contrariwise, Protestant teaching knows of no punishment that must be removed by the good works of the believing sinner after his sin has been forgiven.

Another evidence that Luther was fully "Catholic" in 1517 is his total obedience to the pope. Although by April 1518 Luther was beginning to feel the strain between his emerging concept of the passive righteousness of God[75] and the Roman Catholic doctrine of the indulgence,[76] he resolutely held the dogma that the teaching authority of the pope stood higher than his own understanding of Scripture. He believed that Christians were obligated to receive the indulgence sellers respectfully and to accept the apostolic verity of papal indulgences.[77] This fidelity to papal authority made it impossible for Luther to find certainty of salvation until after the fires of controversy had changed his whole outlook. If Luther had not been relentlessly attacked by men like Tetzel, Eck, and Cajetan, he might never have struggled through to his evangelical understanding of justification or to the conviction that the authority of the Bible is higher than that of the church. In fact, Melanchthon asserted the Protestant position of the superior authority of the Scriptures earlier than Luther.[78] Before 1519 Luther still regarded churchly authority over that of the Bible. This is why he defended indulgences.[79] His statements in the *Theses* should not be interpreted as satirical, as some have understood them, but should be received at face value. Testimonies from 1517–1518 as well as from later years show that Luther saw himself as a loyal "Catholic" at the time of the Indulgence Controversy. His view of justification was still based on works of faith. The controversy was the cause, not the result, of his evangelical discovery.

Notes

[1] In my dissertation of 1955, op. cit., I pointed out the need to study the reformers in the light of their medieval background (pp. 71ff., 86ff., 119ff.). Although earlier writers such as Hunzinger, R. Seeberg, Holl, Scheel, and Link had laid the groundwork, information on the "forerunners" of the Reformation was scarce at that time. The increase of such studies since then has been gratifying.

[2] The number of recent studies which have closed the gap between medieval and Reformation leaders is so great that we can only refer to a few. First and foremost, one thinks of Heiko A. Oberman, *The Harvest of Medieval Theology: Gabriel Biel and Late Medieval Nominalism*, 2nd ed. (Grand Rapids: Eerdmans, 1967), and then of the following works by his pupils: Reinhard Schwarz, *Fides, spes und caritas beim jungen Luther unter besonderer* Berücksichtigung der mittelalterlichen Tradition (Berlin: DeGruyter, 1962). Jane Dempsey Douglass, *Justification in Late Medieval Preaching: A Study of John Geiler of Keisersberg* (Leiden: Brill, 1966). David C. Steinmetz, *Misericordia Dei: The Theology of Johannes von Staupitz in Its Late Medieval Setting* (Leiden: Brill, 1968). Steven E. Ozment, *Homo Spiritualis. A Comparative Study of the Anthropology of Johannes Tauler, Jean Gerson and Martin Luther (1509–16) in the Context of Their Theological Thought* (Leiden: Brill, 1969). James Samuel Preus, *From Shadow to Promise: Old Testament Interpretation from Augustine to the Young Luther* (Cambridge: Harvard University Press, 1969). Scott H. Hendrix, *Ecclesia in Via: Ecclesiological Developments in the Medieval*

Psalms Exegesis and the Dictata super Psalterium (1513–1515) of Martin Luther
(Leiden: Brill, 1974). Besides the Oberman school, see the following: Lewis
W. Spitz, *The Religious Renaissance of the German Humanists* (Cambridge:
Howard University Press, 1963). Quirinius Breen, *Christianity and Humanism:
Studies in the History of Ideas* (Grand Rapids: Eerdmans, 1968). Wilhelm
Maurer, *Der junge Melanchthon zwischen Humanismus und Reformation,*
2 vols. (Göttingen: Vandenhoeck & Ruprecht, 1967–69). Bengt Hägglund,
The Background of Luther's Doctrine of Justification in Late Medieval Theology,
No. 18 in Historical Series, Facet Books (Philadelphia: Fortress, 1971).

[3] WA 56:172, 3.

[4] WA 54:185.

[5] Ibid., p. 186.

[6] Heinrich Bornkamm, "Zur Frage der Iustitia Dei beim jungen Luther,"
ARG 52 (1961): 16–44; ARG 53 (1962): 1–60. Revised and reprinted in Lohse,
pp. 289–383. My citation is found on the first page of each edition.

[7] This mistake of interpreting Luther's term, "the righteousness of God,"
was of course aided by a certain lack of clarity in his *Preface* of 1545. Previous
to 1518–1519 Luther had known of a saving righteousness which justified
by creating good works (*opera fidei*) within the believer, as Karl Holl had
pointed out. A confusion of this point is almost general in the Luther literature, and this mistake has often been the cause for the rejection of the later
dating of the evangelical discovery. For example, Gerhard Pfeiffer thinks that
the "righteousness of God" of Luther's *Preface* means "that the righteousness
of God is the basis of our salvation. Then however the righteousness of God
must not be conceived as that in which God himself is just, but as that through
which we are justified by him." Pfeiffer documents this out of the lectures on
Romans (WA 56:171f.). His interpretation of the lectures is correct, but this
was not what Luther intended to give as his discovery in the *Preface* of 1545.
See Pfeiffer, "Das Ringen des jungen Luther um die Gerechtigkeit Gottes,"
LuJB 26 (1959): 43; reprinted in Lohse, p. 186.

[8] WA 56:254f., 264f.

[9] Ibid., p. 252, 17.

[10] WA 54:186, 5.

[11] WA 56:252, 17.

[12] WA 2:749, 10.

[13] WA 6:444–45.

[14] TR II:11, 5.

[15] DZLE:111, 23; 207, 11.

[16] WA 21:486.

[17] Kurt Aland, *Der Weg zur Reformation,* pp. 6, 51-2.

[18] WA 56:10–11, 171–73; WA 57/I:14, 133–34.

[19] WA 57/II:23.

[20] See ibid., p. 80; WA 57/III:226.

[21] WA 57/III:60–61.

[22] Ibid., p. 60, 20.

[23] On the early distinction between *opera legis* and *opera fidei*, see the *Disputatio contra scholasticam theologiam* (1517): "Maledicti sunt omnes, qui operantur opera legis. Benedicti sunt omnes, qui operantur opera gratiae dei" (WA 1:228, 3). Cf. my dissertation, op. cit., pp. 35ff., 90f.

[24] WA 57/III:iv–v, xviii–xix.

[25] Ibid., pp. 60–61.

[26] WA 54:185, 13.

[27] WA 57/III:xv.

[28] Ibid., pp. xxiv–xxv.

[29] For the reader without access to the volumes of the Wittenberg edition, its contents can conveniently be identified by referring to Aland, *Hilfsbuch*, pp. 549–67.

[30] WA 54:179–80.

[31] Ibid., p. 180.

[32] Ibid., pp. 183–84.

[33] See the fine study by Beate Köster, "Bemerkungen zum zeitlichen Ansatz des reformatorischen Durchbruchs bei Martin Luther," ZKG 85 (1975): 208.

[34] WA 40/I:63, 19.

[35] TR II:281, 11.

[36] WA 5.

[37] WA 2.

[38] WA 1.

[39] WA 18.

[40] WA 54:186.

[41] In his essay, "The Doctrine of Justification in the Light of the History of Protestantism" (1906, 1922), Holl wrote: "The point at which they all [scil., the nineteenth-century thinkers] took offense was the concept of the righteousness of God that had come out of Melanchthon's teaching. (For they only knew the Melanchthonian form; Luther himself was no longer understood, even by the 'Lutheran' theologians). This concept was the unreasonable demand that one subject God to a judgment [scil., that the unrighteous was righteous] which denied the obvious facts" (Holl, *Gesammelte Aufsätze*, Vol. III, pp. 550–51). But Holl here betrays that he has overlooked the real significance of Luther's *simul justus et peccator* in the later, fully Reformational connotation; in the eyes of man or for human reason the justified sinner is really a sinner, but simultaneously and in the divine dimension that same sinner is fully just and free of sin. This view of Melanchthon was also upheld by Luther. See esp. his many sermons on Luke 18:9–14: after God declared the filthy publican righteous, he should no longer be called a sinner (WA 17/I:404, 3–5; WA 27:315f.; WA 15:675, 19).

[42] See Holl, *Gesammelte Aufsätze*, Vol. I, pp. 193–99; Vol. III, p. 187.

[43] August Wilhelm Hunzinger, *Lutherstudien*. Erstes Heft: *Luthers Neuplatonismus in der Psalmenvorlesung von 1513–1516* (Leipzig: A. Deichert, 1906). This book has been undeservedly neglected by Luther scholars who have overlooked the fact that the Young Luther was strongly dominated by Neoplatonism. Among the many criticisms, see Gerhard Ebeling, "Die Anfänge von Luthers Hermeneutik," ZThK 48 (1951): 188–89; Seils, op. cit., p. 34. Another assertion of Neoplatonism in the Young Luther is given in Will-Erich Peuckert, *Die großes Wende*, Vol. II (Darmstadt: Wissenschaftliche Buchgesellschaft, 1966), pp. 534–44.

[44] Link, op. cit., pp. 31f. Heiko A. Oberman, "Simul gemitus et raptus: Luther und die Mystik," *The Church, Mysticism, Sanctification and the Natural in Luther's Thought*, ed. Ivar Asheim (Philadephia: Fortress, 1967), p. 46, f.n. 92. Oberman's essay presents some problems. The title itself is an unfortunate parody of Luther's famous paradox and, despite Oberman's hopes, really cannot be made a new parallel to the *simul justus et peccator* (p. 59). In his attempt to level off the differences in the attitude toward mysticism in the Young and Mature Luther, Oberman constantly begs his question. He writes: "Bernd Moeller collected a list of 26 references to Tauler from 1515–44, all of which are positive. We believe that Tauler was and remained highly significant for Luther . . ." (p. 37). However, the evidence goes against Oberman. Twenty-three of the references are confined to 1515–1522, and of the other three, all of which come from the hands of men other than Luther, two are noncommittal (WA 40/I:520, 2; 37:314, 14ff.) and one rejects Tauler (WA 52:179, 22). These three references to Tauler between 1523–1546 can hardly be called a whole-hearted endorsement. My thanks to Moeller in kindly sending me a photocopy of the quoted essay, "Tauler und Luther," *La Mystique Rhéenane* (Paris, 1963), pp. 157–68; the references to Tauler are given p. 158, n. 3, to which Moeller added two references he had discovered prior to 1522.

[45] Hunzinger, p. 73.

[46] Ibid., p. vii.

[47] Ibid., op. cit., pp. 4–5.

[48] Ibid., p. 3.

[49] Ibid., pp. 5–7.

[50] Cf. ibid., pp. 65–72.

[51] WA 5:163, 17–29; 503, 9–15.

[52] WA 3:124, 29–35; Cl V:94, 14–21; WA 55/II/1/ii:138, 5–12.

[53] Elsewhere I have pointed out that Luther's *Theology of the Cross* of 1518, although it had some brilliant thoughts, is partially pre-Reformational and is not to be confused with his later preaching of the cross. In the explanation of Thesis XX of the *Heidelberg Disputation* (1518), Luther spoke of God's being "hidden in the Passion" (WA 1:362). This seems to diverge from his mature

teaching of the hidden and revealed God, the God of wrath and God of love, hidden in the Law and revealed in the Gospel. From this a strange construction of God as hidden in His revelation has been developed by Walther von Loewenich, *Luther's Theology of the Cross* (Minneapolis: Augsburg, 1976), pp. 21, 29–30. See the more extensive criticisms in my review of this book in LQ 29 (1977): 196–99. I think that von Loewenich has exaggerated the hiddenness of the revelation of God in Christ, perhaps partly under a certain Barthian influence, but one cannot completely deny the presence of a Neoplatonic understanding of hiddenness in the *Heidelberg Disputation*.

[54] WA 5:503–6.

[55] WA 3:167, 14–16; WA 55, ib.:166, 18–20.

[56] Hunzinger, p. 8.

[57] Ibid., p. 68.

[58] WA 7:21, 12–17.

[59] Ibid., pp. 21–2.

[60] Maurer, *Der junge Mel.*, Vol. I, pp. 84–98.

[61] *Wilhelm Maurer, Von der Freiheit eines Christenmenschen; Zwei Untersuchungen zu Luthers Reformationsschriften 1520/21 (Göttingen: Vandenhoeck & Ruprecht, 1949)*, pp. 118f.

[62] This is treated more fully in Maurer, ibid., pp. 38f. See also his programmatic essay, "Die Einheit der Theologie Luthers," ThLZ 75 (1950): 245–52; reprinted in *Kirche und Geschichte: Gesammelte Aufsätze*, Vol. I (Göttingen: Vandenhoeck & Ruprecht, 1970), pp. 11–21.

[63] WA 7:25–6.

[64] WA 8:126, 21–32.

[65] Bengt Hägglund, "Die Rechtfertigungslehre in der frühen Reformationstheologie," *Theologische Beiträge*, Vol. VIII (1977), p. 113.

[66] WA 56:272–73.

[67] WA 8:109, 27–31.

[68] See my articles: "Faith, Righteousness, and Justification: New Light on Their Development Under Luther and Melanchthon," SCJ IV, 1 (April 1972), esp. pp. 67–9; "The Influence of Erasmus upon Melanchthon, Luther and the Formula of Concord in the Doctrine of Justification," ChH XLIII, 2 (June 1974), esp. pp. 193–95; and "Erasmus, Luther, and Melanchthon on the *Magnus Consensus*: The Problem of the Old and the New in the Reformation and Today," LQ XXVII, 4 (November 1975), esp. pp. 368–76.

[69] WA 1:525–628.

[70] AE 31:25.

[71] §§ 39–40.

[72] §§ 8–19, 22–9, 35, et passim.

[73] §§ 39–40.

[74] §§ 92–5.

[75] Cf. WA 1:370, 9-13.

[76] Cf. Theses §§37-49.

[77] Theses §§9, 25, 38, 50, 69, 71, 73, 81, 90-91.

[78] In his theses for the Baccalaureate in Bible (September 9, 1519) Melanchthon had stated: "§16. It is not necessary for a Catholic to believe any articles beyond those of which Scripture is witness. §17. The authority of councils is lower than the authority of the Scriptures" (SA I:24; MSW:18). In his letter to Johann Hess of February 1520 he defended this revolutionary position and stated that it was because of the primacy of Scripture that he rejected transubstantiation but not the Real Presence (SA I:44f., 47-52; MSW:48f., 51-5). "... The judgment of all sacred things should be sought from the Sacred Scriptures alone (*e solis divinis literis*), and not on the things which please men" (SA I:47; MSW 51). The concept of Scripture as the Lydian stone (a norm), suggested already by Erasmus in his Paraclesis of 1516, *Christian Humanism and the Reformation*, ed. John C. Olin (New York: Harper & Row, 1965), p. 100, was introduced by Melanchthon in 1519-1520 (SA I:18; 50 = MSW:53). It was mentioned by Luther in 1519 (WA 2:579, 12). It was borrowed by Calvin in the *Institutes*, IV, 1, xi. It reappeared in the prolegomenon to the *Formula of Concord*. Critical notes on the above Melanchthon documents in *Suppl Mel* VI/1:70-74, 77-9, 87-9; cf. MBW 1:68-9.

[79] Theses §§ 71, 73, 81, 90-91.

Augustine

3

The Doctrine of Justification in the Young Luther as Pre-Reformational

Luther's Doctrine as a Confounding of Law and Gospel

Regarding his situation prior to 1518–1519, the later Luther remarked: "Before this, I had lacked nothing except that I made no distinction between Law and Gospel. I held it all for one and said that Christ and Moses did not differ except in time and completion."[1] Is there really any basis for this, or is it but a failure in an older man's memory as some scholars keep insisting? Actually, Luther's memory was very accurate, for we read the following in the *Dictata super Psalterium*:

> The Law of Christ, the law of peace, the law of grace, the Gospel, is called by many other names . . . It is therefore an astonishing thing how grace or the Law of grace (which is the same thing) is judgment and righteousness. . . .[2] Wherefore the castigation and crucifixion of the flesh and the condemnation of all who are in the world are the judgments of God. He works these things in them through judgment, that is, the Gospel and his grace. And this is how righteousness comes to pass. Because he who is unrighteous in his own eyes and is therefore humble before God, to him God grants his grace.[3]

The Mature Luther insisted that Law and Gospel or wrath and grace were opposites and should in no wise be mingled. Nevertheless, some prominent scholars have failed to see this. In attempting to extract his doctrine of Law and Gospel out of the early lectures, they have arrived at some strange conclusions. From Luther's first lectures on the Psalter one writer claims that the "strange work" (*opus alienum*) of the Gospel is to show sin and announce divine wrath. Another writer says that Luther called the Gospel "the most profound revelation of sin and the wrath of God."[4] Such statements are of course valid in regard to the Young Luther, but they serve our purpose in showing the deep gap between the reformer's early works and the Mature Luther. Anyone acquainted with his position on Law and Gospel in the later lectures on Galatians and Genesis, the sermons, the *Table Talk*, and the *Preface* of 1545 will immediately see the difference.[5]

The distinction between Law and Gospel goes back to the writings of Paul in the New Testament. The Young Luther owed his first understanding of the dialectic of Law and Gospel to Augustine. It is curious that of all the Pauline statements on the subject, Augustine should have based his system on II Corinthians 3:6: "[He] also hath made us able ministers of the new testament; not of the letter, but of the spirit: for the letter killeth, but the spirit giveth life." In rather allegorical fashion Augustine developed this passage in his *Treatise on the Spirit and the Letter* (*De Spiritu et Litera*), which appeared in 412.[6] Augustine wrote: ". . . Through the Law a man is shown his weakness, that through faith he may flee to God's mercy and be healed."[7] The distinction in Augustine often appears as one between Law and Grace. ". . . He is led to grace, through which alone that which the Law commands can be fulfilled. . . ."[8] Here, as is to be expected, grace is the medicinal substance by which the sin-sick patient is nursed back to health. It remained for the Reformation to uncover grace as solely an attitude on the part of God—the mercy in which He freely forgives. Closely related is Augustine's distinction between the Law of works (*lex operum*) and the Law of faith (*lex fidei*). He wrote:

> . . . We conclude that a man is not justified by the precepts of a good life, except through faith in Jesus Christ; that is, not by the Law of works, but by the Law of faith; not of the Letter, but of the Spirit; not through the merits of things done, but by grace, freely.[9]

Augustine went on to attribute this to Scripture: ". . . as it is written, not to the Law of works, from which no one is justified, but to the Law of faith, from which the just lives. . . ."[10]

The widely-held opinion that Luther came to fully evangeli-cal insights in 1513–1514 does not correspond to what is found in the sources of his teaching. Nevertheless, there is good reason for believing that he had an important breakthrough at that time—a breakthrough which was to be a decisive step along the road to his final discovery in 1518. The breakthrough appears to coincide with Luther's assiduous study of Augustine. This is reflected in frequent quotations from the Bishop of Hippo. In the exposition of Romans Luther quotes from *De Spiritu et Litera* twenty-seven times and intersperses other works of Augustine at frequent intervals. Luther's interest in the Latin Church Father is also shown in Augustine's obvi-ous influence on the reformer's thought.

Augustine's dialectic of the Law of works and the Law of faith (*lex operum seu fidei*) is not hard to trace under the formulation, "works of the Law" and "works of faith" (*opera legis seu fidei*), in the early Luther. This primitive form of Luther's doctrine of Law and Gospel is especially found in his lectures on Romans and Galatians (delivered between 1515 and 1517), where Luther distinguishes between works evoked by the Law (*opera legis*) and works evoked by faith (*opera fidei*). Here, to be sure, he finds "works of the Law" damnable, but "works of faith" prove to be the basis for an analytic justification. He makes the following points. (1) "Works of the Law" are done under compulsion, but "works of faith" are done freely. (2) "Works of the Law" originate in the selfish desire to win one's salvation, but "works of faith" originate in a pure love for God—a love willing even to suffer hell if God so willed (*resignatio ad infer-num*). (3) "Works of the Law" are directed merely toward satisfying the Law, but "works of faith" are concerned only with pleasing God. (4) "Works of the Law" boast of a righteousness that is imagined to be already present, but "works of faith" are done out of the longing of faith for a more perfect righteousness lying in the future.[11]

"Those are not called works of the Law (*opera legis*) which are done as preparation for acquiring justification," Luther declares, "but those which were done as if they in themselves were thought suf-ficient for righteousness and salvation." He goes on to explain this rather un-Protestant statement as follows: "He who operates thus, that he may make himself disposed to the grace of justification, is already in a manner just. For the main part of being just is to wish to be just."[12] Luther says that this is the meaning of both the Old and New Testaments and the presupposition for all admonitions to repent and seek God. Then he continues:

> Therefore those works are good, not because their doers trust in them, but because by means of them they prepare themselves for justification, by which alone they place their confidence in their future righteousness. For those who do works thus are not under the Law, since they desire grace and hate it that they are sinners.[13]

If works are offered with the intention of fulfilling the Law and being made just by those works, they are wrong. According to the Young Luther, this is the repudiation of divine grace. Luther struggles with this concept. At times his final solution seems to glimmer through. His closing statement in this paragraph is unable to overcome the medieval concept that it is not faith alone, but faith formed by love or works (*fides caritate formata*), which prepares for the acquisition of justification. Still, in language which sounds much like statements of the later Luther, Melanchthon, and the *Formula of Concord*, he concludes:

> On the contrary, neither works that go before nor that follow justify, how much less works of the Law! Certainly those which go before, because they prepare unto righteousness; truly those which follow, because they require previously effected justification. For it is not by doing just works that we are made just, but it is in being just that we perform just works. Therefore, grace alone justifies.[14]

Let us not be misled by the last sentence, which sounds completely Reformational out of its context. If we inquire into what Luther meant by "grace" at this stage of his development, we will find that he still held to the medieval view of grace as a medicinal substance which heals man of the sickness of sin and produces good works. Hence, righteousness here is the good works within the transformed believer. This finding is confirmed when we analyze what Luther understood by "justify."

It seems clear that Luther here still thinks of the word "justify" in the old sense of "to make just" (*justum efficere*), somewhat as Reinhold Seeberg understood him.[15] Luther says that works prepare the way for justification—not that the individual trusts in the Law, but that the individual wants to be saved. While justification depends upon faith alone, it is a faith made effective through love or works, as taught by the medieval schoolmen. *Quia magna pars Iustitiae velle esse Iustum:* "The main part of being just is to want to be just." Thus, works must precede and works must follow justification. As Holl might have added at this point, justification is here seen "analytically." The believer cannot do good works until he is declared just. The declaration of justification is not only the presupposition for the works that follow it, but the works that follow it are seen in the foreknowledge of God and therefore compose the basis for "analytic" justification.

True believers, who do good works for the sake of their justification (*ut justificentur magis ac magis*), do not despise grace in seeking to fulfill the Law so that they may boast of their own sanctification (thus the hypocrites), but they seek to be found righteous before God. The Young Luther does not deny that good works may contribute toward justification. But he is intent on stressing that works valid for justification are performed not for the Law's sake (*opera legis*) but from an inward longing after righteousness (*opera fidei*).

While some Luther scholars have sought to explain this phase of the younger Luther in a different light, Karl Holl readily admits: "Luther has absolutely no objections to employing the scholastic formula that through penance one 'prepares' himself for grace."[16] This point ought to be clear to all but the hagiographers of Luther. The peril of Luther's position here is that he stood at the brink of an anthropocentricized justification. The Gospel was in danger of being confused with the Law. In terms of Martin Seils' study, the work of God had become confused with the work of man. The whole system teetered precariously on the brink of synergism. Thus, Luther could define saving righteousness as "the very inclination unto good and disinclination from evil, inwardly bestowed through Grace."[17] In this context of justification as a long process of healing in which God proleptically declares the patient well, Luther concluded: "Thus in ourselves we are sinners, and still by the reckoning of God we are just through faith."[18] Let us note the advances Luther had made up to this point. He considered divine assistance the absolute prerequisite for works of righteousness. Only God could infuse the faith which performed works, not for the sake of the Law or for the sake of personal ambitions toward salvation, but out of a sincere love for God and a deep longing to be found righteous in God's sight.

Also in the lectures on Galatians, Luther describes the place of works in salvation. He attempts to explain Galatians 2:16: "Knowing that a man is not justified by the works of the Law, but by the faith of Jesus Christ." With approval he quotes Jerome: "Here, it is not so much works of the Law which condemn as those works of the Law from which they expect to be justified."[19] The works in themselves are often things wanted and commanded by God. It is a false trust in works that condemns. Spurious works of the Law are seen when they are done only outwardly without inward willingness.

> Therefore neither without works, neither out of works, but with works, is it possible to have salvation and righteousness, with this difference, that the more they grow inwardly and increase, so much the more the outward works are diminished.[20]

The works may consist of fastings, prayers, vigils, labors, worship, or even keeping the Ten Commandments. No one can be saved merely by the outward performance of such works. What is needful is that they be kept from the heart, from within. Without true willingness such works are condemnable works of the Law. "But on the other hand, those are called 'works of Grace' or 'works of the Spirit', which are done by the Spirit and by Grace," Luther states, acknowledging his debt to Augustine.[21] Hence, it is grace and faith that constitute the difference between works of the Law and works of faith.

In words which show an ever-increasing perception of how Law and Gospel are to be distinguished, Luther comments on Galatians 1:11 as follows:

> The Law and the Gospel differ in this regard, for the Law preaches what is being done or being omitted, or rather, what has been committed and what has been omitted, and through this it gives solely the consciousness of sin. But the Gospel preaches the remission of sins and the fulfillment that is accomplished over the Law, namely through Christ. Therefore the voice of the Law is this: Pay back what thou owest! But the Gospel says this: Thy sins are forgiven thee![22]

Commenting on Galatians 2:3, Luther gives further clarification to his view on the right and wrong place for works of the Law.

> The strength of this controversy does not lie exactly in works of the Law, but in the needfulness and the benefit of works of the Law. For works of the Law are put to death in Christ, not in the sense that they ought not to be done, but rather that aside from such works, a man should believe himself saved through Christ alone, whether they are worked or are not worked.[23]

Where this all-important truth is overlooked, man becomes guilty of presumption and pride. Works of Grace are thereby transformed into works of the Law, and the righteousness of God is distorted into the righteousness of men. Luther saw unbelief as essentially identical with pride (*superbia*). Through pride the unbeliever opposes God and changes God's gifts of grace into his own works. These, however, condemn rather than save him before God.[24]

It is completely different with the believer. He has learned to despair of finding salvation through "works of the Law."[25] But now because Christ has fulfilled the whole Law, He makes it possible for the believer to perform "works of faith." With such works, salvation and righteousness are possible. Thus, Luther rejected any righteousness from the Law but found room for a righteousness from "works of faith." It is clear that this could pave the way for justification on the basis of what Holl called "analytic" righteousness. Nevertheless, in justice to Luther we must note two important limiting factors in this primitive form of his doctrine of justification. First, God's declaring the believer just was the necessary prerequisite for true good works.[26] Righteousness in justification did not begin with good works that already existed. Rather, righteousness created good works. And second, when such "works of faith" were manifest, they were not called a human but a divine accomplishment, made possible solely by infused grace and infused faith.[27]

Justificatio and *Justitia*

Luther research remains baffled by the usage of such basic terms as justification (*justificatio*) and righteousness (*justitia*). Strange as it may seem, the terms have been interchanged promiscuously even by careful scholars, while more subtle variations such as active or passive justification and active or passive righteousness have often been completely overlooked. Luther's own usage varied between his earlier and his later works, and thoughts occur even in a year like 1530 that apparently were not thoroughly integrated into his thought or ever used again.[28] When one considers this fact and then ponders the attitude of many Luther researchers who refuse to see any difference between the Young and the Mature Luther, it immediately becomes apparent how detrimental this confusion can become. When one further recalls the complicating of the terminology through the independent usages of scholars like Melanchthon, Brenz, Amsdorf, Flacius, or Osiander and then recalls the further development these terms assumed in the events that led up to the framing of the *Formula of Concord* and in subsequent reinterpretations, the complexity of the situation emerges. It therefore becomes clear that the doctrine of justification cannot be delineated until this chaotic terminology is clarified. Nevertheless, the greatest scholars have faltered here. Thus, Friedrich Loofs experienced difficulties in distinguishing *justificatio* and *justitia*. One of his troubles was in wrongly stating the question. He thought that the question was whether the works that made the believer righteous (*justum effici*) were worked by the believer himself or by God. Loofs found that the works in Luther's view of justification in the *Lectures on Romans* were worked by God, not by man. Perfectly correct! But then he wrongly assumed that this was Luther's final doctrine of justification on the basis of passive righteousness. Consequently, Loofs concluded that passive righteousness was worked within man by God in opposition to active righteousness, which man in sinful pride imagines himself able to offer God for his justification. Loofs claimed that the passive righteousness of God was to be found in the *Lectures on Romans*. But the passages he cited spoke of the *justificatio passiva* rather than *justitia passiva*.[29] As we shall see, these terms are entirely different. Hirsch was right in affirming that the term *justitia passiva* does not occur in these early works of Luther, nor does the concept behind it. Nevertheless, Erich Seeberg made a similar mistake in confusing the terms "passive justification" and "passive righteousness." Speaking of "Luther's scientific experience," Seeberg contrasts "passive righteousness" with

". . . active righteousness, by which God is righteous and punishes the sinful and the unrighteous." Passive righteousness then becomes, according to Seeberg, that righteousness ". . . by which the merciful God makes us righteous through faith."[30] But Seeberg, like Loofs and others, is on the wrong track. Long before Luther, righteousness had been seen as that which justifies. Luther's real discovery came later and consisted in the insight that passive righteousness is the extrinsic righteousness given the believer through faith in Christ. The expression *justitia passiva* is an anachronism for Luther's theology of 1515, and in its connection with forensic justification it harks back more to Melanchthon than to Luther. Discussions on Luther's *Lectures on Romans* might better be spared this additional ballast, which does not at all divulge the meaning of Luther's view of "passive justification."

In seeking an alternative to Loofs and Seeberg, one might be tempted to imagine that active justification was the sinful self-justification of the individual before God, while passive justification was the willingness of the individual to accept God's grace. This again would miss the mark. When Luther speaks of passive justification, he means the act of submission on the part of the believer in which he affirms the unfavorable judgment placed upon him by God's Law and thereby accepts God. Active justification, in turn, means that God subsequently reputes the sinner just who has thus acknowledged Him.

Luther develops this in his interpretation of Romans 3:3, 4: "For what if some did not believe? Shall their unbelief make the faith of God without effect? God forbid." When Luther speaks here of active or passive justification, he does not mean active or passive righteousness. Luther wants to say that the unbeliever is not willing to acknowledge his sin but instead tries to boast of his own inherent righteousness. Since God in His holy Law has already condemned the sinner, man's self-righteousness constitutes the denial of both the authority and justice of God. If God tells him, "Thou art a condemned sinner," the unbeliever replies, "No, I am righteous, but Thou, O God, art an unrighteous Judge, for Thou dost seek to condemn me." Such an individual makes it impossible for God to justify him since he denies God this right in claiming that God, in the act of uncovering his sin, is an unfair judge.[31] This shows that there is really no sin apart from unbelief. Unbelief opposes God and makes God a liar in order that man may be justified in himself. But with the believer it is quite the opposite. He does not boast of his supposed intrinsic righteousness but instead admits his guilt before God. When God says to the believer, "Thou art a sinner," he answers with the confession of his guilt: "Yea, God, Thou art right; Thou art a righteous Judge." Thereby the sinner has declared God to be righteous—that is, he has justified God—as Paul noted when he cited Psalm 51:4 in Romans 3:4: "That thou mightest be justified when Thou speakest, and be clear when Thou judgest."[32] This is the moment of silence that God needs in order to justify the sinner.[33] Active justification follows immediately upon passive justification. The believer has justified God in declaring Him righteous.

> Moreover, through this 'justifying of God,' we ourselves are justified. And that passive justification of God, by which we are justified, is the same as our active justification at the hand of God, for he regards that faith which justifies his words as righteousness. . . .[34]

Faith pays God the honor due Him. It lets God be God. When the believer has such a faith, he lacks no further righteousness.[35] But paradoxically, he is still unrighteous. He is saint and sinner at the same time (*simul justus et peccator*). God's word of justification is an anticipation of the final justification.

Justification as Humility

What has been said about "passive justification" leads logically to the consideration of humility as justification. This is true because Luther saw justification as the act in which the individual dethrones himself and gives all the glory to God. It is humility that denies one's proud and sinful self and justifies God both in His holy sinlessness and in the fairness of His condemnation of the sinner. Thus, according to the Young Luther, man, in justifying God through humility, justifies himself. Where humility dwells in the heart, there can only be a genuine relationship with God, bringing life and salvation. Humility is therefore nearly identical with faith. Hence, we see that, years before Luther had successfully defined faith, through the term *humilitas* (humility) he had come to some of the basic insights of the *sola fides, sola gratia* (faith alone, grace alone). This is a station along the way to full Reformation that has not excited the fullest attention and yet represents a permanent motif around which subsequent clarifications gathered.

The opposite of humility is pride (*superbia*), which is the same as sin and unbelief. Pride asserts itself against the justice of God and thereby leads only to God's condemnation and rejection. In his great *Heidelberg Disputation* of 1518 Luther developed his view on humility and pride with remarkable perception. "The only merit is humility and fear of God," he asserted.[36] Luther spoke of a positive danger in good works when they become the occasion of self-confidence. Man thus makes of himself an idol and rejects God. Good works thereby become mortal sins. They cannot be meritorious ". . . except through the fear of humble confession. . . ."[37]

Luther found a similar thought in his earlier treatment of Galatians 3:22: "But the scripture hath concluded all under sin, that the promise by faith of Jesus Christ might be given to them that believe." Luther supplied this comment:

> [The Law] . . . is not against the promises of God, because through the Law . . . all men discover themselves humiliated and sinful; thus they are humiliated by the Law and receive righteousness by grace. Thus for the humble, the Law precedes the promises of God, but for the proud it is 'against the promises of God,' because it makes them sigh after grace, but it puffs them up instead in their own righteousness and against grace.[38]

In a further discussion of this same text Luther shows how the proud are reckoned sinners because they ". . . claim that they are righteous through the 'works of the Law.'"[39]

This conception of humility bears certain resemblances to Luther's later doctrine. Nevertheless, we must be cautious against blurring the distinction between the early and the more mature phases of Luther's thought. This is evident when we carefully read what Luther wrote concerning Romans 4:7: "Blessed are they whose iniquities are forgiven, and whose sins are covered." Luther begins one paragraph as follows: ". . . The righteousness of God is imputed to those who believe without works."[40] This sounds like Luther fifteen years later. But the argument immediately following reveals the "analytic" justification that still lodged in Luther's mind during the *Lectures on Romans*. Luther discusses the question whether the saints were not an exception, since ". . . we read in the stories of many of the saints that in some way or other their works or prayers were reputed by God and commended to others as an example, and therefore they were justified by works in this manner." Surprisingly, Luther does not deny that they were thereby justified. He does not attack the error that they were justified by such works of faith, but that others out of pride sought to imitate the saints! They perhaps imitated the works, but not the humility, of the saints. It was completely different with the saints of old.

> For certainly those unto whom such works were reputed and commended had not performed them for the reason that they might be reputed; on the contrary, they did not know whether they had been reputed by God, but they did what they were able, in humble faith, always praying that God would be gracious according to his mercy to that which they did. So it was on account of the humble sigh of faith that they were reputed at first, and afterwards their works were reputed and approved.[41]

It is clear that Luther at this stage did not possess assurance of his salvation. He exhorted his hearers not to expect their works to be reputed unto righteousness lest this lead to spiritual pride. They should first see their unworthiness and offer God the humble sigh of faith.

Both Martin Seils and Ernst Bizer have pointed out the synergistic character of justification through this early doctrine of humility. In commenting on Psalm 71:19, "Thy righteousness also, O God, is very high," Luther in 1513 had said that this is the distinction between divine and human righteousness.[42] Divine righteousness reaches into the highest, while human righteousness reaches into the lowest. As Bizer has noted, righteousness here is obviously not an attribute of God but the way that leads to God. Therefore, when Luther then says, "All righteousness of God is this, namely, to humble one's self in the depths. Thus indeed he comes into the highest," this means that human humiliation is the indispensable condition for salvation.[43] Seils observes that this agrees with Luther's pre-1518 understanding of justification, in which man cooperates with God. Luther was unable to avoid humility as a kind of synergism until he came to his fully Reformational teaching.[44]

Christology and Justification

At every period of his life Luther's doctrine of justification was strongly linked to the doctrine of Christ. This is also true of his early years between 1508 and 1518. During a period of spiritual conflict, his friend Johann Staupitz had brought him peace by bidding him to relate his dread of God's wrath to the wounds of the Saviour.

Luther's first great Biblical lecture was strongly Christocentric. Erich Vogelsang has shown how this was presented as the twofold advent of Christ in the *Dictata super Psalterium*[45] The first advent lay in the Incarnation (*adventus in carnem*). The second took place in the faith of the individual (*adventus spiritualis*). Both were linked together with the significant word *simul*.[46] Luther commented:

> For what good did it do for God to become man unless we are saved by believing it? Wherefore Christ is not called our righteousness, peace, mercy, or salvation in his person unless he effects these. But it is the faith of Christ by which we are justified and given peace as he reigns through faith in us.[47]

In his expositions of Romans, Galatians, Hebrews, and the Penitential Psalms, Luther developed his views of justification within a Christological framework. When he spoke of grace, it was grace given man for the sake of Christ.[48] When he described faith, it was a faith whose content was Christ.[49] When he treated the subject of righteousness, he spoke of a righteousness worked within the believer by Christ.[50] When he pictured the forgiveness of sins, this was something made possible by the sufferings and death of Jesus Christ.[51] The goal of justification was nothing other than the uniting of the believer with Christ in this life and in all eternity.[52] Such a Christocentric basis could only help lead Luther to overcome the more legalistic aspects of his early doctrine of justification. Thus, he commented on Galatians 2:16: "Therefore, he who believes in Christ not only satisfies all things, but makes it that all things are due him, because by faith he is made one with Christ."[53]

An increasing tension appeared in Luther's theology between 1515 and 1518. It was marked by the view of Christ as the Good Samaritan (Luke 10:25–37) or the Great Physician, who heals the sin-diseased individual with the medicinal substance of grace until eventually the sinner is completely purged in heaven.[54] This notion would be eventually overcome. Grace would be seen as divine favor rather than as a medicinal substance. Saving righteousness would be detached from the God-given accomplishments of the believer and be attached to the merits of Christ on Calvary. Accordingly, when the concept of Christ as Good Samaritan would later recur, as in the polemic against Latomus of 1521, healing would be related to sanctification, which follows justification, rather than to the act of justification itself.[55] Meanwhile, an important change was to take place in Luther's thinking on Christ's role in justification. Instead of the Good Samaritan or Great Physician justifying the sinner by healing or changing him within, Christ becomes the One who makes available an extrinsic righteousness by His substitutionary sufferings and death. Within a declarative or forensic justification, this extrinsic righteousness would then be reckoned to the good of the believing sinner. We shall see, however, that in the Mature Luther the faith of forensic justification did not coexist with a life of wickedness. Good works were inevitable, or else the "faith" was not authentic.[56] Nevertheless, it is not correct to call Luther's later view "effective justification" on that account, because he had learned to distinguish justification from sanctification even if that terminology did not always appear explicitly in his works. Nor is the recent term "synthetic" justification completely satisfactory. As Elert has shown, in Luther's day the German word for justify, *rechtfertigen*, meant that the criminal was not excused but paid for his crime with his life. He "paid his debt." For Luther justification meant that the old man was put to death. Paradoxically, the person still lived. But he did not live unto himself. Christ had taken up His dwelling within.[57]

Summary of the Young Luther

I have shown that Luther's early doctrine of justification must be studied in the light of his development as a theologian and reformer. This means that one must beware of uncritical assumptions. If elements of forensic justification or the imputation of the extrinsic righteousness of Christ are postulated for the reformer's early period, their presence must be found explicitly in the works of the Young Luther and not merely in those of the Mature Luther. The attempt to treat the sources objectively has led to a rather perplexing diversity of concepts and insights. (1) Luther's later doctrine on the distinction of Law and Gospel was present at first only in rudimentary form with a number of weaknesses. "Works of the law" were rejected as the basis for justification, but "works of faith" were regarded as essential. Not only did they dispose the individual to the grace of justification, but they also provided the righteousness which God used to declare the believer just. (2) In the *Lectures on Romans* (1515–1516) Luther taught a twofold justification—active and passive. Active justification meant that the sinner accepted God's adverse judgment on his life and thereby established the jurisdiction of God. Passive justification meant that God in turn regarded this faith of the individual which acknowledged the sovereignty of God and, in that act, declared the believer just.[58] (3) Luther furthermore described justification as the result of humility. Humility was the virtue which God acknowledged under active and passive justification. On account of humility the sinner was first reputed just, and then, unknown to him, his works were approved by God. In humility the believer denied his prideful self and enthroned God in his heart. He thereby justified both God and himself, and good works followed. (4) Last but not least, justification was intricately linked with Luther's understanding of the person and work of Christ. At times Christ was seen as the heavenly Physician who little by little purged sin from the life of the believer until at last the believer, in heaven, found himself sinless. Again, Christ was seen as the One who dwelt within the heart of the believer through faith and thereby provided the basis for a favorable sentence from the judicatory of God. Or the atoning work of Christ itself was seen as the basis on which the believer was justified.

The temptation has always been present for the Luther scholar to absolutize whichever one of these aspects he chanced upon. The result has been an almost chaotic disagreement among schools of Luther interpretation. It ought to be apparent, however, that we do not really have the right to choose among Luther's insights. To choose one and reject the rest is a highly arbitrary and narrowing procedure that cannot lead to a dependable picture either of the development of Luther or of the course of the Reformation. But then we are confronted with the question whether it is possible to construct a system on the basis of these varied and even conflicting concepts in the Young Luther. Or perhaps the question must be raised whether Luther himself was even coherent. We can be sure that Luther was capable of coherent thinking, although in his earlier years he was consciously burdened with the realization that there were inconsistencies he needed to resolve. The task of constructing a system is difficult because Luther did not teach systematic theology but rather courses on the Old and New Testaments. Careful analysis reveals that a wonderful consistency underlay his thought in later years. Tracing the systematic assumptions behind Luther's mature theology is like constructing a fine mosaic work. Much diligence and great patience yield rewarding results. However, seeking to do the same with the early works of Luther is a much more formidable undertaking. Nevertheless, I shall try to trace a few relationships among the seemingly disparate insights on justification in the Young Luther.

What, then, is the relationship among humility, passive justification, the work of Christ, and works of faith? To begin with, the Young Luther acknowledged the fundamental importance of Christ's atoning death on the cross. This was basic with Luther even when he was unable to trace a direct line between the atonement and justification. If the Mature Luther saw justification as the work of the atonement brought into the present and applied, the Young Luther saw the work of Christ in a rather different light. Although his definition of faith was somewhat variable, faith for the early Luther was the acceptance as valid of what the church taught about God and salvation (*credulitas*). Humility, sometimes nearly identified with faith, was also at times distinguished from faith and nearly identified with justification. In any case, faith or humility "let God be God." In the moment of active justification of God, which proved to be the passive justification of the believer, not only was God acknowledged as God, but Christ entered into the heart to begin His work. By means of substantial grace Christ began a transformation of the heart and life of the believer so that genuine good works appeared. If the individual placed his confidence in the works instead of in Christ, he was guilty of the sin of pride (*superbia*), and the process of justification was interrupted. The process of justification showed that the individual did not consciously perform his good works in order to win favor from God. If he did, then humility was not present, and all was in vain. Where works were done in order to gain justification, they were works of the law (*opera legis*) and only condemned. But where they were done in humility without the thought that they were pleasing to God, they became works of faith (*opera fidei*).

> Therefore, salvation and righteousness are to be had neither without works nor out of works, but with works. Yet there is this difference: the more salvation and righteousness grow within and increase, the more works decrease outwardly.[59]

Despite all the criticisms directed against Karl Holl's interpretation of justification, and despite the denials of many Luther scholars, Luther here speaks of an incipient justification. God declares the believer righteous (*justum reputare*), but that declaration is only the anticipation of what God will make of the believer (*justum efficere*). In an act related to God's foreknowledge and predestination, God declares the believer just on the basis of a righteousness He foresees that Christ will accomplish within the believer.[60]

Notes

[1] TR V, No. 5518; WA 48:617, 12.

[2] WA 3:462, 15.

[3] Ibid., p. 462, 34.

[4] Philip S. Watson, *Let God be God! An Interpretation of the Theology of Martin Luther* (Philadelphia: Muhlenberg Press, 1950), p. 156. Warren A. Quanbeck in *Luther Today*, Vol. I in Martin Luther Lectures (Decorah: Luther College Press, 1957), p. 55. See also Heiko A. Oberman, "'Iustitia Christi' and 'Iustitia

Dei' . . . ," HTR 59 (1966): 1–26. He has identified Luther's use of the *lex vetus seu lex nova* with the later distinction between Law and Gospel (pp. 13, 15–17). But the early formulations which make of the Gospel a new law or Christ the giver of the new law are irreconcilable with Luther's later teaching on Law and Gospel. For Luther's later denial that Christ was the giver of a *nova lex*, see n. 5.

⁵ For a good contrast of Luther's pre-Reformational and Reformational thought on Law-Gospel and Christ's role, see F. Edward Cranz, *An Essay on the Development of Luther's Thought on Justice, Law, and Society*, pp. 14–20 and pp. 94–111 respectively. The later Luther emphatically denied that Christ could be called the giver of the new law (p. 97). Cf. the following statements of Luther: WA 2:494, 9; 575, 37 (1519); WA 10/I/1:458, 6; 469, 14 (1522); WA 40/I:562, 1; 563, 15 (1531); WA 43:180, 25; TR VI:76, 38; 134, 20; 136, 16; 141, 28; et passim. See also Paul Althaus, *Die Theologie Martin Luthers* (Gütersloh: Gerd Mohn, 1962), pp. 218–27; Eng. tr. Robert C. Schultz, *The Theology of Martin Luther* (Philadelphia: Fortress, 1966), pp. 251–60.

⁶ CSEL VIII/1:153–230.

⁷ Ibid., p. 167, 21.

⁸ Ibid., p. 168, 19.

⁹ Ibid., p. 176.

¹⁰ Ibid., p. 178.

¹¹ The above instances from WA 56:254–55; WA 57/II:59–60, 68–69, etc. Cf. his explanation of Heidelberg Thesis XXV (WA 1:364, 7). This distinction between *opera legis* and *opera fidei* occurs frequently in the Young Luther. See for example his exposition of Romans 3:20: "The Apostle distinguishes between Law and Faith, or between the Letter and Grace, and thus between their works. Works of the Law, he says, are those which are done aside from faith and grace, and out of the Law, planned through fear or else enticed by the promise of temporal things. On the other hand, works of faith he calls those which are done solely through love of God and out of a spirit of freedom. And these things cannot be done unless by those justified by faith, to which justification the works of the Law can cooperate not a bit, but rather they savagely hamper it, while the man himself fails to see that he is unjust and in need of justification" (WA 56:248, 10). ". . . The apostle does not say that faith justifies without its proper works, but that it justifies without the works of the Law. Therefore justification does not require the works of the Law, but a living faith, which operates by its own works" (WA 56:249, 7). See also the following: WA 56:264, 21; 276, 20.29; WA 57/III:70, 14.

¹² WA 56:254, 19.

¹³ Ibid., pp. 254–55.

¹⁴ Ibid., p. 255, 15.

¹⁵ Seeberg wrote that being justified is ". . . the movement and the course to righteousness. But now this process is never closed and can never reach its end in this life . . . Therefore the danger arises that the sinner might never

come to the certainty of receiving grace. Therefore, in order to free men from such fears, God established the order that, insofar as they battle against their sins and Christ remains active within them, their sins should not be reckoned against them." Reinhold Seeberg, *Lehrbuch der Dogmengeschichte*, Vol. IV/1, 5th ed. (Darmstadt: Wiss. Buch-Gemeinschaft, 1953), pp. 299f. There can be no doubt that *justificare* means at times for the Young Luther *justum facere* (to make just), an "analytic" concept. But when Seeberg overlooked the fact that Luther later turned his back on this view, he failed to do Luther full justice.

[16] Karl Holl, *Gesammelte Aufsätze*, Vol. I, p. 133.

[17] WA 56:271, 11.

[18] Ibid., p. 271, 29.

[19] WA 57/II:68.

[20] Ibid., p. 68, 28.

[21] Ibid., p. 69.

[22] Ibid., pp. 59–60.

[23] Ibid., p. 63, 8.

[24] WA 56:259, 9. Cf. Luther's *Heidelberg Disputation* of 1518 and particularly his explanation of the eighth and ninth theses (WA 1:358–59), where he finds works done without Christ or fear of God to be "dead." A helpful discussion of the *opera dei* and *opera manuum eius* is offered by Erich Vogelsang, op. cit., pp. 52–3.

[25] WA 56:248, 13; WA 57/III:88, 15.

[26] Thus, Luther comments on Galatians 5:13: "Justification by grace is necessary for works and prior to all works" (WA 57/II:100, 1). Cf. thecommenton Hebrews 1:3 in WA 57/III:101, 15.

[27] Luther developed this thought in his important debate at Heidelberg (1518) in the twenty-fifth thesis: "Not he is just who works much, but he who without works believes much in Christ." Luther then gave this explanation of the thesis: "This is how I want the phrase 'without works' to be understood: Not in the sense that he who is just does no works, but rather, that his works do not accomplish his righteousness, but instead his righteousness accomplishes his works. Yes, without our works, grace and faith are infused, from which infusion works simultaneously follow" (WA 1:364). Christ is mentioned as the object of belief, yet it is not the merits of Christ that justify but, we might say, the righteousness that is inspired by faith.

[28] If we are willing to accept the text transmitted only by Veit Dietrich, Luther in 1530 called faith "the active righteousness" of works (i.e., that which renders works acceptable to God) and consequently speaks of works as the "passive righteousness" of faith (WA 30/II: 659, 32). This is found in his *Rhapsodia seu concepta in librum de loco iustificationis cum aliis obiter additis* as it was edited by Veit Dietrich. In this curious notation it was difficult to find a direct link with Luther's other pronouncements. Calling faith that

which makes works pleasing to God does not conflict with either Luther's early or his mature theology. But the naming of works as the "passive righteousness" of faith is difficult to harmonize with the usage in Luther's *Commentary on Galatians* (1531ff.), where the imputed righteousness of Christ is called "passive," although there is no actual conflict involved. This is all a reminder of the fact that while the scholar must try to distinguish terms immaculately, mere analysis of terms does not provide the key to Luther's theology. Unlike others, Luther used a term to express an insight of the moment, often later discarding the usage. Apparently, he did not expect twentieth-century readers to press his terminology!

[29] Loofs tended to devote chief attention to the Young Luther. He quoted Luther thus: ". . . gerecht soll hie nicht verstanden von der Gerechtigkeit, damit Gott richtet . . ." Instead, the righteousness of God in this case meant ". . . die ausgegossene Gnade und Barmherzigkeit Gottes . . ." and therefore ". . . Gottes Gerechtigkeit oder Frommkeit," "dass nicht wir sondern Gott sie wirket in uns." See Fr. Loofs, "'Iustitia dei passiva' in Luther's Anfängen," *Theologische Studien und Kritiken* 84 (1911): 466–67.

[30] Erich Seeberg, *Luther's Theologie in ihren Gründzugen* (Stuttgart: Kohlhammer, 1950), p. 19.

[31] WA 56:226.

[32] Cf. Luther's comment on Romans 3:7: "Therefore we conclude that God in his words cannot be wise, just, truthful, powerful, and good, unless we believe him and yieldingly confess that we are foolish, unjust, untruthful, powerless, and bad. Therefore the work is done by humility and faith" (ibid., p. 218).

[33] In his dogmatics Werner Elert speaks of the individual's being put to silence before God, his Judge, as an indispensable part of justification (Elert, *Der christliche Glaube*, pp. 474f.). Cf. Elert's presentation on justification, and particularly man "Under the wrath of God," in *The Structure of Lutheranism*, Vol. I, pp. 18ff.

[34] WA 56:226, 23.

[35] Cf. a sermon of 1525 (WA 17/II:203f.). Luther comments on Romans 3:4: "Therefore God is justified in his words when belief is manifested in him and in the Gospel in regard to the fulfillment of that which has been promised, so that God is held to be truthful and just. These words therefore are the word of the Gospel, by which he is justified, when he is believed in . . . Justification of God and faith in God are the same" (ibid., pp. 225f.).

[36] WA 1:357.

[37] Ibid., p. 358.

[38] WA 57/II:26-7.

[39] Ibid., p. 84.

[40] WA 56:276, 20.

[41] Ibid., p. 276, 29.

[42] WA 3:457f.

[43] Ibid., p. 458, 4.

[44] Bizer, *Fides ex auditu*, p. 15. Seils, *Zusammenwirkung*, pp. 58–61.

[45] *Erich Vogelsang, Die Anfänge von Luthers Christologie nach der ersten Psalmenvorlesung, insbesondere in ihren exegetischen und systematischen Zusammenhangen mit Augustin und der Scholastik*, No. 15 in Arbeiten zur Kirchengeschichte (Berlin: De Gruyter, 1929), pp. 71–4.

[46] WA 4:19, 31.

[47] Ibid., p. 19, 36.

[48] WA 56:37, 26.

[49] WA 57/III:114, 2.

[50] WA 57/II:80, 26.

[51] WA 1:189, 19.

[52] WA 57/II:69, 23.

[53] Ibid.

[54] WA 56:272–73.

[55] WA 8:109.

[56] The classical statement of Luther is that in the *Smalkald Articles*, Part Three, XIII: "What I have hitherto and steadily taught I know not how to change in the least. That is, that 'through faith' (as St. Peter says [Acts 15:9]) we get a new and clean heart, and God will and does regard us as completely righteous and holy, for the sake of Christ, our Mediator. And although sin in the flesh is still not completely gone or dead, he nevertheless does not will to reckon it or know it. And good works follow such faith, renewal, and forgiveness of sins. Moreover, what remains sinful or deficient shall for the sake of Christ not be reckoned as sin or a deficiency. Instead the person shall as a whole, both as to his person and his works, be spoken and be righteous and holy, out of the pure grace and mercy that are poured out and spread upon us in Christ. Therefore we can boast little of the merit of our works if they are seen apart from grace and mercy. Instead it is as written: 'He who boasts, let him boast in the Lord,' that is, that he has a gracious God. Thus everything is good. We say further that where good works do not follow, such faith is false and not right" (BekS:460f.; BC:315).

[57] See Werner Elert, "Deutschrechtliche Züge in Luthers Rechtfertigungslehre," 1935; reprinted in *Ein Lehrer der Kirche* (Berlin: Lutherisches Verlagshaus, 1967), pp. 23–31 (cf. Rom. 6:3–11; 7:4–6; Gal. 2:19–20).

[58] WA 56:225–31.

[59] WA 57/II:68, 28.

[60] WA 56:272.

How Melanchthon Helped
Luther Develop His Views

〰〰〰

PART II

Introduction to Part II

Philipp Melanchthon has been severely judged for being a humanist and for injecting intellectualism and legalism into Protestant theology.[1] Emotions have been so deep and bitter that they have hindered scholars, especially from the Lutheran camp, in reaching an objective appraisal of Melanchthon. The result has been a serious gap in secular and ecclesiastical history. Perhaps Melanchthon's place in history would be more accurately portrayed if it were realized that he wanted to be and was first of all a philologist and an educator and that his contributions toward theology, no matter how awesome, were secondary to his life's work. Like no other man from the past, he succeeded in changing the humanist pursuit of the classics from an elitist into a popular movement and in paving the way for the modern public-school system.[2]

Melanchthon was a humanist. But as Werner Elert has shown, his humanism made important contributions to the Reformation not only in providing the philological resources for opening the Holy Scriptures and the pedagogical institutions for disseminating religious and secular knowledge among an entire population, but especially in expounding the meaning of the doctrine of justification itself.[3] He gave the sixteenth century an authentic understanding of the nature of man in his strengths and weaknesses. Luther had come from the protective cloisters of monastery living. Melanchthon came from the world of Petrarch, Boccaccio, and Machiavelli.

> His anthropology was that of antique humanity, formed by him in absolute personal purity, but still only a worldly existence—looking optimistically toward the future, self-conscious, progressive, and idealistic. Man was the measure of all things.[4]

Melanchthon brought to Wittenberg this understanding of man together with his interest in Biblical studies. Deeply impressed by Luther, he quickly became his follower and was involved in the life-long pursuit of clarifying the doctrine of justification.

> . . . In the language of the doctrine of justification, this meant that man was no longer the measure of all things, but God instead, and that did not exist on the basis of how he judged himself, but of how God judged him instead. This meant that it was not before himself, but before God [coram Deo] that he was responsible and had to justify himself. In Melanchthon the humanistic anthropology capitulated before the divine judge.[5]

Thus, Melanchthon saw man as totally responsible before God both for his justification and for his consequent life in society. All that he did stood *sub judicio Dei*—under the judgment of God. Elert asserts, "Only in the purely forensic understanding of our justification before God, as we owe it to Melanchthon, is the full hardness of the situation preserved, that we have to answer for everything before God."[6] When we add to these contributions the fact that Melanchthon was also Luther's teacher in Greek and Hebrew and assisted him in his Biblical studies, including the great Bible translation, it becomes doubly apparent that we cannot irresponsibly dismiss him as a harmful humanist as many have done.

Notes

[1] Among American writers who strongly opposed Melanchthon we note especially the following: Gerhard Friedrich Bente, "Historical Introductions to the Lutheran Symbols," in *Concordia, or Book of Concord.*

The Symbols of the Ev. Lutheran Church (St. Louis: Concordia, 1922 et sqq.), Part One, pp. 1–266. Richard C. Caemmerer, "The Melanchthonian Blight," CTM 5 (1947): 321–38. Jaroslav Pelikan, *From Luther to Kierkegaard* (St. Louis: Concordia, 1950, 1963). Robert C. Schultz, "Melanchthon after Four Hundred Years," *The Cresset* 23 (April 1960): 13–14. Schultz concludes: "American Lutheranism will not particularly note the anniversary of Melanchthon's death [scil., April 19, 1960]. The memories of the great reformer who himself needed reform is too painful" (p. 14)—a judgment which echoes the opinion of the other three men, all from the Missouri Synod.

² The standard work on Melanchthon as a humanist and educator is by Karl Hartfelder, *Philipp Melanchthon als Praeceptor Germaniae*, No. VII in series, Monumenta Germaniae Paedagogica (Berlin: A. Hofmann, 1889; reprint, Nieuwkoop: B. De Graaf, 1964), including important appendices with bibliographical and biographical data. For a brief treatment, see my article, "Philipp Melanchthon," ELC II: 1517–27. A longer discussion is my essay, "The Bible in Sixteenth-Century Humanist Education," *Studies in the Renaissance* 19 (1972): 112–34.

³ Werner Elert, "Humanität und Kirche. Zum 450. Geburtstag Melanchthon," in *Zwischen Gnade und Ungnade: Abwandlungen des Themas Gesetz und Evangelium* (Munich: Evangelischer Presseverband für Bayern, 1948), pp. 92–113. The quotations from Elert in the ensuing text bear references to this essay.

⁴ Ibid., p. 103.

⁵ Ibid.

⁶ Ibid., p. 101.

MELANCHTHON

THE TRIUMPH OF REUCHLIN

4

The Contribution of
the Biblical Humanists

Faber, Reuchlin, Erasmus, and Melanchthon

The southern and northern humanists prided themselves on their remarkable recovery of skills in the use of the Latin, Greek, and even Hebrew tongues. Not only did they thereby recover forgotten treasures of the Greco-Roman civilization, but they opened up forgotten riches of the Biblical world. Many humanists as well as reformers were deeply religious and yearned for the assurance that God would be gracious to them. Beyond question, the greatest theologian among these was Melanchthon. But his greatness was deeply indebted to those who went before him. Faber, Reuchlin, Erasmus, and Melanchthon all played an indispensable role in Luther's evangelical discovery and emergence as the reformer of the Western Church.

Faber Stapulensis, as he was known to scholars, or Jacques Lefèvre d'Étaples (c. 1460–1536), was a French Biblical humanist whose contributions toward the theological development of the early Luther are beyond calculation. Faber's *Quincuplex Psalterium* in its first edition of 1509 seems to have come into Luther's possession in 1513 or during the preparations for his first lectures on the Psalms. He was deeply impressed by Faber's commentary and referred to it frequently. We possess this copy with many annotations from the hand of Luther.[1] These annotations not only reveal his interest in the work of the French humanist, but give us valuable information

on his own development. Faber had rejected the medieval hermeneutics of a fourfold interpretation of Scripture and had focused on
the *sensus literalis* or literal meaning. However, he wanted to understand the Psalms not in any historicizing manner but as prophetic
witnesses to Christ. This hermeneutic interested Luther greatly and
guided him in his early Biblical studies.[2]

Johannes Reuchlin (1455–1522) apparently influenced Luther
even earlier than did Faber, for Luther started using Reuchlin's *De
rudimentis linguae Hebraicae* about 1509. Thus, Luther acquired a
working knowledge of Hebrew prior to Greek. Although he preferred the Latin Vulgate to the Hebrew text in his earlier years, he
later came to recognize the priority of the original text. His ability to
read the Scriptures in the original tongues was extremely important
to his Biblical studies and emergence as a reformer.[3]

Desiderius Erasmus (c. 1469–1536) provided Luther with an
important tool when he published the *Novum Instrumentum omne* in
1516, containing the Greek text of the New Testament. Almost immediately Luther obtained a copy and on May 1, 1516, began using it
in his lectures on Romans.[4] In what seems to be a word of acknowledgment regarding Reuchlin and Erasmus, Luther praised "the
most learned men who have taught us Greek and Hebrew."[5] This
was in 1518, at a time when in his letters to friends he was already
expressing doubts regarding the intentions of Erasmus. Shortly after
this, Reuchlin broke relations with his grandnephew Melanchthon
because of his close ties with Luther. Both Reuchlin and Erasmus
remained aloof from the Reformation and maintained their ties with
the old church until their death. Aside from his many other contributions to the Protestant movement, Erasmus would deserve undy-
ing fame for provoking Luther to write one of his greatest books, *De
servo arbitrio*.[6]

Philipp Melanchthon (1497–1560) was already an acknowledged humanist leader when he arrived at Wittenberg in August
1518. But unlike Faber, Reuchlin, or Erasmus, he quickly formed a
close relationship with Luther, became his friend and fellow worker,
and in a unique manner placed the tools of humanism at the dis-
posal of the University of Wittenberg, Luther, and the Protestant
Reformation. He was one of the greatest classical philologians of the
Renaissance, and under Luther perfected his facility in the Biblical

languages, especially Greek. Since Melanchthon is one of the major subjects of this book, we end our sketch on the contribution of the Biblical humanists to dwell on him in greater detail. Without him, Faber, Reuchlin, Erasmus, or other Biblical humanists, it would be very difficult to imagine the Protestant Reformation taking place. They gave the reformers the tools for studying the Bible and discovering its insights, especially on justification.

When the University of Wittenberg was rebuked in 1523 for its hospitality toward humanism, Luther sprang to its defense.[7] He insisted that evangelical theology could not flourish without the languages, poetry, and rhetoric. A competent pastor must have a thorough knowledge of Latin, Greek, and Hebrew. "So dearly as we love the Gospel, let us also cling to the languages in which the Scriptures were written," Luther wrote in 1524 as he admonished the town aldermen of Germany to provide schools to further Biblical and secular studies.[8] Melanchthon found in Luther a tireless supporter for his program of Biblical humanism.

Notes

[1] WA 4:466–526.

[2] On Faber, see esp. Eugene F. Rice, Jr., *The Prefatory Epistles of Jacques Lefèvre d'Étaples and Related Texts* (New York: Columbia University Press, 1971). A good historical orientation is given in the introduction (pp. xi–xxv) and Faber's preface to the *Quincuplex Psalterium* is reprinted (pp. 192–201) with critical notes. On Luther's use of Faber, see the introductory article preceding his annotations of Faber (WA 3:463–66). For an account of Faber's influence on Luther's Biblical hermeneutics, see Gerhard Ebeling, "Die Anfänge von Luthers Hermeneutik," *Zeitschrift für Theologie und Kirche* 48 (1951): 182–230. Faber's relationship to the Reformation and its theology is taken up in Henry Heller, "The Evangelicism of Lefèvre d' Étaples: 1525," *Studies in the Renaissance* 19 (1972): 42–77. Additional bibliography is listed in Rice, op. cit., pp. xxiv–xxv.

[3] There is little recent work on Reuchlin. The best material in English is in Lewis W. Spitz, *The Religious Renaissance of the German Humanists* (Cambridge: Harvard University Press, 1963), pp. 61–80, 306–12 (notes). Reuchlin is related to Melanchthon and given considerable illumination thereby in Wilhelm Maurer, *Der junge Melanchthon zwischen Humanismus und Reformation*, Vol. I (Göttingen: Vandenhoeck & Ruprecht, 1967), pp. 14–44, 215–18 (notes), et passim. See also the volume of essays produced on the five-hundredth anniversary

of Reuchlin's birth, *Johannes Reuchlin 1455–1522: Festgabe seiner Vaterstadt Pforzheim zur 500. Wiederkehr seines Geburts-Tages* (Pforzheim: Selbstverlag der Stadt Pforzheim, 1955).

[4] WA 56:29, 400.

[5] WA 1:525, 24.

[6] WA 18:600–787. It is not my intention to give even an overview of the immense bibliography on Erasmus but to mention several titles relating him to the Wittenberg Reformation. In this connection, see my article, "The Influence of Erasmus upon Melanchthon, Luther and the Formula of Concord in the Doctrine of Justification," ChH 43 (June 1974): 183–200; bibliography is listed there, esp. in nn. 2–5, pp. 183–84, et passim. On the controversy over the will between Erasmus and Luther, see the notes to *De servo arbitrio* by the editor, A. Freitag (WA 18:551–99). On the controversial question of Erasmus' skepticism, see Wilhelm Maurer, "Offenbarung und Skepsis: Ein Thema aus dem Streit zwischen Luther und Erasmus," *Kirche und Geschichte: Gesammelte Aufsätze*, Vol. II (Göttingen: Vandenhoeck & Ruprecht, 1970), pp. 366–402. Maurer devotes a chapter to Erasmus' influence upon Melanchthon in *Der junge Melanchthon*, Vol. I, pp. 171–214, 240–47 (notes).

[7] WA Br III:49f.

[8] WA 15:37f.

5
The Advent of Melanchthon in Wittenberg and His Early Relationship with Luther

Luther and Melanchthon first met in the last week of August 1518, when the twenty-one year old humanist arrived in Wittenberg to take up his duties as professor of Greek at the university. Soon the new Greek instructor would find himself teaching theology as well as philology, inextricably bound with the fate of Luther and the Reformation. The relationship between these two men formed an important factor in the Reformation and remains a major historiographical and theological problem. In contrast to some past writers, the scholar today must ask such questions as these: To what extent did Melanchthon bring pre-Reformational or Reformational concepts to Wittenberg? In what respects was he influenced by Luther? In what areas did he influence Luther? In order to deal with these important questions it is absolutely necessary to ascertain Melanchthon's development before he met Luther.

Before-1955 the early Melanchthon had been much neglected. At that time my doctoral dissertation was accepted at the University of Erlangen. I had concentrated on the period 1518–1521, had offered some new positions, and had thereby generated discussions and controversies which lasted for twenty years.[1] I had lamented the uncritical stance in which Melanchthon had been placed under the shadow of Luther, and had called for new studies dealing with his independent development before August 1518. The response was gratifying. The two-volume study of the young Melanchthon by

Wilhelm Maurer offered an intensive study covering the years 1508–1529. Fully at home in Renaissance humanism as well as Reformation theology, Maurer was eminently qualified to fill this gap. In this and succeeding studies, he has made an indispensable and imperishable contribution to the subject of the relation between Melanchthon and Luther, upon which much of our understanding of the Reformation movement depends.[2] This can be said even if Maurer does not always succeed in overcoming his bias against Melanchthon. Especially important was his finding that although Melanchthon was regarded as a disciple of Aristotle in rhetoric, logic, and physics, in his metaphysical outlook he was, like Reuchlin, decidedly influenced by Plato or Neoplatonism.[3]

In his inaugural address on Sunday, August 29, 1518, Melanchthon announced that he would immediately begin with two Greek courses. In one he would offer a study in Homer, and in the other Paul's Epistle to Titus. We cannot follow the common assumption that Melanchthon had never studied the Bible before he met Luther, for his preparation in a Pauline Epistle obviously extended back into his previous life at Tübingen. Little is known of his Biblical studies before August 1518, although there is an anecdote that he had been denounced for reading from the Holy Scriptures while attending mass at Tübingen. It also appears obvious that he must have heard about Luther and the Indulgence Controversy before moving to Wittenberg. The *Ninety-Five Theses* of October 31, 1517, had traveled through all of Germany within fourteen days and all of Christendom within four weeks.[4] Even if these reports have been exaggerated, it is hard to understand why the prominent young humanist at Tübingen should not have heard of the *Theses*. For example, Erasmus, with whom he corresponded,[5] had commented on the *Theses* and sent a copy to Thomas More in England.[6] Moreover, when Luther engaged in the Heidelberg Disputation in April 1518, three onlookers won by him—Johann Brenz, Theobald Billicanus, and Martin Bucer—were old friends of Melanchthon, and he remained in touch with them through the years.[7] Melanchthon had defended the beleaguered Reuchlin by writing the preface for the *Clarorum virorum epistolae* of March 1514.[8] Did he know that in February 1514 Luther had written a letter to Spalatin, with whom Melanchthon corresponded, in which he had likewise defended Reuchlin and his Hebrew studies?[9] Of course, we are here following the *argumentum e silentio* since letters and documents which could confirm these conjectures have not come down to us. Yet we know that when a professor receives a call to another university, he informs himself as well as possible regarding its various tendencies and the important men with whom he will be associated. Melanchthon's widespread connections through correspondence made it possible for him to be well informed about the University of Wittenberg, Luther, and the Indulgence Controversy before making a final decision. And it is unlikely that he would have made so crucial a move without thus surveying the situation in advance.

Melanchthon's call to Wittenberg had been arranged by his great-uncle, Reuchlin. Frederick the Wise, Elector of Saxony and distinguished patron of the humanities, had founded the university in 1502 and continuously exerted himself to make it a center for Northern Humanism. The three ancient languages of Latin, Greek, and Hebrew were to be taught by outstanding scholars. He had consulted one of the foremost humanists when in a letter dated March 30, 1518, he asked Reuchlin for advice on whom to call to the chairs for Greek and Hebrew.[10] In reply Reuchlin had recommended several men for the chair in Hebrew but only his relative, "Philipps Schwarzerd von Bretten," for the chair in Greek.[11] For he knew no one among the Germans, unless the Dutchman Erasmus, who could excel Melanchthon in Greek.[12] Actually, this opinion was well justified. Moreover, for a young man who had just turned twenty-one years of age, Melanchthon's record in publishing about thirty books was remarkable. Frederick the Wise promptly gave him a call. Reuchlin jubilantly wrote his grandnephew:

> I say farewell to you, using the promise of God to the faithful Abraham: get thee up out of thy country, from thy kindred and from thy father's house, and come into the land that I will show thee, and I will make of thee a great nation, and I will bless thee, and I will make thy name great, and thou shalt be a blessing. Thus Genesis XII. Thus my spirit prophesies and thus I hope for thee, my Philipp, my accomplishment and my consolation.[13]

An amazing prophecy! This removal would indeed make of young Philipp the *Praeceptor Germaniae*, the second leader of the Wittenberg Reformation, the chief of the German humanists, and the leading systematician of a Lutheran theology from which Lutheranism would not separate itself until the nineteenth century.

Melanchthon's inaugural address was very important because it announced his entire program for the future. In typical humanist fashion he decried the decadence and barbarity of the Middle Ages and called for a reform of school, church, and society by a return to the true sources of knowledge and wisdom—*ad fontes*.[14] Aristotle had been corrupted by the pupils of Thomas Aquinas, John Scotus, and others.[15] These must be exorcised and the true Aristotle restored. The result would be that dialectic and rhetoric would no longer seem to be two separate things, as the schoolmen thought who misinterpreted Aristotle, but that the two belonged together. Dialectic (logic) stood in the service of rhetoric.[16] Thereby, theology as well as the liberal arts would be set free. He forecast that all this would take place in his career at Wittenberg as he announced two Greek courses, one interpreting Homer, representing the Greek tradition, and the other dealing with Paul's Epistle to Titus, presenting the Christian Scriptures.[17]

> And when we devote our minds to the sources, we begin to have a taste of Christ, his command is made clear to us, and we become steeped in the blessed nectar of divine wisdom.[18]

Some modern historians delight in debunking Melanchthon. It has become almost commonplace to belittle this oration as the mere reechoing of words from more gifted scholars and as empty dreams he would soon relinquish. But who were those greater minds, and what if the dreams really came true? Those criticisms betray an incredible ignorance of the subsequent history of Germany and its schools. Melanchthon's *Instructions to the Visitors* (1528) was one of his many sequels to his inaugural address, and its school plan was implemented in literally thousands of German schools during the sixteenth century.[19] While humanist ideas of education were carried out in dozens of schools under the effort of men like Guarino, Vittorino,

Vives, or Erasmus, these same ideas were carried out in thousands of schools under the efforts of Melanchthon and his pupils. Contrary to the opinions of historians who feel that Renaissance humanism was dealt its deathblow by the Reformation simply because the influence of Erasmus was damaged by Luther, we find that the ideals of Northern Humanism reached the dimensions of a mass movement in the German Reformation, and there alone. Melanchthon's oration on August 29, 1518, therefore takes on the character of a document which changed the course of history.

All this was not lost upon Martin Luther, who was a keen discerner of historic events as well as of human character. Two days after the inaugural address, he wrote to Spalatin that as long as they could keep Melanchthon, he desired no other teacher of Greek.[20] Two days later he reported glowingly that Melanchthon's classroom was jammed full.[21] Others reported that about four hundred students came to hear the new professor, including Luther himself.[22] In the following four decades Melanchthon actually brought about a unique development in which humanistic learning provided the means for studying and proclaiming the message of the Reformation. It was always his aspiration that the humanist form must never alter the evangelical content. One of the important tasks of the scholar today is to determine how successfully this program was carried out by Melanchthon and his followers.[23]

The relationship between Melanchthon and Luther remains a crucial problem. There were several stages in their association. The early friendship, beginning in 1518, was followed by a cooling in 1522 after Melanchthon's indecisiveness during the Wittenberg Disturbances. After 1527 this coolness gave way to a friendlier relationship which endured until Luther's death.[24] In later years Melanchthon's Gnesio-Lutheran opponents[25] tried unsuccessfully to destroy Luther's confidence in him, but every evidence indicates that Luther trusted him almost to a fault. While others saw false doctrine in Melanchthon's views on free will and the sacrament after 1531, Luther saw no cause for suspicion. His attitude toward Melanchthon is therefore an important factor for the historian or theologian to remember when dealing with the controversies of the last twenty years of Melanchthon's life. We must, of course, not exclude the possibility of gross error or misconduct on Melanchthon's part.

Notes

[1] Much discussion was evoked by an article which was largely drawn from my dissertation, "Die exegetischen Vorlesungen des jungen Melanchthon und ihre Chronologie," KuD 3 (1957): 140–49 =Hammer 3684. Responses to my dissertation or this article included the following: Adolf Sperl, "Nochmals zur Chronologie der frühen exegetischen Vorlesungen Melanchthon," KuD 4 (1958): 59–60 =Hammer 3728. Wilhelm Maurer, "Zur Komposition der Loci Melanchthons von 1521. Ein Beitrag zur Frage Melanchthon und Luther," *Luther-Jahrbuch* XXV (1958): 146–80 =Hammer 3720. Adolf Sperl, "Eine bisher unbeachtete Vorlesung Melanchthons über den Römerbrief im Herbst 1521," ZKG LXIX (1958): 115–20 =Hammer 3727. Adolf Sperl, *Melanchthon zwischen Humanismus und Reformation* (München: Chr. Kaiser Verlag, 1959) =Hammer 3765. Peter F. Barton, "Die exegetische Arbeit des jungen Melanchthon 1518/19 bis 1528/29. Probleme und Ansätze," ARG LIV (1963): 52–89 =Hammer 4040. Ernst Bizer, *Theologie der Verheißung. Studien zur theologischen Entwicklung des jungen Melanchthon 1519–1524* (Neukirchen-Vluyn: Verlag des Erziehungsvereins, 1964) =Hammer 4083. Maurer, *Der junge Melanchthon*, op. cit.

[2] Besides his two-volume study of the young Melanchthon, Maurer has published collected essays in *Melanchthon-Studien*, No. 181 in SVRG (Gütersloh: Gerd Mohn, 1964). As a Lutheran from the union church of Hessen, his aversion toward Melanchthon can be understood by reading his essay, "Das Bild der Reformationsgeschichte bei August Vilmar und Heinrich Heppe," *Kirche und Geschichte: Gesammelte Aufsätze*, Vol. II (Göttingen: Vandenhoeck & Ruprecht, 1970), pp. 78–102. The attempts of the Reformed churchman, Heppe, to discredit Luther and install a Calvinized Melanchthon in his place had serious repercussions in Reformation historiography of the past century. In order to overcome historical distortions as a Luther researcher, Maurer later found it hard to gain sympathy for Melanchthon.

[3] See Maurer's impressive chapter, "Melanchthons philosophischer Ausgangspunkt," in *Der junge Melanchthon*, Vol. I, pp. 84–98.

[4] KK I:162.

[5] Erasmus certainly knew Melanchthon as author of the preface to the *Clarorum virorum epistolae* of 1514 (CR I:5–6). In the annotation to I Thessalonians 2:7 (written in 1515) Erasmus had commented: "Immortal God, what hope does not that mere youth or even boy, Philipp Melanchthon, hold out, undertaking both literatures equally well [i.e., Latin and Greek]. What acumen of invention! What purity of word! How great the memory of treasured thoughts! How varied his readings! In short, what splendor of this modest and princely talent!" *Novum Instrumentum omne* (Basel: Froben, 1516), Part II, p. 555. Melanchthon had responded with similar compliments.

[6] See Roland H. Bainton, *Erasmus of Christendom* (London: Collins, 1969), p. 189. The letter is in EE 3, No. 785, p. 239, 37.

[7] On Melanchthon's friendship in youth with these men, see Karl Hartfelder, *Philipp Melanchthon als Praeceptor Germaniae*, Vol. VII in *Monumenta Germaniae Paedagogica* (Berlin: A. Hofmann, 1889; reprint, Nieuwkoop: B. De Graaf, 1964), p. 25. On the presence of Brenz, Billicanus, and Bucer at the Heidelberg Disputation, see KK I:175.

[8] CR 1:5-6.

[9] WA Br I:23-4.

[10] Suppl Mel 6/I:29.

[11] CR 1:29-30.

[12] Ibid., p. 34.

[13] Ibid., pp. 32f.

[14] CR 11:23; SA III:40.

[15] CR 11:17; SA III:32.

[16] CR 11:19; SA III:34f.

[17] CR 11:25; SA III:41.

[18] CR 11:23; SA III:40.

[19] SA I:267-71; WA 26:236-40.

[20] WA Br I:192.

[21] Ibid., p. 196.

[22] Ibid., p. 197.

[23] An important investigation of this problem is Peter Petersen, *Geschichte der aristotelischen Philosophie im protestantischen Deutschland* (Leipzig: Felix Meiner, 1921).

[24] The best treatment of the relationship between Luther and Melanchthon is that by Gustav Mix, "Luther und Melanchthon in ihrer gegenseitigen Beurteilung," *Theologische Studien und Kritiken* 74 (1901): 458-521. See also my discussion of this, *The Mature Luther*, pp. 133-53.

[25] After the death of Luther in 1546, the Lutheran movement gradually divided into two rival parties: the Philippists, who considered themselves followers of Melanchthon, and the Gnesio-Lutherans (from Greek *gnesios*, genuine), a strict party which included such men as Amsdorf, Flacius, Wigand, Gallus, Judex, Mörlin, Hesshus, Westphal, Hunnius, and Poach. Ironically, the Gnesio-Lutherans, who often attacked Melanchthon and his circle, had been more strongly influenced by the great humanist than they realized, so that they frequently betrayed his influence and depended upon his contributions.

6
The Early Biblical Works of Melanchthon

For some twenty years the early Biblical works of Melanchthon have been subjected to scrutiny as never before in recent times. Unfortunately, the principles of scientific research have not always been followed. Works of dubious reliability have jostled works of unquestionable authenticity and often won the victory. For example, in a work of unimpeachable authority, the *Baccalaureate Theses* of 1519, Melanchthon presented the earliest Reformational assertion of justification by the free imputation of Christ's merit.[1] But this source was simply dismissed by some writers as inconclusive because of seemingly conflicting testimony from texts of uncertain transmission. Because the early Biblical works of Melanchthon are still comparatively unknown, it will be well for us to review them and establish useful categories regarding their nature and reliability. Beyond this brief survey, readers may consult my more detailed analysis elsewhere.[2]

It must first be kept in mind that Melanchthon served in two departments of instruction now known as foreign languages and theology. His call to Wittenberg had been to teach Greek, but Luther soon involved him in teaching theology. In September 1519 he won the *Baccalaureus Biblicus* degree, which gave him the right to give Biblical courses in theology as well as in philology. Both before and after that date Melanchthon used the Bible as teaching material in his Greek courses. After that date he gave extended expositions of Scripture, especially in Matthew, John, Romans, I Corinthians, II Corinthians, and Colossians. In addition he gave systematic studies of Romans which soon evolved into a course in dogmatics or Christian doctrine. When we are trying to establish the place of a given work on Romans, we must therefore decide whether it was Class A, a course in liberal arts, Class B, an exegetical offering, or Class C, a lecture in systematic theology. Failure to observe this kind of distinction has led to the confusion of important issues in the past.[3]

We must next determine the delivery and reliability of the work we have before us. Very few holographs are known, and except for the rare exceptions, the best-attested sources are therefore those which Melanchthon himself prepared for publication and acknowledged as his own. Under Class A, belonging to the arts, come the works he edited in Rhetoric (1518–1519), the Dialectic (1520), and a few letters and declamations.[4] To Class B can be assigned only the *Disputation Theses*, a few autograph marginal notations, and letters and declamations.[5] For Class C we have, besides the *Loci communes*, marginal notations to various works, letters, and the *Baccalaureate Theses* of 1519.[6] The *Baccalaureate Theses* also provide source material for Class B, the exegetical works. This completes the list of works which Melanchthon acknowledged from the Biblical studies of 1518–1521. The rest are only secondary sources at best—that is, materials which have come secondhand. These include copies of his lectures which Melanchthon never saw, pirated editions (Luther himself was the "pirate" who published the lectures on Romans), and even forgeries, of which there have been many.[7] Assuming that such secondary materials can be shown to actually go back to Melanchthon, they can have only corroborative weight. In no case can evidence from these poorly-attested works, and certainly not an item which Melanchthon himself repudiated, be cited in preference to a well-attested work.

Notes

[1] SA I:24.

[2] See my article, "Formgeschichtliche und inhaltliche Probleme in den Werken des jungen Melanchthon: Ein neuer Zugang zu seinen Bibelarbeiten und Disputationsthesen," ZKG 84 (1973): 30–48. This does not completely replace my earlier essay, "Die exegetischen Vorlesungen des jungen Melanchthon und ihre Chronologie," KuD 3 (1957): 140–49. In the later

article I made necessary corrections such as changing the exegetical *Lectures on Romans* from the summer to the fall of 1519 (ZKG, p. 33) and reassigning the course on Galatians to Class A, philological exercises (ibid., p. 32).

[3] Adolf Sperl, "Eine bisher unbeachtete Vorlesung Melanchthons," ZKG 69 (1958): 115–20, called for a lecture by Melanchthon on Romans from July 1521 until January 1522. However, his documentation, "Philippus praelegit . . . ad Romanos Graece . . ." (p. 119), clearly points to a Greek exercise rather than an identification with the *Annotations . . . ad Romanos*, which Luther published in 1522 (Nürnberg: Stuchs, 1522). His attempt to thereby show an advance in predestination by these *Annotations* over the *Loci communes* of 1521 is not convincing (pp. 116–17). The discussion in Sperl, *Melanchthon zwischen Humanismus und Reformation* (pp. 123–25) seems to miss the mark. On p. 25 he cites the "Lucubratiuncula" (CR 21:15–16) with the same assurance as the later *Loci* although Melanchthon rejected the former and accepted the latter as his own work.

[4] The Rhetoric, which originated in the Tübingen period (see Maurer, *Der junge Mel.*, Vol. I, pp. 187ff.), was written in 1518 and appeared in early 1519. The first edition was published by Johannes Rhau-Grunenberg in Wittenberg as *Philippi Melanchthonis De Rhetorica libri Tres . . .* (Beuttenmüller No. 58). This has never been reprinted in modern times. The Dialectic was first published in Leipzig by Melchior Lotther the Elder as *Compendiaria Dialectices Ratio* (Beut. No. 64); in CR 20:711–64. Examples of Greek text editions are in my article in ZKG, op. cit. Further examples are in Ernst Bizer, ed., *Texte aus der Anfangszeit Melanchthons*, No. 2 in Texte zur Geschichte der evangelischen Theologie (Neukirchen-Vluyn: Erziehungsverein, 1966). Two declamations on Paul are in CR 11:34–41; SA I:27–53.

[5] The declamations listed in the preceding note are applicable here. In addition are several well-documented series of disputation theses—the *Baccalaureate Theses* of 1519 (SA I:24–5), the *Themata circularia* of 1520 (SA I:54–5), and the *Propositiones de missa* of 1521 (SA I:163–67). The polemics against "Thomas Placentinus" of 1521 (SA I:56–140) and against the University of Paris of 1521 (SA I:141–62) round out the primary documents in this class. Most of these works are in English translation in *Melanchthon: Selected Writings*, tr. Charles Leander Hill, ed. Elmer E. Flack and Lowell J. Satre (Minneapolis: Augsburg, 1962). This welcome volume is flawed by some faulty renditions—e.g., "D. Hieronymo Bronner, Divi Caroli Caes. Aug. a secretis, Philip. Melanchthon S." is translated as "To Doctor Jerome Brunner, confidential advisor of the late [!] Charles Caesar Augustus, greeting from Philip Melanchthon" instead of as "To Doctor Jerome Bronner, privy counsellor of Charles, Holy Roman Emperor, greeting from Philipp Melanchthon."

[6] The best edition of the 1521 *Loci communes* remains that edited by Gustav Plitt and Theodor Kolde, *Die Loci communes Philipp Melanchthons in ihrer*

Urgestalt, 3rd ed. (Leipzig: A. Deichert, 1900). See also CR 21:81–228; SA II/1:3–163. The best English translation is that by Lowell J. Satre and Wilhelm Pauck in *Melanchthon and Bucer*, Vol. XIX in LCC (Philadelphia: Westminster, 1969), pp. 18–152. The important marginal notations are largely unedited, but see my article in ZKG, esp. pp. 45–7 and the table on p. 48. See also Bizer, *Texte*, op. cit.

⁷ An unusually large amount of forged documents and book annotations exists of works attributed to Melanchthon. For more information, see my article, "Unpublished Autographs of Melanchthon and of the Grynaeus Family in the University of Chicago Library," ARG 65 (1974): 161–71. There I have cited the following pertinent entries in Hammer, Nos. 1723, 1747, 1753, 1763, 2065, 2236, 2374, 2699, 2827, 2829, 2916, 2949, 3403, 3413, 3669, 3671.

7

The Early Doctrine of Justification in Melanchthon's "Theological Institutes"

Although the *Theological Institutes* have come to us in a strange handwriting, they are in a volume bearing Melanchthon's autograph. Therefore, the best source on Melanchthon's earliest doctrine of justification at Wittenberg is this work from 1518–1519.[1] Hence, we shall turn our attention to the teaching found in this early forerunner of the *Loci communes*. Melanchthon asserts that the three main teachings of Romans are on justification, predestination, and ethics. In the *Institutes*, however, he is interested chiefly in justification and its subsidiaries of sin, law, and grace.

Melanchthon undergirded his early doctrine of justification with a concept of sin which went far beyond that of the medieval schoolmen and placed him much closer to Augustine. Melanchthon did not confine sin to isolated acts but led it back to its source in the corruption of the heart or of the affect. Thus, he could define sin concisely as love of self (*amor sui*),[2] and he could see sin in all its depth as original sin. To the question, "Why can we not attain righteousness by our own powers?" he supplied the answer: "On account of original sin. Original sin is inborn passion, a ravaging assault, by which we are dragged into transgressions."[3] This corruption of the heart shows itself as lust or concupiscence, by which all mankind in its sinful desires is consumed as by a fire, leading to countless individual trespasses of the Law.[4] Such a man cannot stand before God.

When man realizes that he is sinful, his first impulse is to flee to the Law for refuge. That is, he tries to overcome sin by a better performance of the outward requirements of the Law. This is the course suggested by the reason of the natural man. But it is a futile attempt. The individual who tries to fulfill the requirements of the Law by keeping each of the commandments is bound to discover that the Law cannot help him but can only lead him further and further into sin.[5] Melanchthon gives two grounds for this inability of the Law to deliver the sinner:

1. That power within man which corresponds to the Law is reason (*cogitatio*). If deliverance were to come through the Law, it would be necessary for the powers of reason to be able to change the affects of the heart. This might be theoretically possible, but in reality it is out of the question, for such power is lacking to human reason. In the fire of temptation the evil desires of the individual overcome the promptings of sober reason. Hence, man does not listen to the Law, as his reason tells him he should, but rather succumbs to his evil desires.[6] Melanchthon admits that he is hereby contradicting the heathen and the scholastic philosophers, but he insists that they were all in error when they thought to improve morals merely by educating the intellectual powers. Indeed, Melanchthon goes as far as to say that the medieval masters with all their Sentences could never change a single human heart for the better.[7]

2. The will of the natural man could provide as little power for fulfilling the Law as could human reason. At best, the will could only assist in producing legalistic works (*opera legis*). Such works, however, do not avail before God since they are performed without love or inward willingness. Because they are done without self-surrender, they are valueless toward justification.[8]

Since the Law, therefore, can operate neither through human reason nor through the will of man, the Law is not only powerless to save but actually leads to further damnation. This is true because the Law cannot eradicate sin committed in the past any more than it can give power to avoid sin in the present or future. Since the Law provides no strength toward its own fulfillment, it actually serves as a scourge (*flagra*), tormenting the tender conscience and bringing the individual untold grief and sorrow. Hence, it is inevitable that, consciously or unconsciously, resentment toward the Law will arise. Since the Law is the Law of God, a burning hatred to God follows. The picture of God is changed from that of a loving God to that of a vindictive God. ". . . From the sweet name of God is made the name of a Hangman and a Revenger, or even harsher than these. For that cause Paul said that the letter kills, and the Law works wrath."[9] The Law, therefore, does not bring man unto righteousness or justification but unto deeper condemnation. Like the bit in the mouth of a horse, the Law can only coerce. Melanchthon conceded that reason was free while the will was in bondage, but he asserted that neither reason nor the will could do anything to alter this damnable condition by cooperating with the Law. If man is to be saved, it must be from some power other than that of the Law.

This brings Melanchthon to the subject of grace. In that moment he breaks forth in the joy of the discovery of the Gospel. First he describes the work of salvation as performed by Christ and worked by the Spirit.

> In truth, Christ died for our justification. All the prophets longed for the time when God would rain forth righteousness upon the earth. It is the troubled desire of pious minds when, having condemned themselves, they realize that they are not able to accomplish that which they strive after, and they sigh from the depths of their hearts that God henceforth for the sake of Christ would richly supply his spirit unto purging, enlightening, and justifying. God indeed did send Christ into the world, who by his death made satisfaction for our offences, and who merited the justifying spirit, that is, the spirit that renews our affects and changes the inner propensity toward sin. For those who believe that he is the author of righteousness, their sins are removed, and the spirit of righteousness is given them. This Christ of our righteousness is proclaimed by Paul before our eyes.

Now Melanchthon can no longer continue in measured scholarly language, but like a Paul he breaks into a song of rapture.

> O mighty Benefice! Thus to know Christ! If you are burdened by the Law, with the evil conscience of your offences, here he bears away

the load and draws you into his arms. If you thirst after righteousness, he supplies it here.

O blessed ones, to whom it is given, thus to know Christ!

O madness, O darkness, to offer other comfort for troubled consciences, other hope for righteousness and perfect goodness, other than from Christ![10]

Christ by his atoning work has thus merited for the sinner the purifying Spirit, by which he is purged from sin.

In this early work Melanchthon, like Augustine and Luther, understands grace as a substance. At times he also identifies grace with the Holy Spirit. Like his two predecessors, Melanchthon begins with the antithesis of the Letter and the Spirit (II Cor. 3:6). The Law is the Letter which kills because, operating only through reason, it cannot change the human heart (affect). Contrariwise, grace is the Spirit through which we are enlightened, purified, and driven toward good.[11] The new affect which drives out the evil passions is given to the believer through the merit of Christ.[12]

No sooner has Melanchthon said this than he speaks of the results of grace as though they were identified with grace. "The parts of grace are: faith . . . , charity . . . , and hope . . ." But what is remarkable is that he does not fall into the medieval distinction and interrelation of these three "virtues." Despite the primitive character of his theology at this point, faith, hope, and charity are described in such a way that medieval views are purposely avoided and the way is cleared for future Reformational development. When it is recalled that Melanchthon had given Luther decisive impulses precisely at this point in September 1518, his treatment of the "virtues" here will appear as the necessary development of his pioneering insight into the nature of faith. "Faith is the firm belief in the divine word; by faith we are enlightened and God is shown to us."[13]

Strangely enough, although Melanchthon together with Luther developed the Reformational idea of faith as trust (*fiducia*), Melanchthon here could still use *fiducia* at times to express a false confidence. This should serve as a warning against making over-hasty decisions as to precisely where fully evangelical doctrine is to be found and should furthermore impress upon us the gradual manner in which such insights came into flower during the Reformation.

This point is startlingly emphasized when we realize that, even in his present writing, Melanchthon has no completely-developed understanding of justification. Instead, traces of the so-called "analytic" view are present just as in medieval theology, the Young Luther, and the later Osiander. Thus, justification is the reception of grace through which the believer receives faith to apprehend Christ as the Author of his righteousness since by His death Christ has achieved satisfaction for man's offences. Christ merits the Holy Spirit for believers and bestows the Holy Ghost, who brings a new affect and thereby works righteousness within the renewed individual.[14] To be justified here means to have the "inborn affections" changed or to have Christ or the Spirit impart new affections. Nevertheless, Melanchthon recognizes sin as the disposition of the heart rather than the mere overt act. Hence, under justification he recognizes righteousness as the disposition of the changed heart from which trusting in self-righteousness has been eradicated. As in Luther, righteousness is therefore the inclination toward good and away from evil.[15]

In his *Theological Institutes* Melanchthon tried to avoid works-righteousness by a careful distinction between the righteousness of the Christian and that of the unbeliever. The so-called righteousness of the heathen and the Jews could never make one just in the eyes of God. Such righteousness stemmed either from fear of judgment (*metus servilis*) or from the desire to benefit thereby (*affectus commodus*). But despite outward appearances, there was no true righteousness in such hearts.[16] As Plato had realized long before, works have no ethical value unless they come from a willing heart. Since the Law could not make the human heart willing, such works came without the participation of the inner man and were therefore valueless in the sight of God.[17] At best, such works could lead to a Pharisaical righteousness, which was actually a vain trust in one's own self rather than in God. The Christian, however, puts his trust not in his own work but in Christ, the Author of his righteousness.[18]

The forgiveness of sins meant the removal of past transgressions. This brought peace (*tranquillitas*) to the heart. All this came about through the merits of Christ (*propter Christi meritum*) so that sins were no longer reckoned to the account of the believer (*non imputari*). This confession Melanchthon called the rock upon which the church was built. Against it not even the gates of hell would ever prevail.

Notes

[1] I usually cite the old copy that Melanchthon himself presented to Johann Hess, from the library of the Christaneum in Altona, *Christaneum Cod. Ms. No. 16, Aa 3/4*, hereafter abbreviated as Cod., p. 5 = CR 21:49. The text given in the *Corpus Reformatorum* has many deviations from this old manuscript, which obviously bears the endorsement of Melanchthon himself. I have devoted some time to the question of whose handwriting is found in the *Codex*, but neither my attempts nor those of several handwriting experts have succeeded in identifying the amanuensis. Although the bound volume in which the *Institutes* are contained bears a dedication to Hess in the hand of Melanchthon himself, the miscellaneous contents of the *Codex*, including the *Institutes* themselves, were written neither by Melanchthon nor his more prominent associates, nor of course by Hess himself. The handwriting has not been successfully identified.

[2] Cod., pp. 31–2 = CR 21:55. Cf. Cod., p. 24 = CR 21:54.

[3] Cod., p. 14 = CR 21:51. Cf. Cod., p. 15.2 = CR 21:52.53.

[4] Cod., p. 14.

[5] Ibid., p. 8 = CR 21:51.50. Cf. the relation between *lex* and *cogitatio* (Cod., pp. 18–20 = CR 21:52–3) and Melanchthon's sharp criticism of philosophy (Cod., pp. 5–6 = CR 21:49).

[6] "The Law indeed is a powerless cogitation, while the affect itself is the life of the mind. Therefore it is not possible that it be overcome by the Law." The work of the Law is "sentencia inefficax quae idipsum non prestet quod mandat" (Cod., pp. 18–19 = CR 21:52).

[7] Cod., pp. 5–6 = CR 21:49, et passim.

[8] "Tum, ad affectus non est Libera, Et sicut adfectus est operis externi pondus, ita membra secum rapit, si ceperit paulo Vehemencius sevire, ita nec in externis operibus erit aliqua Libertas Verum simpliciter Comparata ad opus externum est Libera, sicut perinde Vt intellectus non potest inter contradictorias nisi Vni adsentiri & tamen utramque concipere: Sic Voluntas adfectu in vna aliqua re haeret, potest autem diversum externis membris imperare, Verum sicut alter a Contradiccionis pars mendatium est, ita opus externum quod fit repugnante animi adfectu" (Cod., pp. 16–17 = CR 21:52).

[9] Cod., pp. 20–21 = CR 21:53. This sounds like an echo of Luther before and after his struggle in the monastery and suggests that Melanchthon too had experienced the devastating accusations of the Law.

[10] CR 21:51.

[11] "GRACIA, quam & spiritum Vocat, est spiritus quo illustramur, purgamur, impellimur ad bona . . ." (Cod. pp. 22–3 = CR 21:52).

[12] "Hic affectus meritus est per Christum & GRACIA dicitur . . ." (Cod., p. 24 = CR 21:54).

[13] "FIDES ad sensus Constans Verbi divini & hac illuminamur & deus nobis ostenditur . . ." (Ibid).

[14] "Christus . . . emereretur spiritum iustificantem, hoc est innovantem affectus nostros, et qui intimam propensionem peccati mutet, Vt ipsum qui crederent esse auctorem iustitie illorum peccata abolerentur, ius spiritus iusticiae daretur . . ." (Cod., pp. 12–13 = CR 21:51). "Crede Christo, invoca Christum per fidem, iam spiritus iustificator & purgator adest" (Cod., pp. 34–5 = CR 21:56).

[15] Cod., pp. 27–8 = CR 21:54; see also Cod., p. 30 = CR 21:54f.

[16] CR 21:55.

[17] Ibid., pp. 50–51.

[18] Ibid., pp. 55, 50.

AUGSBURG

8

Toward a Reformational Concept of Faith

The key to understanding any of the various forms of Christian theology is to grasp what its formulators are trying to say when they use
the word "faith." The inability of some Roman Catholic theologians
to understand Luther's theology may be largely due to their failure to
grasp what he meant by the word "faith." Judged by Tridentine definitions of faith, Luther's view of justification would indeed be faulty.[1]
This is also true of subsequent Protestantism. Some of the pietists lost
their continuity with historic Christianity not so much in denying
specific doctrines as in an anthropocentric view of faith that unwit-
tingly changed the article of justification by supplying it with a new
content. Likewise, much of the lack of clarity in interpretations of
Luther's theology may be due to a lack of attention to what he meant
at a given time by the word "faith." Luther underwent a transition in
the year 1518 that was to have far-reaching effects on his doctrine of
justification and, with it, on his entire theology.

Development of the Faith Concept

Many Protestants think that a peculiar contribution of the Reformation
was that it uncovered the doctrine of subjective faith (*fides qua creditur*) at a time when only objective faith (*fides quae creditur*) was
known.[2] This is not at all true. That important distinction had not
been lost in the interval between Paul and Luther as many believe.
Augustine taught the distinction clearly enough,[3] and Luther himself
confessed his indebtedness to Augustine in this respect.[4] It is therefore not true that Luther discovered the doctrine of subjective faith.

A perusal of his earlier works will likewise show that he used much of the medieval terminology for a long time. In his marginal notes on the Sentences of Peter Lombard (1510–1511) Luther knows of an unformed and a formed faith (*fides informis* and *formata*), plays the infused against an acquired faith (*fides infusa* and *fides acquisita*), and speaks of a love (*caritas*) that renders the believer acceptable (*gratum*) in the eyes of God.[5] These concepts persisted in his lectures on Romans, where Luther criticized the idea of an unformed faith but still held to the idea of faith formed by charity.[6] Even in the later lectures on Hebrews he still clung to the received construction.[7] The old notion of the cardinal virtues of faith, charity, and hope lingered on together with their respective coordination with the verb tenses of past, present, and future. This was completely eliminated only after the transition of 1518–1519. Faith in the present tense was pressed with a Latin word meaning to believe in the sense of accepting in the present as true that which one was told to believe (*credulitas*). The concept of trust (*fiducia*) in medieval thought was linked with hope and the future.[8] This accorded with medieval views that justification lay only in a future completion and that one could therefore not be certain in this life of his salvation.[9] Legalism still marked the doctrine of justification in Luther. The insight that faith brings full salvation at the present moment belonged to his mature theology. Until the transition of 1518–1519 Luther was still groping for it.[10] As late as his lectures on Hebrews (1517–1518) Luther followed Jerome in interpreting the word *hypostasis* in Hebrews 11:1 as "substance."[11] Luther's interpretation of the verse as *eine gewisse Hoffnung* (a steadfast hope) belonged to his development after Melanchthon moved to Wittenberg.[12]

With the help of medieval writers, Luther had long been clear that faith was the gift of God. The medieval schoolmen had distinguished between an infused faith (*fides infusa*), which was an inceptive faith given by God, and an acquired faith (*fides acquisita*), giving undue recognition to the latter, of course.

Luther rejected acquired faith as dead.[13] He developed the concept of infused faith in his doctrine that faith is not the road that man builds toward God but is the result of God's act without human cooperation.[14] Faith may also be described as the flight of the sinner to God for refuge and forgiveness. "Since man's weakness is shown him through the law, he is healed by fleeing in faith unto divine mercy."[15] Hence, Luther also characterized faith as the means of approaching to God,[16] without, however, losing sight of its origin in the work of God within man. The believer always realizes that his flight for refuge has been made possible only by God. Luther is still the monk. He can still speak knowingly and forcefully of human responsibility. But this does not confuse his conviction that faith is the work of God—something his medieval predecessors and pietistic successors overlooked. Instead, in ascribing the development of faith to God, Luther points out that he is taking salvation from the uncertain hands of man and placing it in the unfailing hands of God. This is hurtful to human pride but comforting to the contrite sinner. In his lecture on Hebrews 10:38 (1518) Luther still followed the text of the Vulgate, *Justus autem meus ex fide vivit*, which can be translated: "My righteous one lives out of faith" (my translation). Over the phrase, "My righteous one," he wrote the comment: "He who fulfills the commandments of God"[17]—a comment still lacking the insight that faith is righteousness. In the margin he added:

> These are truly words of consolation, a needed explanation for those who suffer the torturing thought that theirs might be insufficient, when in reality faith, i.e., the life of the Christian, is more the working of God than of us, our truest passion.[18]

"Faith is the life of the Christian." And the life of the Christian is the performing of the Ten Commandments by faith—by God working in him. If faith is life, unbelief is death, not only because it leads to eternal death after life in this world, but especially because getting along without God in this world is already spiritual death— death in its deepest sense. Over against this the life of faith is in itself everlasting life. Whoever lives in faith lives in God. Moreover, whoever lives in God cannot possibly be a sinner but is just, for God is holy. It is therefore clear that God must sanctify him. According to Hebrews 11:7, the heart of the believer is separated from all visible things and rests in the invisible things of God.[19] Luther at this time sees in faith a good work, for faith is obedience[20] which fulfills God's law. There is no more sin in the believer who through faith acknowledges God as Judge and Saviour, because on account of his faith he has been acknowledged as just by God.[21]

Some Terms for Faith in the Early Luther

It is important to acquire a precise understanding of Luther's terminology. He used various terms for faith. The most familiar of these
was *fides*, but Luther also spoke of acceptance (*credulitas* as well as
credere), adherence (*adhaesio*), and faithfulness (*fidelitas*).

One of the most important words for faith in both the lectures
on Romans and Hebrews was *credulitas*. Especially in its English
derivative, *credulity*, this seems an unfortunate choice of words.
Luther scholars in the past have virtually ignored this term. Just how
did Luther come to employ such a strange concept? He was following a long tradition.[22] A scanning of the history of dogma reveals the
use of *credulitas* among such scattered writers as Cyprian, Sedulius,
Anastasius, Chrysologus, Gregory of Tours, Theodolfus, Gregory
the Great, Hugo of St. Victor, Alcuin, Hrabanus, Thomas Aquinas,
Alexander of Hales, and others. The term was used to express subjective faith or ". . . subjective faithfulness over against the delivered
objective faith . . . ," as Reinhold Seeberg expressed it in his interpretation of Zenos.[23]

In the early Luther this understanding of *credulitas* as compliance with the teaching authority of the Catholic Church persisted.
This accounts for the fact that he refused to reject such medieval
concepts as the threefold concept of penance, the indulgence, and
purgatory long after they contradicted his findings in Scripture. But
alongside this ecclesial understanding of *credulitas* was emerging an
application of it to God Himself. It became paired with *incredulitas*—
the rejection of God in His majesty and in His Word. To comprehend Luther's meaning we must dissociate these two Latin terms
from their English derivatives, *credulity* and *incredulity*, terms with
negative values which in meaning approach the words *gullibility*
and *ingullibility* and thereby reverse the values. Instead, we must
see them in Luther as the virtues of faithfulness toward the creedal
authority of the church and toward the divine authority of God.[24]

Credulitas means faith. It is the recognition of the majesty
of God. It dethrones the ego of the sinner (*se esse deum*) and gives
God the honor due Him (*deum esse deum*). The grace to let God
be God does not come naturally, for natural man wants to be both
God and Judge. It is the gift of faith.[25] Natural man glorifies not

God but himself. This is *incredulitas*. But the contrast between faith and unbelief goes still further. Since in his faith the believer denies himself and glorifies God, he is thereby invested with true humility (*humilitas*).

The relation between the humility of faith and the peril of pride in the attempt to become just by doing justly was a problem for the Young Luther. He asserted: "Without works, the righteousness of God is imputed to those who believe."[26] At first reading, this seems to express the full content of the doctrine of justification of the Mature Luther, but a more careful study disappoints the evangelical reader. Luther is answering the question whether the good works of the saints are reckoned by God as righteousness unto justification, and he must answer in the affirmative. Now the point of this passage becomes clear. Their works are accepted by God unto justification not because the saints intended them so (*opera legis*), but because God was pleased to accept them in view of faith (*opera fidei*). Nevertheless, the godly men did not do good works in order to be justified but because they longed after righteousness. They themselves did not realize that God was pleased with them. Their works were as nothing in their own eyes. This constituted their humility. They cast themselves before God, never certain whether God accepted their works or not, concerned only with finding the mercy of God.[27] This was true faith (*credulitas*). This was humility, and it stood in sharpest contrast to the cold calculation of the proud unbeliever who presumed to stand before God on the basis of his own works of righteousness. ". . . Humility and the fear of God is the only merit," Luther asserted at Heidelberg in April 1518.[28]

The importance of humility was further expressed in the *Heidelberg Disputation* under the eighth thesis: "Far more works of men are dead because they are performed without fear, in unadulterated and evil security." Luther then commented: "For where there is no fear, there is no humility; where there is no humility, there is pride, there is the wrath and condemnation of God. . . ."[29]

There are three other aspects of *credulitas* in Luther's early theology. It expresses the relationship of man to God. While unbelief separates from God, faith joins the believer with God.[30] Again, *credulitas* contains the concept of the indwelling of God and His activity in the heart of man. Through His Word in the believing heart, God dwells therein.[31] *Deus nobiscum*—Immanuel—God with us! Finally, from the antithesis of *credulitas* and *incredulitas* Luther derived the thought that the unbeliever knows no fear of God, but the believer lives under the true fear of God.[32]

Faith is described under a different aspect by the word *adhaesio* (adherence). By faith the Christian clings to Christ as though he were glued tightly. Indeed, faith is even likened to glue or a coupling.[33] This concept includes several ideas which it expressed more suitably than other terms. Luther used it not only to describe faith as a personal clinging to God, but also as clinging to the Word of God.[34] It could also express the thought of compliance with the will of God and obedience to His commandments.[35] This clinging by faith to Christ therefore means the renovation of the believer. He is totally changed both inwardly and outwardly so that he conforms to the pattern of Christ. Luther describes this in his comment on Hebrews 2:10:

> In this, the way in which we are saved is beautifully shown, namely through Christ as the idea and example, to whose image all who are saved are conformed. For God the Father made Christ to be a sign and idea, in whom those who cling by faith are transformed into the same image, and thus drawn away from the images of the world.[36]

Thus, it is clear how this concept of faith related to Luther's doctrine of justification at this time. Faith was the organ by which that inward transformation was effected through clinging to Christ. The individual was thereby made more and more Christlike until at length he was truly justified.

This concept of faith had certain points in common with Luther's view of the *fröhlicher Wechsel* or the "marvellous exchange" of the righteousness of Christ for the sin of the believer. Calling faith a coupling agency and comparing it to glue suggests the mystic qualities of Luther's theology. As the forerunners of the later Orthodox doctrine of the mystical union, these qualities differed from the mysticism of the Middle Ages. Then, mystical contemplation had sometimes been a justificational approach to God. But in Luther's theology, as in later Lutheran Orthodoxy, mysticism was not the attempt to achieve one's own justification.[37] It was the experience of justification. In other words, the mystical union was not the cause but the result of justification.

Still another word for faith was fidelity or *fidelitas*, which expressed the faithfulness of the believer over against the promise of God in contrast to faithlessness or *infidelitas*.[38] By his *fidelitas* the believer fulfilled the Law, just as all sin could be traced back to unbelief or *infidelitas*.[39]

The Emergence of Fiducial Faith

Nevertheless, the Latin term *fiducia* or trust was destined to become the distinctively Reformational view of faith. In the history of dogma *fiducia* had been employed somewhat sparingly and had often been used in an unfavorable sense. *Fiducia* had been associated with *spes* (hope), which necessarily had futuristic connotations. This made faith a trust in God that hoped for future fulfillment.[40] Augustine used *fiducia* to express the confidence of the belief that God in His grace would bring him at length to eternal salvation.[41] This idea was corrupted after Augustine's time. In the period of high scholasticism *fiducia* was connected not only with God's promise but also with the good conscience of man.[42] In late scholasticism, especially in the theology of Gabriel Biel, *fiducia* was not only trust in the grace of God but also the confidence of the believer in the value of his own merits (*merita*).[43] Where it was understood that justification rested upon the intrinsic righteousness or merits of the believer, *fiducia* became the hope that God would declare one righteous for the sake of these merits. Sometimes justification was even seen as theodicy—that is, God showed that He was just when He rewarded the believer for his merits.

From this it is clear that we must not confuse every occurrence of the word *fiducia* with its Reformational usage as saving faith. Reuchlin had written in his *Vocabularius breviloquus* (1504): "*Fiducia* is used of good things and evil things, but more often regarding good things."[44] It is likely that the Reformational usage first occurred to Melanchthon from reading Erasmus, who used the term both positively and negatively. In his *Enchiridion* of 1501 Erasmus had combined the word with *opus* in disparaging the Jewish confidence in good works (*fiducia operum*).[45] However, in his annotation to Hebrews 11:1 for the *Novum Instrumentum omne* (1515–1516), he defined faith as *fiducia*, albeit in the futuristic connotation.[46] In his *Ratio seu Methodus compendio perveniendi ad veram Theologiam*

(1518) Erasmus treated *fiducia* as a synonym for faith.[47] The same usage was suggested in his 1522 *Paraphrase of Romans 3:22*[48] and his later *Annotations*.[49] Although justification by faith alone does not seem to have played a large role in his thinking, it is likely that Erasmus guided Melanchthon toward his Reformational concept of faith and, through him, Luther as well.

The term *fiducia* occurred in Luther's first *Lectures on the Psalter*,[50] but not in the sense in which he was later to employ it. In his marginal notations to the sermon of Tauler (1516) he warned against *fiducia* as false, carnal security.[51] At the same time, he could use *fiducia* positively.[52]

Among medieval writers it had been common to speak of the three "cardinal virtues" of faith, hope, and charity in terms of a temporal sequence. Derived from I Corinthians 13, the Biblical order of these words was rearranged to fit the order of current views of justification as faith, charity, and hope (*fides, caritas et spes*). Faith, which corresponded to the preterit, was the intellectual assent to past truths as professed in the teaching authority of the church. Love took the present tense and embraced good works by which faith was "formed" (*fides caritate formata*) and thereby made effective toward justification. And hope was the trust (*fiducia*) that God, who was a just Judge, would fittingly reward the merits of the believer with justification and salvation in the hereafter. The Young Luther had been trained in philosophy as a modernist and had studied the great nominalist, Gabriel Biel. Biel had intellectualized faith as the acceptance of doctrine, with the emphasis upon hope as far as salvation was concerned.[53] Hope was the waiting for the fulfillment of God's justifying promises. But the believer could not enjoy the certainty of his justification in this life. Between him and his final arrival into heavenly bliss lay a long and complicated system. It was a way of seeking after merits in this life through his own deeds and through the supererogatory works of the saints, and a way of seeking grace during the intermediate state of purgatory. Faith was ". . . the *substance* of things hoped for . . ." In the present tense one spoke more of love (*caritas*). It was the function of love to form faith until the hope was achieved.[54]

One of the few Luther scholars who has recognized the change in Luther's concept of faith during the 1510's has been Walther von Loewenich of Erlangen. His early work, *Luthers Theologia crucis*, took note of these problems as early as 1929. But although this book was much admired and passed through five German editions and also appeared in English, its important section on faith has not received the attention it deserves. Von Loewenich warns against letting the Young Luther suppress the Mature Luther and points to the change of 1518–1519 in Luther's concept of faith. At that time the eschatological (futuristic) concept had made way for the soteriological (present-tense) aspect. Faith now involved an existing possession rather than a future hope.[55] It is this insight that I intend to develop.

Luther had previously understood justification not as a present reality but as a hope for something in the future (*non in re sed in spe*).[56] Or as Holl so clearly described the "analytic" position, justification was the act of God in declaring the sinner just on the basis of the anticipated righteousness which God in His foreknowledge knew He would bring to pass within the believer. When did Luther overcome this early view and reach the Reformational concept of faith—that needful prerequisite for the later doctrine of justification by faith alone?

Luther still clung to the more traditional position in the *Lectures on Hebrews* as late as the winter of 1517–1518. In the gloss to Hebrews 11:1 he followed the *Novum Instrumentum omne* of Erasmus:[57] "It seems that with some, *fides* here is understood more as *fiducia* than as *credulitas*."[58] Faced with the choice of faith as assent to doctrine or hope that God would grant him salvation, Luther chose the eschatological possibility. In basing his interpretation upon Jerome's rendition of the Greek word *hypostasis* with the Latin *substantia*, Luther followed Erasmus. Luther followed the same understanding in the scholium on Hebrews 3:14. "By faith we begin to possess that which we shall possess completely by sight,"[59] he writes as he proceeds to explain that faith is a substance. "Through faith Christ is our 'substance,' that is, our riches, and simultaneously we through the same faith are his 'substance,' that is, we are made a new creature."[60] Luther seems rather confused in the scholium to Hebrews 11:1. Whereas in the gloss to this passage he chose *fiducia*, he now suggests that *fides* really means *credulitas*[61] and then subsequently equates it with *adhaesio verbi Dei*.[62] He refers to the position of Chrysostom, who had understood the Greek word *hypostasis* as a faculty such as "conviction," but Luther fails to grasp what this involves.[63]

But in August 1518 Melanchthon came to Wittenberg, and a few days later Luther began to study Greek under the young humanist. This instruction was to have far-reaching results, for it brought Luther clarity concerning faith. He wrote in 1519:

> Jerome understood faith as described by the apostle in Heb. 11 as the "substance of things, hoped, for" . . . I was also of this opinion for a long time, because I had observed that *substantia* was commonly employed in various parts of the Holy Scriptures to denote capabilities and possession. I held tenaciously to the authority of Jerome on this doctrine. For who would dare to change what the writers of the Sentences, in writing on faith, had put within the term *substantia*? But more recently I have followed Philipp Melanchthon as my teacher in Greek. He is a young man in respect to his body, but a hoary-headed old sage in regard to his intellectual powers. Melanchthon would not let me understand it thus, and showed me that when *substantia* refers to "goods," the Greek equivalent is not *hypostasis* (the word used by the apostle [for faith] in Hebr. 11, 1) but *ousia* [possessions], *broton* [food] or *hyparxin* [goods]. Then I changed my mind, and conceded that *hypostasis* or *substantia* means "existence" or the essence of which anything subsists in itself, as Chrysostom thought, or even as a promise, an agreement. . . .[64]

Before this discovery Luther had regarded faith as a "substance," as the believer's present riches and hope of future reward. Faith had been the virtue of assent directed toward the past teachings of the church. From now on faith would instead be "assurance," confidence, trust that God is favorable and forgiving. Faith would entail the certainty that the believer is at the present moment completely justified by the gracious verdict of God[65] and that he has complete assurance of his eternal salvation.[66] Of course, Luther did not immediately state all this, but the basis for all his future theology had now been provided.

The first major opportunity for Luther to engage in a debate on his new discovery came in the meeting with Cajetan in October 1518. During the time Luther and Melanchthon were becoming acquainted, and while Luther was joining the students in learning Greek at the feet of the humanist, the chain of events that had begun in the conflict with Tetzel was rapidly involving Luther more and more deeply.

In July 1518 Pope Leo X had ordered a trial for Luther. On August 7 Luther had received the summons to appear in Rome within sixty days. Through the diplomacy of Luther's prince, Frederick the Wise, the meeting place was changed to the city of Augsburg in Germany. Luther arrived in Augsburg on October 7 to discuss matters relating to the *Ninety-Five Theses*. He met with Cajetan and Prieras in discussions that lasted three days. On October 20 Luther left Augsburg and arrived safely again in Wittenberg on the first anniversary of the *Ninety-Five Theses*. We know what took place at Augsburg from his published report, the *Acta Augustana*.

To this Luther was attacked at Augsburg on the following two points: (1) He had taught that the treasure of the church, the key to heaven, was not the merits of Christ but was procured by the merits of Christ. (2) Luther had taught that every individual who went to the Lord's Supper must have faith.[67]

To this Luther now added the assertion that justification itself could not take place without faith. Such faith was faith in the sense of certainty of one's salvation—a notable advance over his earlier position. Luther now overcame the medieval teaching which described faith either as general faith (*fides generalis*) or as specific faith (*fides specialis seu particularis*). Only specific faith was genuine. General faith was an illusion. Luther cites the centurion as an example (Matt. 8:8). "Speak only a word," he pleaded, "and my servant will be healed." Luther said: "This was certainly not a general faith, but a specific faith, believing in and accomplishing its result in the present moment."[68] Citing numerous other examples from Scripture, Luther concluded:

> And briefly, whatever clear case we choose from the old or the new law, we read that it was accomplished by faith, not by works nor by general faith, but by faith linked with a result in the present. For in Scripture, nothing else is commended as faith.[69]

Luther called faith indispensable to justification.

> . . . No one can be justified except through faith, so namely, that it is necessary that he, with a certain faith, believes that he is justified, and by no means doubts that grace will follow. If however he doubts and is uncertain, he is then not justified, but he vomits forth the grace.[70]

Luther's allegory of Christ as the Good Samaritan is an espe-cially clear example of the pre-Reformational concept of a futuris-tic justification. Christ binds up the wounds of the believing sinner, takes him to the inn, and restores hope to him with the promise of future healing. In Luther's thinking before 1518–1519, this meant a justification which would not be completed until the next world, when one's earthly record of good works was completed. Thus, the sinner in this life was justified only in hope (*in spe*), while in reality (*in re*) he remained a sinner.[71] The noted paradox, *simul justus et peccator*, had an entirely different content from its later meaning. For the Young Luther it meant that the viator was actually a sinner but proleptically righteous—i.e., just in view of what God would make of him.[72] In Luther's later theology the simultaneity was entirely differ-ent. In the eyes of man or from the standpoint of human reason, the believer was not righteous but covered by sin. But by virtue of God's forensic declaration or of faith, the believer was totally righteous and without sin.[73] In 1533 Luther wrote: "If I am a sinner, I am still no sinner. I am a sinner in myself aside from Christ, but I am no sinner if I am in Christ, aside from myself."[74]

Summary

It is in the *Acta Augustana* of October 1518, then, that we find the first clear delineation of faith in the fully evangelical sense.[75] The importance of this discovery for Luther can scarcely be over-estimated. Here he speaks of faith as active in the present (*fide ad praesentem effectum destinata*).[76] The discovery of the righteousness of God in the evangelical sense was closely linked. Now Luther came to understand what was later called passive righteousness—that is, righteousness reckoned to the believing sinner not on the basis of any condition within, but on the basis of the merits of Christ, the *jus-titia aliena*, grasped by faith. It is true that this new insight only grad-ually appeared in Luther's theology. After another decade it would find its definitive development. But the year 1518 marks Luther's entry into a fuller and more evangelical understanding of faith and justification, of Law and Gospel.

In coming to his new understanding of faith and justification, Luther explicitly says that he was aided by the young Melanchthon.

Many scholars have been unwilling or unable to consider the degree of influence Melanchthon might have had upon Luther.[77] Yet the impartial student must never close his mind to such a possibility. The discussion on faith that Luther mentions[78] evidently took place during the first weeks that Melanchthon was at Wittenberg. Would it be unreasonable or even impious to assume that Melanchthon came to the Reformational view of faith before his association with Luther? If so, could it be that here new light might be given to the animated discussions on the relationship of Luther and Melanchthon?

Notes

[1] Schmaus, *Katholische Dogmatik*, Vol. III/2, p. 227.

[2] The twofold usage of an objective and a subjective faith extended far back into the history of dogma. Objective faith was the doctrine itself as it was proclaimed by the church. In the phrase, *fides quae creditur*, the relative pronoun, *quae*, is feminine nominative singular, so that the literal translation is "the faith which is believed" in the sense of accepted. Subjective faith was the attitude within the believer who accepted the doctrine of the church. In the phrase, *fides qua creditur*, the relative pronoun, *qua*, is feminine ablative singular, yielding the literal translation, "the faith by means of which is believed." In the latter usage faith is "subjective"—the attitude of the individual believer. In the former usage faith is "objective"—a teaching which remains unchanged even where unbelievers refuse to believe it.

[3] See esp. Augustine's book, *De Spiritu et Litera* IX, 15, in CSEL VIII/1:167, 13–18; XXXII, 55, in CSEL VIII/1:212, 24–7; XXXII, 56, in CSEL VIII/1:214, 13–19; XXXIII, 58, in CSEL VIII/1:216, 16.

[4] Luther mentioned this in the *Preface* to the first volume of the Wittenberg edition of his Latin writings (1545) (WA 54:186). See also a remark in the lectures on Romans (WA 56:36, 11). Cf. TR V, No. 5247; WA 56:7, 7; 36, 11; 37, 1; WA 57/III:208–9.

[5] Luther against this in 1531ff. (WA 40/I:226, 13).

[6] WA 56:173–74.

[7] WA 57/III:187, 11.

[8] Augustine had applied the tenses of past, present, and future to the concept of faith. See his *Enchiridion*, II (8): "Est etiam fides et praeteritarum rerum et praesentium et futurarum." He then says faith in the death of Christ is related to the past, faith in the *sessio ad dextram* to the present and, in the future, to the coming judgment. However, Augustine did not penetrate to the evangelical insight that faith brings justification into the present aside from any futuristic perfection.

[9] Thus, Luther writes in the scholia on the Psalms: "Nova autem lex proprie de futuro Iudicio et Iustitia prophetat" (Cl V:156, 32). This is in the context of a discussion of Romans 3:21f.: "But now the righteousness of God has been manifested apart from the Law, although the Law and the prophets bear witness to it—the righteousness of God through faith in Jesus Christ for all who believe." Luther here obviously does not come to an evangelical penetration of the text.

[10] This development in Luther is commonly overlooked. Thus, Warren Quanbeck writes: "Faith . . . is *fiducia*, an attitude of trust, which is God's work in the sinner" (*Luther Today*, p. 58). His dating here is vague, but the context suggests that Luther had arrived at this understanding by 1514. Luther of course had not come so far at this time; Quanbeck is apparently smuggling this in from a later period.

Years later Luther rejected his earlier view as that of a "sophist." In a sermon of 1530 he related: "The sophists jabbered much [concerning faith], and so did I, when I was still a sophist, but we understood nothing . . ." (WA 32:98; from DZLE, No. 140).

[11] Curiously enough, the English Authorized Version of 1611 anachronistically preserved this pre-Reformational understanding: "Faith is the substance of things hoped for, the evidence of things not seen."

[12] Thus, in the *Heidelberg Disputation* (April 1518) Luther said: ". . . We live in the Hidden God, that is, in naked confidence (*nuda fiducia*) of his mercy" (WA 1:357). This usage of *fiducia* is evidently futuristic, linked as it is not with the Revealed but the Hidden God (*Deus absconditus*) and looking for delivery at some future point. The context that follows: ". . . We have in ourselves the answer of sin, folly, death, and hell."

[13] WA 57/III:233, 5.

[14] Ibid., p. 143, 1.

[15] WA 56:36, 20.

[16] WA 57/III:63, 1.

[17] Ibid., p. 60.

[18] Ibid., pp. 60–61.

[19] Ibid., p. 235, 13.

[20] Ibid., pp. 151, 9–18; 178, 11f.

[21] WA 57/II:70, 5.

[22] In his great glossary Du Cange lists a great number of theologians who used the term. Du Cange himself distinguishes four different meanings for *credulitas*: (1) *professio*, (2) *fides data*, (3) *mutuum*, (4) *opinio* or *sententia*. In the writings of the ancient fathers and the medieval schoolmen *credulitas* nearly always meant *professio*. See Carolo Dufresne Domino du Cange et al., *Glossarium mediae et infimae Latinis*, Vol. II, s.v. *credulitas*.

[23] Reinhold Seeberg, *Dogmengeschichte*, Vol. II, 3rd ed., p. 376; cf. Vol. III, 4th ed., p. 348. A perusal of the second and third volumes of this work will yield a survey of the usage of this term.

[24] Cf. the gloss to Romans 1:17: "ex fide non nisi ex credulitate in Deum" (WA 56:10, 9). To Romans 4:5: "fides talis credulitas" (WA 56:41, 12). ". . . fides seu credulitas . . ." (WA 56:227, 18, et passim). In the lectures on Hebrews, cf. scholium on Hebrews 11:1: "Sic enim fides aliud nihi quam credulitas" etc. (WA 57/III:227, 4;234, 9, et passim). "Credere enim in Christum est in ipsum toto corde intendere et omnia in ipsum ordinare" (WA 56:252, 5).

[25] WA 1:225, 1; WA 57/III:90, 21.

[26] WA 56:276, 20.

[27] Ibid., p. 276, 30.

[28] WA 1:357, 17.

[29] Ibid., p. 358, 28.

[30] WA 57/III:19, 4.

[31] Ibid., p. 143, 1.

[32] Ibid., p. 19, 22. The use of antitheses in Luther's theology has been shown with particular clarity by Swedish theology. See Gustaf Aulén, *Das christliche Gottesbild in Vergangenheit und Gegenwart*, pp. 164–75, as well as his short English work, *Christus Victor*. A convenient resumé of this in Swedish theology is given by Edgar Carlson, *The Reinterpretation of Luther*, pp. 48ff.

[33] WA 57/III:157, 1.

[34] Ibid., pp. 143, 3; 159, 15; 228, 17.

[35] Ibid., p. 178, 10.

[36] Ibid., p. 124, 9.

[37] Cf. Adolf Köberle, *The Quest for Holiness*, pp. 6ff.

[38] Scholium to Galatians 5:22: "Si autem 'fides' pro 'fidelitate' acciperetur . . ." (WA 57/II:105, 2). Cf. WA 56:223, 13. See also the gloss to Romans 3:3: "fidem fidelitatem in promissis exhibendis dei" (WA 56:30, 11).

[39] Scholium to Galatians 2:16: ". . . omne peccatum reducitur ad infidelitatem, qua non creditur in Christum . . ." (WA 57/II:70, 5).

[40] This view was refuted very clearly by Melanchthon in 1520 in one of his preliminary studies for the *Loci communes*. See CR 21:45. Cf. CR 21:788 (1559).

[41] Reinhold Seeberg, *Dogmengeschichte*, Vol. II, p. 544.

[42] Ibid., Vol. III, pp. 478–79.

[43] Ibid., p. 783.

[44] WA 56:280, 10, note.

[45] AS 1:208, 216.

[46] Part II, p. 595.

[47] AS 3:296–98.

[48] Cler. 7:786E.

[49] Cler. 6:562F.

[50] Instances are WA 4:531, 632, et passim. See Seeberg, *Dogmengeschichte* IV/1, pp. 120–22.

[51] "Quia confessio saepe nocet, dum fiduciam praebet peccati dimissi, ubi tamen cautio futuri non faciendi vera non fuit ex corde" (WA 9:104, 12). See similar negative use in WA 56:280, 10; 503, 4; cf. 510, 18.

[52] Cf. WA 56:387, 21; 510, 18; 297, 5. Luther writes in 1518: "Et omnino in vetere testamento quomodo fiducia potuisset consistere . . ." (WA 1:542, 15). "Cui qui crediderit eum fiducia, vere obtinuit pacem et remissionem apud deum (id est, certus fit se esse absolutum) non rei sed fidei certitudine propter infallibilem misericorditer promittentis sermonem . . ." (WA 1:542, 15). Note esp. the words: "not in actuality but in the certainty of faith." Here again faith is not present (*non rei*).

[53] See Reinhold Seeberg, *Dogmengeschichte*, Vol. III, p. 783. Cf. Heiko Oberman, *Harvest*, pp. 68–84; Bengt Hägglund, *The Background of Luther's Doctrine of Justification in Late Medieval Theology*, Facet Books, No. 18 in Historical Series (Philadelphia: Fortress, 1971), pp. 16–34.

[54] I developed this thought in my doctoral dissertation, completed late in 1954. But little was available on this subject until the appearance of Reinhard Schwarz, *Fides, spes und caritas beim jungen Luther* (Berlin: DeGruyter, 1962), 444 pp., a work which breaks off with the year 1518. See also Otto Ritschl, *Dogmengeschichte des Protestantismus*, Vol. II/1, pp. 85ff.

[55] Walther von Loewenich, *Luthers Theologia crucis*, 4th ed. (Munich: Chr. Kaiser, 1954), pp. 105–7; tr. by Herbert Bowman, *Luther's Theology of the Cross* (Minneapolis: Augsburg, 1976), pp. 84–6.

[56] WA 56:269, 30; 272, 19.

[57] Part II, p. 595.

[58] WA 57/III:61, 17.

[59] p. 152, 11.

[60] p. 153, 9.

[61] p. 227, 4.

[62] p. 228, 17.

[63] pp. 227–28.

[64] WA 2:595, 15.

[65] In his exposition of Psalm 121 (1532) Luther commented thus on Hebrews 11:1: "Fides autem est noticia rerum invisibilium ex expectandarum, quae haeret in promissione et verbo Dei" (WA 40/III:46, 23). Luther here has completely overcome any futuristic understanding of faith and regards faith in Hebrews 11:1 as referring to the hiddenness (*absconditas*) of one's help as it comes from the Lord, who made heaven and earth. Over against the visible power and terror of the pope, Luther trusts the invisible power of God (pp. 50–51). See also pp. 59, 21–6; 124, 19–23.

Also, in his *Commentary on Galatians* (1531ff.) Luther speaks against the idea of a *fides caritate formata* when he writes: "Haec fides sine et ante charitatem iustificat" (WA 40/I:240). Cf. Melanchthon in 1554 (CR 21:788).

[66] In 1543 Luther presided at the disputation of Johann Marbach. Not Luther but Melanchthon drew up the theses. The tenth read: "It is an impious error to teach that we must doubt whether we are in grace. Such doubt is actually sin, for it is inflamed by the law, as Romans 7 says, and it impedes and falsifies prayer" (WA 39/II:207). Cf. the nineteenth thesis!

[67] WA Br I:214, 216. Cf. *Ninety-Five Theses*, Nos. 58, 60.

[68] WA 2:14, 24.

[69] Ibid., p. 15, 21.

[70] Ibid., p. 13, 7. Someone might object that some of this material was in his *Resolutions* on the *Ninety-Five Theses*, which in all likelihood had been composed during the spring of 1518, and that therefore the *Acta Augustana* offered no advance. It might further be objected that we are consequently unjustified in deferring this change in Luther until the autumn of 1518. It is true that the assertion that he who disbelieves thereby vomits up again the substance of grace had appeared in Thesis VII of the *Resolutions*. But in the earlier work the certainty of salvation was not grounded in the doctrine of justification but in the absolution by the priest. To believe meant to accept the absolution of the priest according to Matthew 16:19 (WA 1:541, 22). ". . . A person is more uncertain about grace when it is present than when it is absent," Luther commented, and showed how the visible and audible promise of the priest alone could bestow a certainty that was efficacious. Grace was a substance. Faith was the confidence that, subsequent to absolution, grace was infused, thereby bringing about an analytic justification. He who believed the absolution truly received peace from the priest and forgiveness from God. However, this forgiveness was not in reality but in faith, which was conceived futuristically (*non rei sed fidei*) (WA 1:542, 15).

Therefore, when in the *Acta Augustana* Luther said that he had taught justification by faith alone in Thesis VII of the *Resolutions*, he in his own mind had filled the older words with a new content. He had gained this new insight into faith in the summer of 1518. He was attempting to bring his hearers up to date.

[71] WA 56:272, 19.

[72] Ibid., pp. 270, 10; 272, 19; 287, 11.

[73] WA 8:67, 32; WA 39/I:564, 3.

[74] WA 38:205, 27. See also the good presentation of this in Paul Althaus, *Die Theologie Martin Luthers* (Gütersloh: Gerd Mohn, 1962), pp. 211–13; Eng. tr. by Robert C. Schultz, *The Theology of Martin Luther* (Philadelphia: Fortress, 1966), pp. 242–45.

[75] It is hardly necessary to document the assertion that the Mature Luther characterized faith as *fiducia*. A few examples may be cited from WA 40/III: 25f.; cf. p. 173, 30. In Luther's later theology the triad of faith, hope, and charity took a completely different direction from that of his earlier view, which had been so dependent upon scholasticism. The Mature Luther thought of

hope as fortitude under tribulation, while faith was the initial relationship to God. Although faith related to doctrine and hope to exhortation, the two were just as inseparable as the two cherubim on the Mercy Seat.

[76] WA 2:15, 23.

[77] Elert wrote many years ago: "What Melanchthon has meant theologically has often enough been investigated. But there is not one single presentation that does not let him appear completely over-shadowed by Luther. This is true even of Melanchthon's opinion of himself. 'I learned the Gospel from him,' he confesses in his testament of 1540. But the other question, whether on the other hand Luther might also have learned from Melanchthon in theological matters, has until now never been raised, let alone answered. It appears to us that this approach could yield very important results for tracing the development of Luther's concept of the church, as well as for his doctrine of justification and the proper relation between Law and Gospel." Werner Elert, "Humanität und Kirche: Zum 450. Geburtstag Melanchthons," in *Zwischen Gnade und Ungnade*, etc., (Munich, 1948), p. 96.

[78] WA 2:595.

9

In Search for the Meaning of Grace

One of the curiosities in modern Protestant theology and liturgical practice is the use of the word "grace." Here, if anywhere, pre-Reformational thoughts are reflected. Some collects, prayers, and hymns ask for the infusion of the regenerating and healing grace-substance. Many Protestants speak of a "state of grace" strikingly similar to the habitus views of medieval theology. Seeing that such lack of clarity still prevails four centuries after the Reformation, it should not surprise us that Luther did not come to a Reformational doctrine of grace at once.

Luther's Early View of Grace

As late as his *Lectures on Hebrews* (1517–1518), Luther quoted the writings of Chrysostom, Bernard of Clairvaux, and Peter the Lombard, among others, without dissociating himself from their understanding of grace.[1] The reason is simply that Luther himself stood close to medieval views at this time. In various utterances between 1515 and 1518, he saw grace as a substance imparted by Christ[2] as a gift[3] or else poured out or infused.[4] This view of grace as a substance can be traced back to Tertullian (c. A.D. 200) and is characteristic of the theology of Augustine, Thomas Aquinas, and many others. In fact, it is the view usually associated with Roman Catholic theology to the present.[5] In Luther's earlier writing the usage of a substantial grace shows his commitment to pre-Reformational thought. Its later appearance can be attributed either to a slip of the tongue or to the attempt to emphasize the theocentric character of grace,

for example, over against the concept of grace as making the sinner acceptable (*gratia gratum faciens*). Thus, when Luther employs
a substantial view of grace in the *Heidelberg Disputation* of 1518, his
primary aim is to emphasize the monergism of divine action. Here
Luther says that true Christian humility confesses that salvation
depends upon a nonhuman, alien, infused substance. This shows the
helplessness of man and the exclusiveness of divine operation.[6] God
seeks out the man, not the reverse. "Without human merit" means
"out of grace alone."[7] Hence, grace is prevenient.[8] Since natural man
resists grace, only the eternal predestination of God can make grace
active.[9] Even the first contrition is the product of God's grace rather
than of man's deed.[10] Salvation could come only through grace without any merits or works of man and without anything lovable in man
that might be the attracting cause of God's mercy.[11] Salvation was not
cheaply procured but was won through the suffering and death of
Christ, for whose sake it is given gratis to the believing sinner. Thus,
justification together with the subsequent works of faith are effected
solely by God's grace.[12] And grace is revealed preeminently in Christ.

In Luther's great works between 1515 and 1518, one finds a
fourfold system of grace:

1. In continuity with medieval thought, Luther described
   grace as the preparation for the production of righteousness in the believer.[13] Luther stressed that grace was freely
   given without any merit or worthiness (*gratia gratis
   data*). In a gloss on Romans 5:15 Luther explains grace
   as a divine gift or "transfusion" originating in the meritorious, saving work of Christ by which He has not only
   made Himself acceptable to the Father, but by which He
   also makes believers acceptable before God.[14] Thus, the
   presence of grace infused into the heart of the believing
   sinner makes him acceptable in the sight of God (*gratia
   gratum faciens*). At the same time, grace prepares the
   way for deeds of righteousness through which the sinner
   may appear righteous before God. In a sermon delivered
   January 1, 1517, Luther says that God's word of justification comes before good works. Nevertheless, works are
   important since they prepare the way for the reception of

additional grace.[15] Continuing this thought in his *Lectures on Hebrews* in the winter of 1518, Luther observes that the believer is made just by faith and grace unto good works. Hypocrites who try to come unto grace by good works can only fail, for this is impossible.[16]

2. A second part of Luther's early view of grace is that this grace brings the sinner forgiveness for the sake of Christ. Here Luther at times comes close to the mature Reformational view of grace as divine goodness.[17] Nevertheless, he fails to overcome his earlier understanding because of the rather mechanical "operations" of his view of grace. Grace is not yet unequivocally the attitude of God toward sinners but is still a substance which does something. Grace brings release from guilt[18] after it has removed the sin and covered the offense.[19] It is significant that by this time Luther had at least discarded the idea of some medieval thinkers that the Sacraments mediated grace which justified the heart without faith.[20]

3. The third usage of *gratia* by the young Luther is of prime significance. He thinks of grace as a medicine. We previously explored the concept of justification as healing. In continuity with medieval theology, the early Luther thought of grace as the medicine which Christ the Physician used to heal the sin-afflicted patient.[21] This marked the beginning of a new habitus.

4. This new habitus brings the believer to the performance of good works. Justification is God's pronouncement that the sinner is righteous. First he is made righteous through justification, and then he does righteous deeds. For righteousness is the inclination to good and declination from evil which brings the believer to good works.[22] The law is thereby fulfilled,[23] and that without coercion.[24] Thus, early in 1518 Luther comments: "It is really impossible that one who is under the grace of God could perform other than a good work, as John writes: 'He who is born of God does not sin.'"[25] Such a man has the "supernatural

qualities" of faith, hope, and charity.[26] At this period
Luther was still bound by the older view, in which faith
was intellectual while hope involved trust and confidence
in one's salvation. It therefore becomes clear that Luther
was here thinking that the man who enjoyed the habitus
evoked by grace was the one fully justified before God. All
this should be accomplished by grace because, after the
analogy of human sperm, grace was the seed of spiritual
life by which natural men were begotten. Luther could
thus say: "It is necessary therefore that we be 'sons of the
highest', for grace accomplishes this. Nature begats men;
grace begats sons of God."[27] It is generally agreed that
the reformers changed the concept of grace from that of
a substance to that of the favor or mercy of God (*favor
Dei*). It is clear that grace as a substance would be an
ingredient of an "analytic" view of justification since God
transforms the individual by grace and produces good
works as the basis of a favorable verdict. It is equally clear
that such a grace-concept is incongruous with a forensic
justification in which God overlooks sin and out of sheer
goodness (divine favor) pronounces the sinner righteous
for the sake of an alien righteousness. We should not be
surprised, therefore, to learn that Luther regarded grace
as a substance until the time of his evangelical discovery
(1518–1519) and that, in fact, the new view of grace did
not appear in his extant works before 1521. Previous writers have neglected this question regarding Luther's first
exhibition of the Reformational concept of grace. As far
as I can determine, he first presented the new concept in
his treatise against Latomus in the summer of 1521. There
he defined grace as the mercy or favor of God (*gratia seu
misericordia, favor dei*).[28] Only two years earlier, in the
shorter *Commentary on Galatians*, he had rejected divine
favor as the understanding of grace in Galatians 3:7.[29] We
are once again reminded that Luther came to his evangelical insights through a process of long duration. In fact,
the concept of grace as divine favor did not become a
dominant feature in his theology until his later years.

Melanchthon on Grace

Melanchthon apparently led the way to the Reformational insight that grace denotes divine goodness rather than a medicinal substance. It is possible that this insight, in turn, went back to suggestions in Erasmus' 1516 New Testament—suggestions which the Dutch humanist himself did not develop further. In any case, Melanchthon's usage can be documented between November 1520 and February 1521, when he defended Luther from the attacks of Thomas Rhadino.[30] In this treatise Melanchthon sharply rejected the medieval construction that the three cardinal virtues (faith, charity, and hope) are achieved in the believer through the infusion of the grace-substance[31]—a construction which had greatly troubled Luther until the breakthrough revealed in the *Acts of Augsburg* (October 1518). Instead of regarding grace as a substance, Melanchthon asserted that it was an attitude of God—His kindness revealed in the Gospel. Grace was the forgiveness of sins and justification. "For where *gratia* [grace] occurs, it is a word which denotes favor in Christ," Melanchthon said.[32] Since this was destined to become the position of Protestant theology, it is of great interest to retrace its development. To do so, however, will take us to two works of lesser authority than the reply to Rhadino.

In the *Annotations on Romans* (1519 or 1520) Melanchthon defined the Gospel as the proclamation of grace, and grace as the mercy of God (*gratia, hoc est favor dei*).[33] He told his students: "In this way we receive these benefits through Christ, the favor of God . . . Wherefore as to those who do not believe, God does not feel graciously disposed (*favet*) toward them . . ."[34] During the winter semester of 1520–1521 Melanchthon again taught from the Epistle to the Romans, but this time he treated it systematically rather than exegetically. Of these studies in Romans only a student's copy, the so-called *Lucubratiuncula* ("Night-Work"), remains. In uncharitably poor Latin the student quoted Melanchthon's doctrine of grace at this period: "Grace is a word that signifies the favor of God, by which God embraces the man whose favor is in God and not in man; and as soon as God regards such a man with favor, he stands very near to him, and holds him in his hands. . . ."[35] There are many parallels in which the same thing is said almost word for word in the *Lucubratiuncula* that is stated in the *Annotations on Romans*.

Except for the *Augsburg Confession*, Melanchthon's *Loci communes* of 1521 were the most important of his writings. Here he developed the new grace-concept into a full system. After a brief word study on the usage in the Hebrew Old Testament, the Septuagint, and the Greek New Testament, Melanchthon asserted: "The word for grace does not signify any kind of condition in us, but rather the same gracious will or benevolence of God toward us."[36] He thus excluded the concept of grace as a substance or quality working within the believer and firmly defined it as relational. As a Biblical humanist, he found that ". . . in the Sacred Scriptures grace denotes favor, and this is the grace or favor in God, by which he accepts the saints."[37] Like Luther, Melanchthon distinguished between grace and the gift of grace—an advance over his position in the earlier *Theological Institutes.*[38] "In conclusion, grace is nothing else than forgiveness or remission of sin. The gift is the Holy Spirit, regenerating and sanctifying the heart."[39] This was the clearest presentation of the grace-concept in the early 1520's. Grace is the attitude of God toward sinners. Good works in the person who has experienced grace are not the result of the outpouring of a grace-substance, but they are the visible fruits of the believer's response to the mercy of God. Justification is the application of the grace, love, and mercy of God to lost, sinful man. For all practical purposes, grace is forgiveness of sin: *Non aliud est gratia nisi condonatio seu remissio peccati.* Subsequent to forgiveness, the heart is sanctified and renewed through the gift of the Holy Spirit.[40]

Notes

[1] WA 57/III:68, 3; 169, 15; 191, 21.

[2] "Christus autem fuit minister gratie . . . et gratiam daret . . ." (WA 57/II:71, 11). ". . . et data gratia . . ." (WA 56:274, 10).

[3] *Gratia*—i.e., *donum* (WA 56:55, 1). Cf. WA 57/II:55, 3.

[4] "Ista autem purgatio est opus Dei et gratiae infusio . . ." (WA 1:118, 15). ". . . cognoueritis sc. per infusionem lucis et gratie spiritus" (WA 57/II:31, 5). This concept of infused grace persists even at a much later date—e.g., in a sermon in the Postille for Advent (1552) Luther is quoted: ". . . gottis gerechtickeytt . . . heyst nach brauch der schrifft die ausagossene gnad und barmhertzickeyt gottis . . ." (WA 10/I/2:37, 1). Here Luther, although he speaks of grace as a substance that is outpoured, evidently has come to the evangelical understanding of grace.

[5] Thus, a current dogmatician writes: "Grace is a supernatural gift, which God bestows freely on rational creatures for the sake of Jesus Christ and according to the example of Jesus Christ, to the end that they may participate in the life of the trinitarian God." Michael Schmaus, *Katholische Dogmatik*, III/2 (München: Max Hueber Verlag, 1956), p. 8.

[6] WA 1:360, 25.

[7] Ibid., p. 191, 22.

[8] "Actus amicitiae non est naturae, sed gratiae praevenientis. Contra Gab" (ibid., p. 225, 7). Cf. the twenty-third thesis also.

[9] "Optima et infallibilis ad gratiam praeparatio et unica dispositio est aeterna dei electio et praedestinatio" (ibid., line 27).

[10] "True contrition comes not from ourselves but from the grace of God. Therefore we must despair in regard to ourselves and we must find refuge in his mercy" (ibid., p. 322, 9).

[11] Ibid., p. 365, 8.

[12] WA 57/III:69, 15. Cf. WA 56:37, 26.

[13] Melanchthon also held this view at first.

[14] Luther's manuscript is given in WA 56:53, 14, while the same thought is preserved in a student's copybook (WA 57/I:53, 7).

[15] WA 1:118, 13–17.

[16] WA 57/III:230, 19.

[17] For example, to the word *misericordia* in Galatians 6:16 Luther supplies the gloss—i.e., *gratia justificans* (WA 57/II:48, 9). Yet too much can be read into this by the scholar who is eager to prove an earlier emergence of fully Reformational views. Luther does not yet say, "Grace is mercy," but he says, "Mercy is justifying grace." Grace in this context must be seen as a regenerating substance that renders the believer acceptable to God and that prepares for further good works.

[18] "Gratia que operatur remissionem culpe" (WA 56:7, 2). "Gratia qua remittitur peccatum" (WA 57/II:6, 4).

[19] "This grace is spiritual and hidden, because it takes away sins and covers the most hidden offenses . . ." (WA 57/II:55, 1).

[20] See WA 57/III:191, 19.

[21] "Quod per gratiam sanari inceptum est" ("Healing is begun through grace"), Luther preached on January 1, 1517 (WA 1:119, 4). This thought was treated elaborately in Luther's exposition of Romans 4:7 (see WA 56:272f.). The medicinal concept of grace is also found in his exposition of Galatians 3:10 (see WA 57/II:80) as well as in the *Heidelberg Disputation* of May 1518 under Thesis XVII, where Luther describes the longing of the sinner for healing grace under the analogy of the sick man who seeks the medicine that he knows will cure him. While vestiges of this concept are found much later in the theology of the Mature Luther, nevertheless medieval views gradually disappeared under the evangelical understanding of grace.

[22] "Thus our righteousness is from God. It consists in the same inclination to good and declination from evil that is given within through grace. Works are more the fruit of righteousness. Sin is the corresponding decaliation from good and inclination toward evil" (WA 56:271, 11). Cf. WA 1:119, 34; WA 57/III:200, 9; 210, 1; 230, 19. "Whoever is under grace works things pleasing in the sight of God" (WA 57/II:55, 4).

[23] Commenting on Romans 3:31, "We establish the law," Luther said: "It is fulfilled through faith and grace" (WA 56:40, 3). "Christ gives grace, which Moses required" (WA 57/II:71, 12). "Therefore the office of the new priest is properly not to teach the law, but to show the grace of Christ, which is the fullness of the law" (WA 57/III:192, 23). Here Luther is on the way to the solution of the problem of Law and Gospel. Christ is seen as supplying through grace that which the Law demands because He Himself has satisfied the demands of the Law.

[24] This point is basic to Luther's view of faith. Grace changes the believer from within so that he does right spontaneously. See again WA 56:271, 11; cf. WA 57/III:69, 15. Cf. also the following citation.

[25] From lecture on Hebrews (WA 57/III:217, 22; cf. 225, 27).

[26] Comment on Hebrews 7:1 in ibid., p. 187, 6.

[27] Ibid., p. 42, 20.

[28] WA 8:106, 10.

[29] WA 2:511, 15; AE 27:252. It is worth noting that by 1523, when Luther published a revision of this *Commentary on Galatians*, he removed this criticism of grace as divine favor. In so doing, he showed the change that had taken place in the meantime in his understanding of the concept of grace (WA 2:511, critical apparatus).

[30] In a letter of Luther to Spalatin of November 13, 1520, he mentions that Melanchthon is preparing a polemic against Rhadino, who mistakenly is imagined to be Hieronymus Emser of Leipzig (WA Br 2, No. 352). Melanchthon's treatise (CR 1:287–358; SA I:57–140) was written between this time and its publication in late February 1521 (Suppl Mel 6/I:116–18). The treatise was a literary as well as theological masterpiece and was ascribed by some to Erasmus, to the latter's amusement (Suppl Mel 6/I:116–18).

[31] SA 1:83, 27.

[32] Ibid., p. 84, 29.

[33] Annot. Rhom., Fol. Aiiii, Bii.

[34] Ibid., Fol. Bii.

[35] CR 21:35.

[36] SA II/1:86.

[37] Ibid.

[38] CR 21:55.

[39] SA II/1:87, 24.

[40] Ibid.

10

Luther's Theology of Justification in Transition

The Reformational doctrine of justification consisted in the insight that one is justified by faith. Two concepts are contained in this familiar statement: faith and justice or righteousness. The doctrine required the Reformational understanding of faith, which Luther first mastered in October 1518.[1] But at that time he had still not arrived at his definitive concept of justice or passive righteousness, which, according to Luther's explicit statement,[2] first gave him the interpretive key to Romans 1:17. It is true that in the Augsburg propositions he had stated: "Therefore the righteousness of the just and his life is his faith."[3] This was like the dawn of a new day just before the rising of the sun. In the earlier breakthrough during his first lectures on the Psalms,[4] he had come to see that the good works for justification are worked by God rather than by the believer. This Christological dimension aided him in making an important advancement. In his new understanding of 1518, faith brought righteousness and life because it united the believer with Christ like the bride is united with her bridegroom. This new understanding was indebted to the bridal mysticism of the Middle Ages, but the debt was mainly one of terminology. In content the new understanding stood much closer to Pauline theology than had its medieval predecessor. However, the newly-won interpretation was not really a forensic doctrine of justification. Its hallmark was not the Christ for us (*Christus pro nobis*) but the Christ within us (*Christus in nobis*).[5]

Changes in Luther's *Sermon on Threefold Righteousness*

In Luther's *Sermon on Threefold Righteousness*, the justifying righteousness which the believer shares through faith is the merit of Christ.[6] It is bestowed when one is implanted into Christ in Baptism,[7] and it confers certainty of salvation, for to doubt that one's righteousness were adequate would be to doubt Christ[8]—a grievous sin. Several important advances are present in this sermon. Justification is the gift of God in Christ, doubtful human efforts at producing saving righteousness are rejected, and in contrast to medieval thought and his own earlier theology, Luther now insists that the believer can be certain that he is saved and will go to heaven.

However, certain statements in the *Sermon on Threefold Righteousness* link it to Luther's pre-Reformational thinking.[9] For example, he described a threefold concept of sin and a threefold concept of righteousness. Sin was seen as some civil offense, as inherited lust, or as actual sin. Civil sin was ". . . obvious wrong-doing, which even the secular power punished . . . ," such as theft, murder, arson, or robbing of churches. Inherited lust (*peccatum alienum*) was the sin transmitted by birth and consisted in concupiscence, which led to transgressions. Luther called actual sin ". . . the fruit of original sin . . ." and defined it as all works done by the natural man ". . . before faith . . . ," no matter how good they might appear to human eyes. But this scholastic analysis of the concept of sin falls far short of Luther's earlier and later dynamic delineation of sin. Such a system inevitably leads to the atomization of one's understanding of sin. Luther did not fully succeed in speaking impressively of sin because such a dismemberment of the concept tends to conceal the real nature of sin. In his later writings he emphasized the utter damnability of all sin and stripped the sin-concept of every comforting suggestion of degrees of sin.

The threefold construction of righteousness as civil, alien, and actual corresponded to the sin-structure. Civil righteousness did not require faith but could be accomplished by Jews and heathen who did not know Christ. And it could appear so excellent that ". . . in the sight of men, a man might appear so good, that no one could accuse him of anything." Yet this man was serving himself, not God. This was not true righteousness, acceptable before God, because it came not from the love of God but more from fear of punishment or from personal, convenience. "This is not the righteousness of sons, but of slaves," Luther commented. He taught a righteousness based on the indwelling of Christ. In other words, the underlying basis is less the *Christus pro nobis* (Christ on our behalf) than the *Christus in nobis* (Christ within).[10] When Luther here speaks of alien righteousness (*iusticia aliena*), he sees it as in Christ in a twofold sense. (1) Through the Incarnation the solidarity of Christ with the human race has been established. "Truth springs up from the earth. . . . And this truth is Christ."[11] (2) This is bestowed on the individual through Holy Baptism, from which springs faith. "This is conferred through Baptism, which is properly that which the Gospel announces, and is not righteousness of the Law but righteousness of Grace."[12] Although the later view of justification is not fully present, Luther is in transition between scholasticism and Reformational thought. Justification is no longer "analytic" to the degree that it was in his earlier exegetical lectures. It is no longer Christ as the Good Samaritan or the Great Physician, who justifies by a moral transformation, as much as it is the Christ who, dwelling within, renders the believer acceptable to God.

Here the second type of righteousness is followed by the third. Actual righteousness comes, ". . . flowing out of faith and essential righteousness . . . ,"—that is, the righteousness of Christ. "Faith is the sole merit. It is most vain if a single deed be called worthy of eternal life. It is needful that the person be worthy. Christ has obtained this for us and has given it to us, and gives it to us daily."[13] In this distinction between alien and actual righteousness Luther was moving toward his later Reformational position and toward the later distinction of the Confessions and Orthodox Lutheranism between justification and sanctification. Justification depended upon alien righteousness. The Christian life that followed (sanctification) was the result of justification, not its cause. Luther asserted that a Christian should therefore never be uncertain whether he is pleasing to God, otherwise he is not of faith and all he does is sin. Luther made an important move toward the Reformation when he wrote that the testimony of a good conscience is that God is pleased to accept a Christian through Christ. Works seen without Christ are sin, no matter how great they appear outwardly. But when works are seen in Christ, they are pleasing to God.

> Righteousness is nothing other . . . than that by which original sin is expunged and the body of sin is destroyed, and so merit is prevalent righteousness, but not an act by which it is obtained, but that which effects the merit.[14]

Through faith, nurtured by the indwelling of Christ, the believer does good works that are pleasing to God. Luther declared that the uncertainty whether one's works are acceptable to God is tantamount to unbelief.

> As therefore concerning Christ you ought not doubt that he is pleased, so also you ought not to doubt concerning your works, that they are acceptable for the sake of Christ in whom you believe; in this way, all are works of such faith, and are most full of grace, no matter how unworthy they appear of themselves in your sight.[15]

It is significant that Luther's opponents at Worms (1521) approved this earlier sermon on righteousness.[16]

A Breakthrough in the *Sermon on Twofold Righteousness*

A few months later Luther preached on a similar topic. This in itself would not prove that he had undergone a profound change. It is conceivable that he was so convinced of his view on threefold righteousness that he presented it again and again. Nevertheless, in examining the later sermon more carefully, we find some important advances. In the *Sermon on Twofold Righteousness* of 1519, Luther no longer discusses sins according to various categories but only as inherited or actual lust. And righteousness is only of two kinds—the righteousness of Christ, alien righteousness, and the righteousness of the believer, proper righteousness. Christ is no longer only the great example to be imitated but is the Lord who shares all His gifts with the believer.[17] The Christological basis of justification is much clearer than in the earlier sermon. Moreover, the aspect of bridal mysticism is developed more fully, and Luther's famous doctrine of the joyful exchange of grace for sin begins to emerge. At times this is delineated under the example of bride and groom as in the present sermon. Luther preaches:

Therefore through the first righteousness the voice of the bridegroom arises who says to the soul, 'I am thine'; through the second comes the voice of the bride who says, 'I am thine.' Then the marriage is consummated, it becomes strong and complete, like in the Song of Solomon: 'My beloved is mine, and I am his.' Then the soul no longer seeks to be righteous in itself, but has Christ as its righteousness, and therefore seeks the salvation of others.[18]

Both the *Sermon on Twofold Righteousness* and the *Commentary on Galatians* utilized concepts which were retrogressive as far as the movement toward an evangelical doctrine of justification was concerned. We have seen that Luther had rejected the proposal that grace might be an attitude of God rather than a gift outside Him.[19] This concept of grace as a gift, an infused substance, was to continue in his thinking. He preached: "Therefore such alien righteousness, without any actions on our part, is infused into us through grace alone."[20] If justification consisted in an infused state or habitus, then what Holl called an analytical teaching had not been fully overcome. Luther continued: "For righteousness is not infused all at once, but it begins, it progresses, and it is perfected only at the end through death."[21] The verb "infuse" and the adjective "alien" are both intended to emphasize that the righteousness which justifies comes from without aside from any actions by us (*sine actibus nostris*). The indwelling Christ works this justification within us, driving out the old Adam and increasing our faith and knowledge.[22]

Luther's New Position in the *Commentary on Galatians*

Similar thoughts are found in Luther's *Commentary on Galatians* in the discussion of "righteousness." Negatively, righteousness is described as follows: (1) Righteousness is not the sum total of works of the Law (*opera legis*) presented by the individual in his own behalf to God.[23] (2) Good works do not precede righteousness but follow it.[24] (3) Righteousness is not something external but something internal.[25] (4) Righteousness is not achieved by man at all.[26]

Positively, righteousness is described as follows: (1) It is calling upon the name of the Lord as in Romans 10:13.[27] Since the name of God consists in "mercy, truth, righteousness, virtue," etc., the individual who calls upon that name participates in these attributes of God. This is his righteousness.[28] (2) Righteousness means to be in Christ and to have Christ within.[29] (3) Righteousness means to be made righteous (*justum effici*).

In his *Commentary* Luther describes how justification takes place. He first begins with the gift of faith which God bestows.[30] Second, sins are forgiven.[31] Third, grace is infused. "Grace is diffused from thy lips . . . Most gracious and joyous are thy words to lost sinners, because they announce remission and grace."[32] Fourth, love (*caritas*) is infused: ". . . through faith is infused love of the Law. . . ."[33] Fifth, the Holy Spirit is given. Through this new spirit the goal is achieved. ". . . Next he sends the Holy Spirit into their hearts, who dilates them with love, and makes them pacified and cheerful. . . ."[34] Sixth, the Law is thereby fulfilled through faith and love.[35] Through faith in Jesus Christ they are made righteous (*iustos fieri*)—that is, fulfillers of the Law (*legis impletores*).[36] Yet this justification in only inceptive and is not as yet complete,[37] just as the fulfillment of the Law is only inceptive.[38] "Every one who believes in Christ is righteous, not yet completely in reality, but in hope (*nondum plene in re, sed in spe*). He has begun to be justified and to be healed, like that man, taken half-alive. Meanwhile however, while he is being justified and healed, that which remains of sin in the flesh is not imputed to him. . . ."[39] What is missing here from the later Protestant position? It is the clear forensic insight wherein justification is actually complete, the Law is really overcome, and the pronouncement of justification means that no one can call the believer a sinner any longer. Thus it was in the Mature Luther, where justification was not merely in hope (*in spe*) but also in reality (*in re*). Yet these remnants of earlier teachings are more the exception than the rule.

Simul Justus et Peccator: Its Altered Meaning

When we examine Luther's use of his old paradox, *simul justus et peccator*, we see how the emphasis has shifted from that of 1515. In the *Lectures on Romans* justified man was a sinner in actuality and righteous only in hope of future achievement of the grace of God within him. But now when Luther brings in this paradox in the exposition of Galatians 2:18, it has a new content despite remnants of his Neoplatonic dichotomy of spirit and flesh. Man is a sinner in regard to his flesh, but he is righteous in regard to his spirit. He is a sinner because a bit of sin remains in him (the flesh), but he is not at all a sinner by virtue of the fact that he is justified by faith, so that sin and the Law are overcome.[40] When Luther criticized his *Commentary on Galatians* of 1519 in later years, it was not because his mature view on justification was not already present but because remains of his older view still occasionally reappeared. Again in his work on Galatians from 1519, we find prominence given to the indwelling of Christ. Justification means that the believer is united with Christ so that his sins are no longer his but Christ's, and righteousness is no longer Christ's but the Christian's.[41] The exchange of places is so complete that Christ even becomes a sinner![42]

To see how far Luther had come by 1519, it is instructive to make a few comparisons with the *Lectures on Galatians* of several years earlier, which have come down only in a student's copybook.[43] Luther had destroyed the earlier manuscript and revised the lectures because of his dissatisfaction with them. This change is evident in his treatment of Galatians 1:4: "[Christ] gave himself for our sins, that he might deliver us from this present evil world, according to the will of God and our Father." In the discussion of this passage in 1516, there is not a word about certainty of salvation (*Heilsgewissheit*). Luther did not possess such certainty until after he came to clarity over justification—something that probably did not take place much before the beginning of the year 1519. But when Luther now returns to his study of Galatians, he cannot help compensating for what was earlier missed. Again and again he brings out the second person pronoun. "This faith justifies you, in you Christ dwells and lives and reigns." Now he scores the view he himself had held three years earlier. "Therefore these are fables of the imaginations of the Schoolmen, teaching that a man cannot be certain whether or not he is in a state of salvation. You beware! Be not uncertain, but certain, that in yourself you are lost. But you must strive to be certain and solid in the faith that Christ was delivered for your sins."[44]

Summary

Luther's depiction of justification under various concepts of Christology and bridal mysticism presented some thoughts of compelling religious beauty. Although the views we have just examined are not those of a forensic justification, and although they tend toward the "effective" or even "analytic" doctrine, they avoid the dangers of the latter positions expressed in the question, "How can I be sure that my good works are sufficient to establish my justification?" They avoid these dangers by pointing to the Christ within and to His promises: Christ comes to take upon Himself your sin and to give you His perfect righteousness. To distrust Him is the greatest sin. Only accept Him and believe in Him, and you will have Him and His gifts. Through His righteousness you are justified and given an unshakable certainty of your eternal salvation. Furthermore, these beautiful thoughts rest upon certain passages of Scripture. But they do not present the whole story. The forensic justification of Paul later made its appearance in Luther's thinking, and although the more mystic doctrine remained in Luther and Lutheranism, the forensic view eventually became prevalent.

Many uncritical readers in the past thought they had found a fully forensic justification in the earliest Luther. The English-language editions of Luther have often aided this misunderstanding by mistranslating sentences and inserting such words as "imputation" and "justification" where the original text did not justify such a rendition. Consequently, students of Luther are sometimes uninterested in retracing the reformer's steps to forensic justification. Or they regard with hostility the possibility that Melanchthon or even Erasmus might have helped Luther take these steps. This development, however, needs to be traced. It is here that the second lectures on the Psalter are of crucial importance. The publication by Vogelsang of "unknown fragments from Luther's lectures on the Psalter," from which the important *Commentary on the Psalms* of 1519 emerged, furnishes an important means of tracing his development (see Table 3).

A remarkable statement from Luther that presents the new views on faith and righteousness (which he called his evangelical breakthrough in the *Preface* of 1545) appears in his interpretation of Psalm 5:9 (in the Vulgate numbering; Psalm 5:8 in the English Bible). This high point is apparently missing in the earlier lecture on the same verse (c. November 15) as well as in the recapitulation of this verse (c. December 17).[45] Commenting on the familiar words, "Lead me, O Lord, in Thy righteousness," Luther twice cites Augustine's

TABLE 3

A Chronology of Luther's Development: 1518-1519

February, 1518; May, 1518: Writing of the explanations of the *Ninety-Five Theses* (WA 1:525–628; AE 31:83–252).

April 4, 1518: Completion of the lectures on Hebrews (WA 57/III).

April 25, 1518: Heidelberg Disputation (WA 1:353–74; Cl V:377–404; AE 31:39–70).

May-December, 1518: Second series of lectures on the Psalter (Unbek F:31–94; WA 5).

Psalms 1–3: May 17, 1518–July 12, 1518.

Psalm 4: August 6, 1518–September 25, 1518.

Psalm 5: November 5, 1518–December 20, 1518.

December 21, 1518–February, 1519: Editing of Psalms 1–5 for *Operationes in Psalmos* (WA 5; *Commentary on the Psalter*).

Older view on faith as a substance, after Jerome (Unbek F:55). Newer view of faith as assurance, after Chrysostom and Melanchthon (WA 2:595), appeared between September 20, 1518 (lecture) and October 12, 1518 (appearance before Cajetan; WA 2:6–26).

August 29, 1518: Melanchthon's inaugural address at Wittenberg.

Autumn (September 14, 1518?): *Sermon on Threefold Righteousness* (WA 2:43–7).

November 5, 1518–December 20, 1518: Lectures on Psalm 5.

January, 1519 (?): *Sermon on Twofold Righteousness* (WA 2:145–52).

January, 1519: *Commentary on Galatians* ready for printing; then withdrawn and revised until April, 1519 (WA 2:443–618; AE 27: 151–410).

December, 1518–January, 1519: Final revision of *Commentary on the Psalter* (WA 5).

On the Spirit and the Letter XIII, "Give me what Thou dost command."[46] He then comments:

> . . . And now [the Psalmist] says, 'Lead,' that is, I beseech Thee with tears for grace, because of myself I would rather fall away from Thy righteousness. I neither trust my powers nor am I able. 'Give me what Thou dost command.' Thou dost command that I be righteous. Do Thou therefore 'Lead me in Thy righteousness,' that is in the righteousness of faith, which comes from Thee through grace, and not in my own or in human [righteousness]. . . .[47]

But although the righteousness of which Luther here speaks is not a punitive but a saving righteousness, and although it is the gift of God and therefore not a human but a divine righteousness, it is still a righteousness within the believer ("analytic," Holl) and not the "passive righteousness" of the 1545 autobiographical *Preface*.[48] This is even clearer in the scholium to Psalm 5:9b of the same date:

> In Hebrew [it says] 'direct Thy way before my face,' and this commends grace even better and more fittingly. It is as if he said: I cannot be saved in my way or in my righteousness, but in Thy way and in Thy righteousness, i.e., which is from Thee, in which Thou dost make me to walk. Therefore as in the first part of the verse he said, 'in Thy righteousness,' it would have been suitable if he had said as in the following part, 'in Thy way.'[49]

As though dissatisfied, Luther returned once more to this verse on December 17 and said: "Lead me, O Lord, in Thy righteousness,' i.e., make me to progress in the righteousness which comes from Thee through grace and justifies all. . . ."[50] Thus, righteousness, although the gift of God, is the life of the believer. He progresses in righteousness by doing more or better works. Soon after these statements of November and December 1518, Luther would label this one's own or proper righteousness (*iustitia propria*) and remove it from the context of justification. In its place he would put the alien righteousness that comes from Christ (*iustitia aliena*), which alone could form the basis for justification. As Cranz has noted,[51] this distinction, obscured in the *Sermon on Threefold Righteousness*, first came into its own in the *Sermon on Twofold Righteousness*. It formed the basis for Luther's fully Reformational views on justification, the distinction of Law and Gospel, and the doctrine of the two kingdoms. But these important views were present only implicitly. Their explicit development was a matter for the future. And as far as justification is concerned, the *Sermon on Twofold Righteousness* accompanied the concept of the Christ within the believer.

Therefore, out of all these works during the crucial year of 1518–1519, it is chiefly the *Commentary on the Psalms* (the *Operationes in Psalmos*) which gathers together the new findings of the reformer and anticipates his fully Reformational teaching. In its outward form this commentary was the first in which Luther abolished the medieval distinction between glosses and scholia and followed instead the practice of the humanists in presenting one unified interpretation. The advances in content are also remarkable. In place of the comments on Psalm 5:9 which we noted in the lectures of 1518, he wrote the following statement, which, as Martin Brecht observed,[52] provided important parallels to the description of the evangelical discovery in the *Preface* of 1545.

> The 'righteousness of God' . . . is not that in which God himself is just and by which he damns the impious, as it is most commonly taken. But, as the Blessed Augustine says in *On the Spirit and the Letter*, it is that with which he clothes man when he justifies him. It is the same mercy or grace which justifies, by which we are reckoned righteous before God . . . [Quotation of Romans 1, 17 and 3, 21]. For it is called the righteousness of God and ours, because his grace is given us, as the work of God which he works in us, the word of God which is spoken to us, as the power of God which works in us, and many others. . . . Whence Psalms [24, 5] was translated skillfully [in the Vulgate]: 'He shall receive blessing from the Lord and mercy from the God of his salvation'; although the Hebrew text has 'righteousness' in place of 'mercy,' the point is that the blessing of God and the righteousness of God are the same thing, namely, the same mercy and grace of God which have been conferred upon us in Christ. And this is an illustration for the righteousness of God . . . in which God is righteous, so that by the same righteousness, God and we might be righteous. Just so, by the same word, God forms and we exist, so that we might be in him what he is, and that that which is his might be ours.[53]

In these words we find the old mixed with the new. The concept that justification is a declaration of righteousness is beginning to appear. It is even more clear in the following statement, in which Luther gives a new twist to an older idea:

> Indeed when we enter the covenant of faith with God, what else are we doing than vowing praise and glory? For we confess that all our things are nothing, and we declare that it is only by his grace that we can be saved. We are avowed debtors in accordance with this covenant, proclaiming and confessing the grace which we receive. We owe, I say, this confession to God: We are ruined by ourselves and saved only by His gift. And this our debt is the vow which we redeem when we thus praise God and accuse ourselves, when we glorify him and confound ourselves, when we justify him and damn ourselves, in such a way that he is justified in his words [Ps. 51:6] and every man is a liar.[54]

Here Luther takes up the earlier teaching about a passive justification of God by the believer. Such a concept had been present in the first lectures on the Psalms.[55] It had been developed further in the *Lectures on Romans*: "That is the passive justification of God, by which he is justified by us, and it is the same active justification of us by God."[56] But the theological framework had been completely changed. Faith was no longer assent (*credulitas in Deum*)[57] but was now trust in the favor of God. Righteousness was no longer meritorious works but the free gift (later, imputation) of the merits of Christ. "Reckoning righteous"[58] was no longer based on intrinsic but on extrinsic merit. Justification now meant that in fiducial faith one had called upon the Lord, whose predicates were righteousness, power, mercy, etc. Faith enshrined that Lord in the believing heart, and with the Lord were enshrined those predicates, especially the righteousness of justification. Just as the believer called upon the name of the Lord and before the world declared Him righteous, powerful, merciful, etc., so God (later, forensically) declared the believing sinner endued with the attribute of righteousness and therefore justified. We shall see how "passive righteousness" became a part of Luther's vocabulary a few years later and how justification became the pronouncement of the verdict of righteousness. These aspects of forensic righteousness were implicit but still undeveloped in 1519–1520. To find these important Reformational ideas in Luther we must move on to his later period.

Notes

[1] §8.

[2] WA 54:185f.

[3] WA 2:13, 14.

[4] An early breakthrough during the first lectures on the Psalter, in which Luther came to understand the "righteousness of God" as that by which God "makes the sinner righteous" in an analytical type of justification, was masterfully portrayed in Erich Vogelsang, *Die Anfänge von Luthers Christologie nach der ersten Psalmenvorlesung*, No. 15 in Arbeiten zur Kirchengeschichte (Berlin: Walter de Gruyter, 1929), esp. pp. 48–55.

[5] In his first disputation against the Antinomians (1537) Luther spoke critically against Neoplatonism and particularly its bridal mysticism (WA 39/I:389, 18).

[6] WA 2:44, 32.36; 45, 1.16.25.29; 46, 6.29.

[7] Ibid., pp. 44, 22.33; 45, 6.

[8] Ibid., p. 46, 16.29.

[9] Kurt Aland, in his provocative little book, *Der Weg zur Reformation*, correctly sees that the "tower experience" could not have taken place before February 15, 1518 (pp. 37f., 102). He is also correct in finding Luther's Reformational view of the righteousness of God in the sermon on *Two Kinds of Righteousness* (WA 2:146; AE 31:298f.). But he seems to miss the mark when he tries to date the crucial sermon at March 28, 1518 (p. 104), in order to locate the "tower experience" in the interval between February 15 and March 28 of that year. Three objections immediately appear: (1) Although the Epistle for Palm Sunday (Phil. 2:5ff.) is prominent in this sermon, this does not prove that it was delivered on any Palm Sunday, and there is insufficient evidence for Aland's dating. (2) This dating obliges him to assert that this sermon was preached earlier than the one on *Three Kinds of Righteousness* (WA 2:43–7), of which the sermon on *Two Kinds* is obviously a revision. (3) Luther cannot have proclaimed the views given in this sermon as early as Aland asserts since the new insight on the righteousness of God is missing in the subsequent *Heidelberg Disputation* and the *Explanations of the Ninety-Five Indulgence Theses*. Therefore, Aland's position needs some modification.

[10] Heiko A. Oberman's article, "'Iustitia Christi' and 'Iustitia Dei' . . . ," HTR 59 (1966): 1–26, raises some interesting points that require at least a brief response at this point since it rejects what I understand by the *Christus pro nobis* (p. 22). The essay attempts to define Luther's evangelical discovery with the following proposition: "the heart of the Gospel is that the *iustitia Christi* and the *iustitia*

Dei coincide and are granted simultaneously" (p. 19). The hypothesis seems incapable of documentation, and the supporting arguments are unconvincing. I have been unable to find the first occurrence of the expression, *iustitia Dei passiva*, in WA 18:769, 1 (p. 24, n. 51). I am also uneasy about several of his supporting arguments: (1) His distinction between the *Christus pro nobis* as *exemplum* rather than as sacrifice can only be supported out of the pre-Reformational works (see pp. 21–3). Luther of course later discarded the *Imitatio Christi* in such a context. (2) The essay appeals to a legal distinction between *proprietas* and *possessio* from Roman law. However, this distinction does not actually exist in such a form in Luther (pp. 21f., 25f.). (3) The attempt to interpret *extra nos* without its forensic value is weakened by the misquotation of WA 39/I:109, 1. That statement should be linked with WA 39/I:83 (Thesis 27) to suppy its context (pp. 21–2). (4) The attempt to dismiss forensic justification in Luther altogether (pp. 21f.) is an extreme position which cannot be reconciled with Luther's later teaching. In conclusion, the inventive statement, *fides Christo pro nobis formata extra nos* (p. 24), is of course Oberman's, not Luther's.

[11] WA 2:45.

[12] Ibid.

[13] Ibid., p. 46.

[14] Ibid.

[15] Ibid.

[16] Ibid., p. 41.

[17] In distinguishing between the sermons on threefold and twofold righteousness, I am standing rather close to Cranz (op. cit., pp. 75–7) and differing with Saarnivaara (*Luther Discovers the Gospel*, pp. 92–101) and with Bizer (*Fides ex auditu*, pp. 106–12). Saarnivaara and Bizer find little difference between the sermons and think that both were fully Reformational.

[18] WA 2:147.

[19] Ibid., p. 511.

[20] Ibid., p. 146, 29.

[21] Ibid., p. 146, 34; AE 31:299.

[22] Ibid.

[23] WA 2:489.

[24] Ibid., p. 492.

[25] Ibid., p. 489.

[26] Ibid., pp. 491, 460.

[27] Ibid., p. 490.

[28] Ibid.

[29] Ibid., pp. 455, 11; 458, 24; 490, 39; 491, 4; 495, 4.13; 555, 20.

[30] Ibid., pp. 518, 563, 502.

[31] Ibid., p. 495.

[32] Ibid., p. 466.

[33] Ibid., pp. 498, 552, 560, 562, 574, 582, 591, 599, 604.

[34] Ibid., p. 490. Cf. pp. 536, 552, 570, 613.

[35] Ibid., p. 490.

[36] Ibid., p. 496.

[37] Ibid., p. 495.

[38] Ibid., p. 497.

[39] Ibid., p. 495.

[40] Ibid., p. 497.

[41] Ibid., p. 504.

[42] Ibid., p. 534.

[43] WA 57/II.

[44] WA 2:458.

[45] It is possible to reconstruct the academic year 1518–1519 at Wittenberg. We know that Luther lectured on Mondays and Fridays, and we can establish with reasonable certainty which days were missed because of holidays, vacations, or journeys. Two or three pages of notes generally constituted a typical lecture. On the basis of information given by Vogelsang in his edition of the second series of lectures on the Psalter (*Unbekannte Fragmente aus Luthers zweiter Psalmenvorlesung 1518*, pp. 13–14), I have attempted the following disposition of the material. N.b.: It is possible that Luther lectured on Monday, December 20. If so, the material could be spread a little wider. However, so late a date seems improbable.

TABLE 4

The Second Series of Lectures in the Psalter:
An Attempt at Dating the Class Periods

Day and Date	Passage	Material	Source in Unbek F (Vogelsang)
Monday, August 16	Psalm 4:1, 2	Gloss	pp. 31–32
Friday, August 20	Psalm 4:2	Gloss	p. 33
	Psalm 4:2	Scholium	pp. 40–41
Monday, August 23	Psalm 4:3	Gloss	pp. 33–35
	Psalm 4:3	Scholium	pp. 41–42
Friday, August 27	Psalm 4:3	Scholium	pp. 43–44

(continued)

TABLE 4 *(continued)*

Day and Date	Passage	Material	Source in Unbek F (Vogelsang)
Monday, August 30	Psalm 4:4	Gloss	p. 35
	Psalm 4:4	Scholium	pp. 45–46
Friday, September 3	Psalm 4:4	Scholium	pp. 47–48
	Psalm 4:5	Gloss	pp. 35–37
Monday, September 6	Psalm 4:5	Scholium	pp. 48–49
Friday, September 10	Psalm 4:5	Scholium	pp. 50–51
Monday, September 13	Psalm 4:5	Scholium	pp. 52–53
Friday, September 17	Psalm 4:6	Gloss	pp. 37–38
	Psalm 4:6	Scholium	p. 53
Monday, September 20	Psalm 4:6	Scholium	p. 54
	Psalm 4:7	Gloss	p. 38
	Psalm 4:7	Scholium	pp. 54–56
Friday, September 24	Psalm 4:8, 9	Gloss	pp. 39–40
	Psalm 4:8, 9	Scholium	p. 56
Friday, November 5	Psalm 5:1–3	Gloss	pp. 57–58
	Psalm 5:1–3	Scholium	pp. 69–71
Monday, November 8	Psalm 5:4, 5	Gloss	pp. 58–60
	Psalm 5:4, 5	Scholium	pp. 71–72
Friday, November 12	Psalm 5:6, 7	Gloss	pp. 60–63
	Psalm 5:6, 7	Scholium	pp. 72–74
Monday, November 15	Psalm 5:8, 9	Gloss	pp. 63–65
Friday, November 19	Psalm 5:10	Gloss	p. 65
	Psalm 5:10	Scholium	pp. 75–78

Day and Date	Passage	Material	Source in Unbek F (Vogelsang)
Monday, November 22	Psalm 5:11	Gloss	pp. 65–67
	Psalm 5:11	Scholium	pp. 78–79
Friday, November 26	Psalm 5:12	Gloss	pp. 67–68
	Psalm 5:12	Scholium	p. 79
Monday, November 29	Psalm 5:12	Scholium	pp. 80–82
Friday, December 3	Psalm 5:12	Corollarium	pp. 83–85
Monday, December 6	Psalm 5:12	Corollarium	pp. 86–89
Friday, December 10	Psalm 5:13	Gloss	pp. 68–69
	Psalm 5:13	Scholium	p. 89
Monday, December 13	Psalm 5:2–8	Recapitulation	pp. 89–92
Friday, December 17	Psalm 5:9–12	Recapitulation	pp. 92–94

[46] In his autobiographical *Preface* of 1545 Luther wrote that right after the break-through of 1518–1519 he again read Augustine's *De Spiritu et Litera* and found many of his new insights in that work (WA 54:186). However, it is questionable whether Augustine really stood so close to the Reformational Luther.

[47] Unbek F:64, 20.

[48] WA 54:186.

[49] Unbek F:74, 9.

[50] Ibid., p. 92, 14.

[51] Cranz, op. cit., pp. 74–6.

[52] See Brecht, "Iustitia Christi—Die Entdeckung Martin Luthers," ZThK 74 (1977):221.

[53] WA 5:144, 1.

[54] Ibid., p. 663, 27.

[55] WA 3:284, 288, etc.

[56] WA 56:226, 23.

[57] WA 56:226, 1.

[58] WA 5:144, 5.

The Reformational Doctrine of Justification

PART III

REGENSBURG

11

The Mature Reformational Teaching

Justification by Faith

If a distinction were to be made between the respective emphases of Luther and Melanchthon, it could be said that Luther stressed justification by faith (*sola fides*) while Melanchthon emphasized justification by grace (*sola gratia*). Justification by faith stressed the responsibility of the individual, while justification by grace emphasized the exclusive operation of God unto salvation. These two were not mutually exclusive but were simply two basic constituents of Biblical justification. We shall now examine these two aspects. In this section I shall discuss Luther's presentation of justification, at times employing terms that were not prominent in Melanchthon. In the next chapter I shall go especially into the problem of forensic justification as it was developed with special interest in Melanchthon. We shall find a strong unity in diversity between the two men.

Justification in the Mature Luther: A Textual Problem

One of the tantalizing things about the Mature Luther's doctrine of justification is that although he can show himself in fundamental agreement with Melanchthon on the idea of forensic justification and the concept of the imputation of Christ's merits to the believer, he often ignores these aspects. Thus, he can simply write in his *Open Letter on Translating* (1530): "The chief article of the Christian faith is that we become righteous through faith in Christ, without any works of the Law."[1] Or he can express himself with easy straightforwardness:

"Faith alone appropriates the death and resurrection of Christ, aside from all works, and this same death and resurrection is our life and righteousness. Thus it is perfectly obvious that faith alone brings, appropriates, and gives us this life and righteousness."[2] This is typical of a statement by Luther which comes directly from his hand. The greater works such as the lectures on Galatians (1531) and on Genesis (1535–1545) often contain formulations which seem to bring him closer to Melanchthon or the *Formula of Concord*. But these are almost always from the hand of a stenographer or editor, and therefore their value as sources needs careful investigation in each instance.

Considering the fact that Luther often insisted that justification is the chief article of the faith, and taking into account his customary verbosity, it seems strange that he devoted comparatively little time or space to leaving posterity an unmistakably clear treatise on the subject. As a matter of fact, he has left no treatise at all on justification. The closest thing that we have to such a work is the strange *Rhapsodia seu Concepta in Librum de loco iustificationis* (1530). It has been transmitted to us by the hand of Veit Dietrich, one of the less dependable editors, and published in a modern edition[3] which leaves a great deal to be desired.[4] Despite the problems of historical criticism involved, it appears that Dietrich simply copied Luther's autograph without changes, and the tampered text in the Weimar edition can be utilized in consultation with the *Revisionsnachtrag*.[5] Furthermore, although most of the "Great" *Commentary on Galatians* of 1535[6] was not edited by Luther, it was prepared by the very reliable scholar, Georg Rörer. The careful scholar will of course utilize the methods of historical criticism in reading this commentary. But to the experienced reader it becomes increasingly clear that it is the irrepressible Luther and not the careful Melanchthon generally speaking from these pages. Greschat's criticism of the authenticity of the commentary is therefore too far-reaching. Furthermore, he is simply not correct in characterizing Rörer as a pupil of Melanchthon, for Rörer had come to Wittenberg in 1522 after virtually completing his education, including a master's degree from Leipzig University. Moreover, we are in the fortunate situation of possessing Rörer's original stenographic copies of the 1531 lectures, printed in the upper third of the page,[7] and can compare his revision for the published *Commentary* of 1535, printed in the lower two-thirds of the page.[8]

As far as the content of the *Rhapsodia* is concerned, Luther emphasizes again and again that it is faith alone which justifies, that faith justifies before any good works have been done and therefore justifies without reference to such works,[9] and that works are the inevitable consequence of justifying faith but must be kept strictly distinguished from justification.[10] This repudiation of works as the basis for justification was Luther's rejection of his earlier "analytic" teaching. Also, the concept of the Christ for us has replaced the Christ within. The topic is not the indwelling of Christ but His meritorious sufferings and death appropriated through faith.[11] Luther rejects the multiplicity of names and concepts of his Roman adversaries, which obscures the Gospel,[12] and insists that only the name of Christ can save.[13] Nevertheless, it is striking to see how Christology has receded and been replaced by the concept of faith and works. We dare not press the new balance, however, because the *Rhapsodia* was only a rough outline. On the basis of this sketch it would be impossible to guess how Luther might have treated these topics if he had actually written his treatise on justification. Furthermore, in the 1535 *Commentary on Galatians* the strong Christological emphasis returns. Here the Christ for us (*Christus pro nobis: propter Christum*) takes its rightful place in a discussion of Pauline theology. We shall return to this *Commentary* later.

"Faith" in the Mature Luther

The Council of Trent (1545–1563) decreed in Canon 9: "If anyone say that the impious is justified by faith alone . . . , let him be anathema."[14] We are not here concerned with the word "impious" but with the phrase, "by faith alone." The tragedy of the sixteenth century was the split in the Western Church. One of the causes for the split was the failure of the Council of Trent to grasp what Luther meant when he said that man was justified by faith alone. We have previously analyzed Luther's early concept of faith. Had this pre-Reformational concept of faith (*credulitas*) been in the mind of the Mature Luther when he proclaimed justification by faith alone, the Council of Trent would have been right in rejecting his teaching. But as we have seen, the word "faith" had changed meaning for Luther. It was no wonder that his opponents, operating with the medieval view of faith, took exception. Had they understood what Luther was trying to say, their rejection—if one had come—might not have been so bitter. Since the contrast between Luther's early and later concepts of faith has been overlooked even by modern specialists, it is important that we now turn to "faith" in the Mature Luther.

Melanchthon and the later dogmaticians thought of faith as *fiducia* or trust preceded by knowledge and assent (*assensus ac notitia*) in inferior order. This was not wrong, of course, but for Luther faith was more dynamic. It was a continuous struggle or wrestling. Strangely enough, this view did not appear during the time of his great struggles in the monastery. Then his faith-concept was expressed as *credulitas*—that is, the acknowledgment of the validity of certain propositions as true. After 1518, assisted by Melanchthon, Luther was led to the insight that faith was a term of relationship to God comprehending some of what medieval writers called *fides, spes et caritas*, and therefore trust or *fiducia*. Only then was he ready to articulate his position fully.[15]

Faith as Submission

In his exposition of Psalm 125:1 (1533) Luther develops the verse: "They that trust in the Lord shall be as mount Zion, which cannot be removed, but abideth for ever." The way to salvation does not consist in works invented by men, but that which leads to God is believing and trusting in Him.[16] "This is the nature of God, as I said before, that he creates all things *ex nihilo*." God meets with him who is harmonious with His nature. This is man with faith—that is, "He who believes that God is aid in time of danger, life in death, strength in weakness, righteousness in sins . . ." Such a man looks upon God aright, and God can neither hate nor abandon such a one. He is a true servant and worshiper of God since he confides in the mercy of God. "God is pleased solely by this worship, because he delights in making something out of nothing. Thus he created the world out of nothing. Thus he raises up the poor and the oppressed. Thus he justifies sinners. Thus he gives life to the dead. Thus he saves the damned."[17]

In this development of the attitude of faith by Luther, we see an organic relation to his theology from various periods of his life. The early exegetical lectures on the Psalms and on Romans developed the concept of *humilitas* as a prominent part of his view of justification. There *humilitas* capitulated before the judgeship of God. Especially in the *Lectures on Romans* (1515–1516) Luther held that such capitulation constituted passive justification. In acknowledging the righteousness of God's condemnation of him, the humble believer acknowledged the proper place of God and was therefore justified (active justification). Luther's view of justification was greatly modified and developed when he came to his Reformational understanding of faith in 1518 and then of passive righteousness. In his sermons on the parable of the Pharisee and the Publican, spanning most of his preaching career, Luther sees the Pharisee damned because of his pride (*superbia*), but the publican is saved because he acknowledges the righteousness of God's condemnation of himself and in faith flees to the mercy of God (*humilitas*). Time and again in these sermons, Luther points to the explanatory words of Christ: "Every one that exalteth himself shall be abased; and he that humbleth himself shall be exalted" (Luke 18:14). In the words of his exposition of Psalm 125:1, we could say that the publican was justified because he thrust himself before God as nothing and asked God to create a new being out of nothing (*creatio ex nihilo*). God does not build on human accomplishments and pride (thus the Pharisee) but on human failure, emptiness, and humility (thus the publican). In the end this is what the Mature Luther had to say about justification. Thus, he eliminated from his earlier position the idea of an intrinsic righteousness as the basis for an "analytic" justification. He had come to see that this was inconsistent with his view of humility. Justification had become "synthetic"—i.e., it was created out of nothing.[18] Luther did not bow to the criticisms of those who say that such a justification involves a self-deception and unrealism on the part of God. God creates out of nothing![19] Nor can this be twisted to imply that God supplies what is lacking in the form of a new, God-worked, intrinsic righteousness in the sense of the *Lectures on Romans*. The righteousness that justifies is a paradoxical righteousness. It is supplied in the mercy of God precisely because it did not exist in empirical reality. Some overly-critical writers have categorically rejected the textual reliability of the *Lectures on Galatians* of 1531. In some cases, however, the texts present holographs of Luther. Thus, he wrote in words unmistakably authentic: "They show themselves to be evil dialecticians who do not distinguish the passages of Scripture which speak about faith which produces works from those about faith which justifies."[20] With these words Luther unshrinkingly rejected his earlier teachings and affirmed that works before, during, or after justification are no part of it.[21]

Sufficient attention has not been directed to the aspect of justification by faith in Luther in which faith justifies the sinner by paying God the honor due His offended majesty. God has delivered His immutable will in the Ten Commandments. The sinner offends against them and thereby against God. He does this not only in transgressing the individual commandments, but he also does it in the hostility of his heart with which he hates the Law and therefore also hates God. In the confusion of his heart he wants to overthrow this God whose Law demands what he cannot fulfill and then so cruelly condemns him. He wants to set himself up as judge in place of God in order that he may praise the supposedly good works he offers in rivalry to what God demands in the Law. The result is idolatry of the worst kind—worship of self.

Such self-idolatry is overcome only by humility and faith. Faith is the attitude in which the sinner acknowledges that God's Law is just and that God has a right to be angry with him because he has broken God's Law. Faith makes no attempt at self-justification but bows in humility before God. But faith is not intimidated by the Hidden God or by the Law. Faith looks beyond the *Deus absconditus* to the *Deus revelatus*—the God who revealed in Christ that He is love and that He does not desire the death of the sinner. The sinner who turns to God in faith and trusts Him to be merciful and to forgive finds that he has not been deceived. For it is the highest glory of God not to condemn but to forgive and to justify the sinner freely by grace alone.

Luther brings this out with great beauty and forcefulness in his preaching. Some researchers have now shown that Luther's devotional material, such as his sermons, must be used with caution in developing theological propositions. There is some truth in this. First, some of Luther's sermons have been delivered from secondary sources. And second, Luther's purpose in preaching was not to construct a technical theological proposition but to edify the congregation. There is a reply, however, to the supposition that Luther's sermons might not be reliable historical sources. Although it was not Luther's purpose to construct a system of justification in his sermons, he was nevertheless a man of integrity, and therefore a system may be reconstructed by exercising due care with the material. It is indeed necessary that much attention be paid to the delivery of each sermon. Historians consider those which have come down from Georg Rörer as highly dependable. They are in the form of a German and Latin shorthand which Rörer himself used. Luther preached in German, and Rörer, who was facile with Latin shorthand, used Latin words and abbreviations to keep up with Luther's delivery from the pulpit. These are therefore direct transcripts that have come down to us in this macaronic form. The printed sermons, prepared by such redactors as Roth, Poach, Dietrich, and others, are more numerous. These are not so direct, at times show much editing, and therefore are to be used with more caution. However, by taking a large number of sermons preached by Luther over a period of years on the same text, a reliable picture can be gained of his doctrine of justification. We shall do this in analyzing about twenty sermons preached by Luther on the parable of the Pharisee and the Publican (Luke 18:9ff.)[22]

Justification in Luther's Sermons on the Parable of the Pharisee and the Publican

In the Pharisee of the parable Luther saw a picture of man both in his conceited self-sufficiency before God and in his desperate need.[23] The Pharisee dared to come before God confident that God could not accuse him of sin. He boasted of his fastings and his almsgiving and painted a picture of himself as one who flawlessly kept the commandments. Luther saw two damnable sins in this action. First, man unconsciously stood in revolt against God, for he rejected the divine judgment that stood against him and tried instead to whitewash himself. He thereby drove God from His judgment seat, placed himself thereon, made an idol of his own self-exalted image,[24] and made of God a devil.[25] This was the sin against the First Table of the Decalogue. The Pharisee also sinned against the Second Table in his attitude toward his fellow man. He bolstered his self-confidence by the epithets he hurled against the publican. He boasted that he was not as other men—extortioners, unjust, adulterers, or worst of all, publicans like the one who stood before him in the temple! Thus, he showed that his heart was evil toward his neighbor.[26] Luther says that he should rather have prayed for the publican, confessing that he was no better than the other man and begging God to help his neighbor and deliver him from his sin. Instead, the Pharisee lifted himself above the publican.

In the attitude of the publican Luther found a beautiful delineation of saving faith. The man took an honest look at himself and was shocked by the evil reflection he found. He did not try to boast of his accomplishments. He saw nothing good in himself, no basis for hope of forgiveness. Stricken with his sins, he smote upon his breast and pleaded the simple prayer: "God be merciful to me, a sinner!"[27] This prayer was not offered in false pathos, but it came from the depth of his heart. Under these words lay the conviction that because of his sins he deserved nothing but eternal damnation. But this was not all. Beside this condemnation of self was the commendation of God. The man had faith. How else would he ever have had the audacity to pray the words, "God be merciful to me"? As he drove God out, the Pharisee had unconsciously said in his heart, "Only God can damn me." The publican said in his heart, "Only God can save me." In this contrast lay the whole weight of Luther's doctrine of justification. It was not faith as a power or virtue that helped the publican. Faith was in no sense something offered to God. It was the denial of self and the affirmation of God. Faith saved, not because it was the most virtuous of all deeds, but precisely because it was the abstention from all virtuous deeds or from the intention of being justified through them.

Hence, the publican was saved because he silently accepted the accusation of God's Law as presented by the Pharisee: ". . . an extortioner, unjust, adulterer, or even as this publican . . ." The publican accepted that cutting judgment of himself even though the Pharisee had no right to offer it. His conscience told him that this was God's inexorable judgment upon his life. And in that moment of submission to God the Judge, he discovered God the Justifier.[28] "This man went down to his house justified rather than the other" (Luke 18:14).

Luther found a reflection of his own case in the publican. It was not that Luther was a notorious sinner. Attempts have been made to besmear his name as a lecherer, a drunkard, a man of vile language, or a psychotic. But Protestant and Catholic scholars today tend to agree that Luther was none of these. His consciousness of sin lay not in the fact that he was empirically an unusually wicked man, but in his unusually deep insight into the nature of sin and its damnableness before God. He struggled with this not only before his arrival at the evangelical doctrine of justification, but all his life.[29] And Luther saw that despite all his accomplishments, the most virtuous man must still stand empty-handed before God and join in the confession, "We have been unprofitable servants." More than this, Luther saw that even the most virtuous man must stand before God confessing his total condemnation in the light of the divine Law. For in the Law God demanded what no man could fulfill. As Melanchthon expressed it in the *Apology*, *Lex semper accusat*.[30] In unreservedly accepting this judgment upon himself, Luther saw the indispensable preliminary for justification not as a meritorious act of the sinner but as the renunciation of all meritorious acts in the total casting of self upon the mercies of God.

Luther impressively described how the publican came to be justified. The publican believed that this divine and wrathful Judge was also the divine and merciful Saviour. The publican had faith in the saving grace of God. Only faith made it possible for him to bring together the paradox of Law and Gospel, wrath and mercy, punishment and forgiveness, sin and grace. Faith taught the publican to do the unthinkable. Faith taught him to rhyme sin and mercy and to seek forgiveness of this wrathful God. He believed that God wanted to save him. "I a damnable sinner, Thou a merciful God," he pleaded.[31] And he appealed to the proper place. For the highest glory of God is not His holy wrath but His forgiving love. In thus renouncing himself, the publican enthroned God in His rightful place—the Judgment Seat. And the paradox occurred when God, accorded his rightful place, became the God of mercy and forgiveness.

Luther at this point says that the rightful comportment of the publican in acknowledging God, in letting God be God, fulfills the First Commandment.[32] This agrees with Luther's classical exposition of that commandment in the *Small Catechism*: "We should fear, love, and trust in God above all things." Of this the publican was a prime example. This was no mere outward behavior but the inner disposition of the heart. This was faith. And only faith could fulfill the First Commandment. Luther treats this in greater detail in the *Large Catechism*, where he shows how faith fulfills all the Decalogue, and again in the *Small Catechism*, where each commandment begins with the shortened form of the First Commandment, "We should fear and love God . . ." In his sermons on Luke 18:9ff. Luther at times speaks of faith as though it were a fulfilling of the Law or a paying to God of the honor due Him. "Thereby he gave God the honor due him, and paid him off through faith. . . ."[33] This raises the question whether Luther had not made a meritorious act of faith, thereby merely substituting faith for good works and still basing justification on human action. But when Luther's theology as a whole is considered, this conclusion is seen to be false. Indeed, Luther does call faith a payment, not to God but to God's honor. In other words, we are dealing with pictorial and not with literal language. We have before us Luther's way of making justification palpable for unsophisticated hearers in the parish church. Faith was not a meritorious act but the denial of meritorious acts. Faith was not a human accomplishment but a divine work in man. Faith was self-damnation, not self-exaltation. It provided God with the moment of quiet needed to speak the word of pardon.

Justification in Luther's Teaching

In a disputation held at Wittenberg University in 1543, Luther provides an important parallel to his view on justification.

> Faith is trust and completed righteousness, but charity is incomplete. But we are not justified by incomplete righteousness. Where therefore is our completed righteousness? It is Christ our Lord; my righteousness is given me. It is absolute righteousness; verily, my charity is not absolute. Faith here is a work, but works of the Holy Spirit are different from those of the Law. The works of the Holy Spirit are the infusion of charity, hope, and faith.[34]

One is justified before God not by good work (charity) but by faith in Christ. Hence, faith is righteousness. Faith, which is the work of the Spirit, is all that could still the demands of the Law, for faith apprehends Christ. Before Him the Law must capitulate.

The justification that takes place through faith in Christ figures prominently in the large *Commentary on Galatians*. Faith saves, not because it is a faculty in man, but because it apprehends Christ. Faith apprehends Christ, who is our Redeemer, Saviour, Fulfiller of the Law, Justifier and Victor over Death. To believe in Christ means to have Him dwell in one's heart. And to have the Forgiver and Justifier dwell in one's heart means to have forgiveness and justification.[35] "This is the beginning of salvation, and in this manner we are freed from sin, we are justified, and given eternal life, not on account of our merits or works, but on account of faith, by which we apprehend Christ."[36] Luther describes faith as the mounting on a golden ring which encloses and holds fast the precious gem.

> . . . He who will be found holding Christ in his heart with such a faith, him God will reckon righteous (*reputat iustum*). This is that merit, by which we came to remission of sins and righteousness. God says: Because you believe in me and your faith apprehends Christ whom I have given for you, believing that he is your Justifier and your Saviour, for this reason you are justified. Therefore God accepts you or reckons you as righteous solely on account of Christ, in whom you believe.[37]

It was the art of the publican that he learned to rhyme sin and grace: "I a sinner, thou a merciful God." His was the conviction that there was forgiveness of sins not merely for the world but also for himself. Luther emphasizes this in discussing Galatians 2:20: "Who loved me, and gave himself for me." He brings out the words, FOR ME, FOR ME! He comments:

> These words, which are the purest preaching of grace and Christian righteousness, Paul contrasts to the righteousness of the Law, as if he said: The Law is sound, divine teaching, it has its glory, but it does not love me nor give itself for me, but it accuses and frightens me. But now I have another One who has freed me from the terrors of the Law, from sin and from death, and has translated me into liberty, righteousness of God and everlasting life, he who is called the Son of God, who loved me, and gave himself for me.[38]

This is of greatest hope and consolation for the troubled conscience.

Justification by Faith in Melanchthon

We have seen Melanchthon's important role in developing the fully Reformational concept of faith. Luther admitted that Melanchthon had been his teacher in finding clarity on this central concept. It is therefore somewhat surprising to note that justification by faith alone became much less prominent in Melanchthon than in Luther in succeeding years. Of course, Melanchthon made ample use of the concept.[39] But at times he was ill at ease with the doctrine of faith. Although he had led the way in defining faith as *fiducia* or trust, Melanchthon's theology was ever in danger of synergism—that is, the view that man cooperates in his salvation. As Melanchthon knew, such a view would be irreconcilable with the Gospel taught by the reformers. There seems, therefore, to have been overanxiety on his part lest faith be regarded as a condition for justification. Luther rejected every form of synergism and taught the bondage of the will. Yet he had no compunctions whatsoever about calling faith a payment made to God in return for which the believer received justification. Luther could do this because in his system faith was worked entirely by God alone. This divine origin of faith was not as consistently developed in Melanchthon's system. He was therefore handicapped at each step. When Luther and Erasmus had their intense debate on the powers of the human will, Melanchthon was unable to accept Luther's clear-cut monergism—i.e., his assertion that God was free and worked in all things and that the human will was in bondage and dependent upon God for all things. Melanchthon attempted to take a mediating position. He was not willing to go as far as Erasmus in teaching the freedom of the will even in spiritual matters. Yet he feared that Luther's view would destroy responsibility on the part of the individual and lead to false security. Ever after the Wittenberg disturbances of 1521, Melanchthon assigned more and more responsibility to the individual and more and more power to the will. Had he, like Luther, accepted the monergism of divine activity and hence denied the liberty of the will, he would have spared himself many problems. And he would also have likely found a more suitable manner of teaching good works in the renovated life of the believer. Through his penchant toward freedom of the will, his faith-concept—one of his greatest contributions to

Reformational theology—was endangered.[40] There was a tendency for his ethics to become autonomous. But his doctrine of forensic justification saved his theology. We shall now turn to this important insight. If justification by faith was not so secure in Melanchthon's thought, the forensic aspect nevertheless sufficiently brought out the teaching of justification by grace alone.

Notes

[1] WA 30/II:640.

[2] Ibid., p. 642.

[3] Ibid., pp. 657–76.

[4] The Veit Dietrich copy of the *Rhapsodia*, in a volume which once belonged to Adam Rudolf Solger, the eighteenth-century Nürnberg collector, is described by Hans Volz in Br 14:118 (No. 255).

[5] The text of WA 30/II:657–76 is corrected in the *Revisionsnachtrag* of 1967 (p. 145), where the following items are described as interpolations of G. Koffmane, editor of the WA edition: WA 30/II:658, 37–659, 37; 660, 4–11; 660, 12–22; 673, 18–34; 674–76. O. Matthes has established that Dietrich's copy was not merely his own transcription from a conversation, but that he reproduced an autograph of Luther and that the date of the *Rhapsodia* was May 1530. This of course renders superfluous the construction of Martin Greschat, *Melanchthon neben Luther* (Witten: Luther-Verlag, 1965), pp. 60–64, with an August dating.

[6] WA 40.

[7] Ibid.; not given in AE.

[8] Ibid.; AE 26–7. Greschat makes sweeping remarks about the supposed unreliability of Rörer's work (op. cit., pp. 11–17). In fact, very critically-minded scholars have found the 1535 *Commentary on Galatians* a useful source, especially because the WA 40 text is accompanied with the original notes of Rörer taken down in the actual lecture by Luther. Moreover, Greschat himself has depended heavily on these same materials! It is also strange that Greschat faults Rörer for having noted parallel statements in Melanchthon on the margin of his manuscript of Luther's lectures (Greschat, p. 15, n. 17). Greschat neglects to mention that Rörer introduced none of these notations into the published commentary, as a comparison will quickly reveal. Since Greschat wants to compare Luther and Melanchthon, one wonders why he should object to Rörer's private comparisons.

[9] WA 30/II:661, 16.19; 662, 9; 664, 9.30.

[10] Ibid., pp. 664, 26; 668, 23.

[11] Ibid., pp. 659, 22; 660, 31; 666, 15; 669, 1.

[12] Ibid., pp. 671–72.

[13] Ibid., p. 673, 6.

[14] Denzinger, No. 819.

[15] For literature on Luther's faith-concept, see esp. the following: Walther von Loewenich, *Luthers Theologia crucis*, 1954, 4th ed.; Eng. ed., *Luther's Theology of the Cross*, tr. Herbert Bouman (Minneapolis: Augsburg, 1976). Werner Elert, *Morphologie des Luthertums*, Vol. I, 1952, 2nd ed., chaps. 1, 4, 12; Eng. ed., *Structure of Lutheranism*, tr. Walter Hansen (St. Louis: Concordia, 1962). Leonart Pinomaa, *Der Zorn Gottes in der Theologie Luthers*, 1938. Pinomaa, *Der existenzielle Charakter der Theologie Luthers*, 1940. Pinomaa, "Die Anfechtung als Hintergrund des Evangeliums in der Theologie Luthers," *Zur Theologie Luthers* (Luther-Agricola Society of Finland, 1943), pp. 98–113. Carl Heinz Ratschow, *Der angefochtene Glaube*, 2nd ed., 1960, chap. IV. Albrecht Peters, *Glaube und Werk*, 1962.

[16] ". . . Sed simplicissima via ducentem ad Deum et primum praeceptum ac pronunciantem, hanc esse summam salutem, confidere ac sperare, Hoc cultu Deum unice delectari" (WA 40/III:154).

[17] Ibid., pp. 154–55. What is the *tertium comparationis* here? It seems to be the power of God's Word. There is action! (Cf. Gen. 1:1; John 1:1–3.) In Genesis 1, when God said, "Let there be light," there was light. It was both a declaration and an action by God's omnipotent word. Here in justification, by a (forensic!) word, God both declares the sinner righteous and thereby simultaneously makes him righteous. The latter is a paradox but is just as real as that the poor, when raised up, are really rich (Luke 6:20: "Blessed be ye poor: for yours is the kingdom of God"). Empirically, the poor are still poor, but in God's sight they are rich, for they inherit the kingdom of heaven. Or the word of justification can be compared to the word by which the dead are raised up. The living must still die, and they which sleep in the tomb are still waiting; but paradoxically, they live even now.

[18] We have noted that Luther calls the divine work of justification a *creatio ex nihilo* (creation out of nothing). By this expression he wanted to stress that justification is totally the work of God and thereby to exclude every kind of synergism or works-righteousness. It is therefore especially ironical when John Henry Newman used the same concept for the opposite purpose—to make justification a matter of keeping the Law. He wrote: ". . . If He blesses, surely it is by making holy; if He counts righteous, it is by making righteous; if He justifies, it is by renewing; if He reconciles us to Himself, it is not by annihilating the Law, but by creating in us new wills and new powers for the observance of it." Newman, *Lectures on the Doctrine of Justification*, 9th impression (New York: Longmans, Green, & Co., n.d.), p. 34. The gross legalism of Newman's doctrine of justification is brought out in the following statement: "The coming of the Holy Ghost, to write the Divine Law in our hearts: that Law then so implanted is our justification [sic!]" (ibid., p. 46).

[19] WA 40/III:154, 30.

[20] WA 40/I:23, 9.

[21] Ibid., p. 225, 23. In his *Rhapsodia . . . de loco iustificationis* (1530) he left some telling remarks which separated justification from works. ". . . We are justified by faith alone and completely aside from works" (WA 30/II:661, 20). "By faith immediately efficacious [*fide presente*] they are righteous prior to works" (WA 30/II:662, 9). "But this promise is not obtained by works, but by faith, before all works. For the heart is justified by faith before there are works" (WA 30/II:666, 1). On the difficult problem of a reward for works he wrote: "These are not said in regard to justification, as though through these works we were justified, but they are promises of works which those already justified will do here, and they do not do them for the promise of gain. Therefore, they shall receive [their reward] in the future" (WA 30/II:667, 27).

[22] In the next several pages I offer a brief summary drawn from Luther's sermons. For a fuller treatment and additional documentation, see my article, "Justification in Luther's Preaching on Luke 18:9–14," CTM 43 (December 1972): 732–47. The study was based on all extant sermons by Luther on this text, drawn from most of his preaching career.

[23] WA 17/I:401.

[24] WA 20:474.

[25] Ibid., p. 475.

[26] WA 11:163.

[27] WA 22:205.

[28] See Elert's *Der Christliche Glaube*, pp. 474f. Justification means that the sinner is put to silence. This is the quiet moment God needs to declare him just!

[29] See Werner Elert's excellent description of Luther's concept of *Angst* in *Morphologie des Luthertums*, Vol. I, pp. 39ff.; in English, *The Structure of Lutheranism*, tr. Walter A. Hansen (St. Louis: Concordia, 1962), pp. 43ff.

[30] BekS:167, 185, 217 (=BC:112, 125, 150).

[31] WA 34/II:145f.

[32] WA 17/I:404.

[33] WA 10/III:299.

[34] WA 39/II:214.

[35] WA 40/I:229; cf. pp. 235, 232–34, 236, 241.

[36] Ibid., p. 232.

[37] Ibid., p. 233.

[38] Ibid., p. 297.

[39] Justification by faith was Luther's specialty. In the following lines I merely wish to show that Melanchthon himself accepted this concept although it was not as central in his thinking. In his *Didymi Faventini adv. Th. Placentinum . . .* (1521): "For the Gospel is the announcement of salvation. By it grace, life and salvation are promised to those who by faith are joined to Christ. Evangelical

righteousness is nothing other than trust (*fiducia*) in Christ" (SA I:104). The following reference offers a significant parallel to the above discussion of Luther: "All this is summed up in the Ten Commandments, for the first commands faith, when God speaks: 'I am the Lord thy God'" (p. 174). From Melanchthon's short summary of the faith, written for Philipp, Landgrave of Hesse: "This is truly Christian righteousness, when the confused conscience is lifted up through faith in Christ, and knows that it receives the forgiveness of sins for the sake of Christ" (p. 181). From his *De ecclesia . . .* (1539): "The beginning of justification by God is faith, which believes in him who justifies . . ." (p. 346).

[40] A difficult problem in Reformation and post-Reformation research is the question whether Melanchthon taught synergism. It is often held against him that he said that three causes concur in conversion: the Holy Spirit, the Word, and the consenting will of man (CR 21:376, 658). On the surface this sounds like a clear case of synergism—that is, cooperation in conversion. However, when we investigate what he understood by conversion, we learn that he spoke of two kinds: (1) that of the unregenerated and (2) that of the regenerated. The latter kind, synonymous with sanctification or good works done by the believer, was intended in the statement about the three causes. Obviously, anyone opposed to synergism would admit that after the initial conversion the believer must be willing to live according to God's Word. Hence, if Melanchthon defined his terms in that way, he was not propounding synergism in that statement. I plan to treat this problem much more fully in a forthcoming article scheduled to appear in the *Luther-Jahrbuch* in 1980.

12

The Reformational Doctrine of Justification as a Forensic Action of God

Law and Gospel and the Problem of Forensic Justification

Only when justification is seen as a forensic action by the divine Judge is legalism overcome. Recent New Testament scholars such as Bultmann and Käsemann have underscored the juridical aspect of Biblical theology.[1] The Law sets forth the requirements of God's righteousness—standards so high that no person can satisfy them. Since the Law thereby discloses one's shortcomings and sins, the Law condemns and places the individual before the judgment. All the world is pronounced guilty before God (Rom. 3:19). But then the Gospel of divine grace is proclaimed in a message which overcomes the accusations of the Law. It reveals that God has met the claims of the Law in the saving work of His Son, Jesus Christ. And in another juridical or forensic announcement, those who in faith accept this favorable verdict are declared just or righteous (*justum pronuntiari*).

Since the accusations of the Law are a given quantity, they extend to every man, woman, or child unless they have been stilled. Theologically, this takes place in forensic justification and only in forensic justification. If it has not taken place in forensic justification, the condemning voice of the Law has not been silenced, and the individual remains in a nomological, not an evangelical existence. Here Luther and Melanchthon's distinction of Law and Gospel is needed. The Law is proclaimed to reveal sin, show the person his dangerous predicament, and make him yearn for help. The Gospel is then proclaimed to show that Christ has made atonement, has stilled the accusations of the Law, has satisfied the demands of justice, has forgiven the believer his sin, and has imputed to him the perfect righteousness of his Saviour. The distinction of Law and Gospel is therefore the basis of justification.[2] And the basic concept of justification, in which the evangelical position is most sharply contrasted and made unmistakable, is forensic. This is paradoxical. Only when justification is seen as a judicial act is legalism overcome. This means that justification is an act that takes place, as it were, before the judgment throne of God (*coram Deo*) here and now. It is an act in which God proclaims that the sinner who has been accused by the Law for his sins is from that moment set free.[3] This important aspect of justification has been misunderstood by prominent contemporary theologians. They claim that Melanchthon, not Luther, taught this and that Melanchthon based his whole system upon the Law. They therefore claim that it is a legalistic view of justification.[4] But they overlook an important paradox, for the forensic view does exactly the opposite. Because of his sins man comes under the condemnation of the Law. And since justification is a forensic or judicial act, the believer is thereby actually freed from the Law. He is freed in a manner in which he could not be freed under a view of justification that overlooked the forensic motif.

A justification described merely in forensic terms falls short of the Biblical insights discovered under the Reformation. The writers who assert that forensic justification is fundamentally Melanchthonian are not wrong until they claim that the judicial aspect of justification is not found in Luther at all. Not only did Luther generously acknowledge Melanchthon's doctrine of justification, whether in the *Loci communes*, the *Augsburg Confession*, or the *Apology*,[5] but he also taught forensic justification explicitly, as we shall presently see. Nevertheless, it was more characteristic of Luther to describe justification under the doctrine of Christ or of faith. At the same time, it would be just as erroneous to deny that faith or the doctrine of Christ was present in Melanchthon. These three aspects of justification will therefore serve to give us a well-rounded picture showing both the contrasts and the similarities between Luther and Melanchthon. It will thus show the essential agreement they both claimed. We shall also explore the possibilities for the agreement in diversity that exists in the ecumenical debates.

The Doctrine of Sin as a
Necessary Component of Justification

Ours is a badly confused age in world history. Countless persons, including trained theologians, feel that the doctrine of justification is no longer "relevant." They fail to see that man needs to be rid of guilt. Concurrently, we hear massive indictments of the barbaric cruelties of our age—the millions of victims of Stalin and Hitler, the atrocities in Vietnam and Cambodia, the rise in juvenile delinquency and adult crime, and the tragic breakdown of sexual morality, marriage, and the family. Never have the misdeeds of the human race been more apparent. Stated theologically, never have the grounds for expecting God's punitive wrath been sounder. Theology today is badly in need of a new study of the doctrine of sin. Such a study will in turn make it clear that forensic justification is neither outdated nor irrelevant but is the needed solution for our getting right with God and making a new beginning.[6]

"Our teaching magnifies sin and grace," Melanchthon wrote in 1543.[7] These words could just as well have been said by Luther. Whoever wills to understand the Gospel at Mount Calvary must first experience the crushing trumpet call of the Law at Mount Sinai, which uncovers his sin and need. Only after Luther had suffered under the wrath of God could the grace of justification come to him. His doctrine of sin was therefore one of his most profound insights. When we reduce sin to something the individual can handle by his own good works, we belittle the saving work of Christ, who thought it necessary to die for the sins of mankind. The more we magnify sin, the more we magnify Christ. The more we belittle sin, the more we belittle Christ.[8] In the 1535 *Commentary on Galatians* Luther asserts:

> Therefore you must not imagine that your sins are small or that you can remove them by your works, nor should you despair on account of their magnitude, if you feel them oppressing you at any time in life or in death. But learn here from Paul to believe that Christ was delivered up not for fictitious or painted but for true sins, not for small sins but for the greatest sins, not for one or two but for all sins, not for sins that have been overcome (because no man nor even an angel could overcome the least sin), but for unconquered sins. And unless you can find yourself in the number of those who say: [He was

delivered up] 'for our offenses' [Gal. 1:4], that is, of those who hold this doctrine of faith and teach, hear, learn, and love it, there is no salvation for you.[9]

Imputation of the Righteousness of Christ

The necessary condition for a favorable judgment before the judicatory of God is the imputation of the righteousness of Another in place of the transgression of the sinner. We have discussed Luther's concept of *der fröhliche Wechsel*—the "blessed exchange" that occurs when Christ assumes the sinner's guilt and gives in exchange His perfect righteousness. There is a certain tension between this concept and the idea of the imputation of righteousness. The former is mystic; the latter is forensic. The former was found in the theology of Luther before he had solved several central points of his theology; the latter was developed especially by Melanchthon. Yet despite the inner tension between the internally or the externally transmitted righteousness of Christ, both have indisputable basis in Scripture, and both are found in the writings of Melanchthon as well as Luther. In any case, imputation is the concept under which the doctrine of Christ is linked with forensic justification.

Historians of the Reformation who lack a grasp of systematic theology and systematicians unacquainted with the historical problem of the Reformation often imagine that imputation is distinctive in Luther's position and that it is found in his earliest writings. It is true that the words "impute" and "repute" are found with some frequency in the *Lectures on Romans*, where these words are used to establish a relationship between the righteousness of Christ and the righteousness of the believer. But a careful study of the context will show that in nearly every case these usages are more closely related to medieval thinking than to Luther's mature position. Another source of confusion is the failure to observe where Luther is merely quoting the Latin Vulgate (especially Ps. 32:2) or an earlier theologian. Still another cause for misunderstanding is the failure to distinguish between three seemingly identical but actually separate terms: *imputare, non imputare,* and *reputare.* It seems simple to assume that *non imputare* is merely the opposite of *imputare* or that *imputare* and *reputare* are perfect synonyms. More thorough analysis will show the fallacy of such premature judgment.

Melanchthon was the first to introduce justification by imputation into Reformation theology when he wrote in September 1519: "All our righteousness is the gracious imputation of God."[10] Writers such as Otto Ritschl have tried to prove that this concept came from Luther and that Luther was the real author of this statement. Ritschl, however, was forced to retract.[11] Melanchthon used this formula earlier than Luther, and the imputation of the righteousness of Christ to the believer is a concept difficult to document in Luther. Melanchthon seems to have found it in the *Novum Instrumentum omne* (1516) of Erasmus. There, in his annotations to Romans 4, Erasmus asserted that the Greek word λογίζεσθαι (to reckon) should be translated as *imputatum est* where the English Bible reads: "Abraham believed God, and it was counted unto him for righteousness" (Rom. 4:3). But what was imputed? Erasmus thought it was Abraham's faith.[12] Melanchthon made a significant advance over Erasmus in this. The ground for justification in Melanchthon's view as well as in Luther's was not the imputation of one's faith but the imputation of the alien righteousness of Christ.

Justification: A Legal Term

It is now fashionable to decry any doctrine of justification as untimely. "Prominent speakers" at popular theological gatherings state with mock regret that it is well-nigh impossible to make justification "relevant" to "modern man" since that exotic creature is more concerned instead with how God may be justified in his sight than with how he may be justified before God. The justification of God in the form of theodicy is common today whether it comes as a detour of some doctrine of the divine Word or whether it occurs in a funeral sermon in which the preacher apologizes for the God who has taken some young person from this earthly paradise to Himself in heaven.

It is difficult, therefore, to make the doctrine of justification relevant to modern man. For one reason, many people have no sense of accountability before God. For another, modern legal usage has changed the term. Today a man proved guilty of committing a crime is not justified in court by being forgiven for that crime. To be justified means to prove that the accused man never committed the crime in the first place. In theological terms, however, a man can be proved guilty of the crime and still be justified. How can he be found just if he is in fact guilty?

Werner Elert clarified this problem in the light of legal history. In the legal code of Luther's day the concept of justification was not applied at all to one who showed himself innocent of a crime.[13] In sixteenth-century Germany, justification ". . . denoted either the painful trial by ordeal, which might go so far as to claim the life of the person being tried, or more commonly the carrying out of a penal sentence, especially the execution of the one convicted."[14] Elert notes that during the seventeenth century it was still common to speak of the expenses to the state for corporal punishment as the "costs of painful justification" and that mention is made of ". . . the body of one justified with the sword."[15] The same usage is found in Hans Sachs and Luther. Luther spoke of "justification" when a merchant was hanged by order of Cardinal Albrecht of Mainz and of the "sharp justification" inflicted on the torture rack—a practice he strongly condemned. The Revised Standard Version renders Acts 12:19 as, "[Herod] examined the sentries and ordered that they should be put to death. . . ." This same text is translated by Luther, "Herod justified the sentries, and let them be put away"—that is, executed. Elert continues:

> Therefore, when the Apology expressly says that the word justification is understood 'according to legal usage' (*usu forensi*), every reader knew that being justified had to do with punishment. The goal of justification was not that the individual was cleared of guilt, but rather that the executioner 'gave him his deserts,' as Luther understood the secular punishment (WA 41: 324). With the presupposition of this linguistic usage, it becomes clear that the forensic doctrine of justification neither veils nor weakens the question of how the Gospel relates itself to the responsibility of every man before his Creator, but rather that it makes it palpable in all its cutting entirety. For the teaching which affirms that man before God faces his Judge who will 'give him his deserts' also says that he has been called by God to give an accounting. This is done in the act in which the final answer is given to the question, 'How can I find a merciful God?'[16]

Several passages in the New Testament likewise describe the way of salvation in terms of death of the sinner in such a way that he is nevertheless forgiven and granted fellowship with God. In Romans 6:3f. Paul writes:

> Know ye not, that so many of us as were baptized into Jesus Christ were baptized into his death? Therefore we are buried with him by baptism into death: that like as Christ was raised up from the dead by the glory of the Father, even so we also should walk in newness of life [vv. 3–4]. For he that is dead is freed from sin. [v. 7].

Here those who have been justified (Rom. 5:1) are said to have experienced the death of the old Adam in order that the new man might come forth to live with Christ. This is a continuation of Paul's thought regarding the first and second Adams in Romans 5, which finds a more succinct formulation in I Corinthians 15:21f.

> For since by man came death, by man came also the resurrection of the dead. For as in Adam all die, even so in Christ shall all be made alive.

In order to be the Saviour, Christ took upon Himself the curse of the Law—that is, death. "Christ hath redeemed us from the curse of the law, being made a curse for us" (Gal. 3:13). "For he hath made him to be sin for us, who knew no sin; that we might be made the righteousness of God in him" (II Cor. 5:21). These parallels from the New Testament indicate Luther's intended meaning of the forensic term, "justification." The sinner was put to death, and the new being emerged.

Through the forensic declaration man is removed from the unjustified to the justified state. This is a profound change. However, justification means no outward change in the qualities of the individual. In justification the "making righteous" of the individual was ". . . the sentence of God that the individual could only have said concerning him, or could only receive. This sentence had declaratory meaning. The 'making righteous' is a speaking righteous or declaring righteous."[17]

Thus, justification by imputation of alien righteousness need not be called a fiction but something that actually takes place in the decision of God, something that alters the destiny of the individual. God regards him as a just person. For the sake of Christ, God is pleased to regard the sinful self as purged. God reckons his faith to him for righteousness. In His love God sees something in the individual that no human eye can see. God declares that the Law, sin, and death can no longer harm him. He has been forensically cleared. He is justified!

Notes

[1] In spite of the fact that some of their work has seemed too "liberal" and unapplicable to church life, many of the insights of these men really clarify Biblical teachings and expose the shallowness of the social gospel and activistic thinking which are rampant in the churches today. See Rudolf Bultmann, *Theologie des Neuen Testaments*, 2nd ed. (Tübingen: J. C. B. Mohr, 1954), §§17–40; Eng. tr., *Theology of the New Testament* (New York: Scribner, 1970). Ernst Käsemann, "Zum Verständnis von Römer 3, 24–26," *Exegetische Versuche und Besinnungen*, Vol. I, 4th ed. (Göttingen: Vandenhoeck & Ruprecht, 1965), pp. 96–100.

[2] Besides the statements of Luther and Melanchthon on Law and Gospel, see the FC III, IV, V, VI. The classical presentation is that by Carl Ferdinand Wilhelm Walther, *The Proper Distinction Between Law and Gospel*, Thirty-Nine Evening Lectures, tr. William Herman Theodore Dau (St. Louis: Concordia, 1928ff.). The great recent exponent who has built an entire systematic theology around the doctrine of Law and Gospel is Werner Elert. A convenient summary in English is his *Law and Gospel*, tr. Edward Schroeder. See also Elert's *Christian Ethos*, tr. Carl Schindler (Philadelphia: Fortress, 1957), and his *Structure of Lutheranism*, tr. Walter Hansen (St. Louis: Concordia, 1962). Gerhard O. Forde has written several significant books, including *Where God Meets Man: Luther's Down-to-Earth Approach to the Gospel* (Minneapolis: Augsburg, 1972). A convenient summary of Paul Althaus's position is given in his *The Divine Command* (Philadelphia: Fortress, 1966). For further information, see my article, "Luther Research in English-Speaking Countries since 1971," LuJB 44 (1977): 112–15, with notes.

[3] For an impressive investigation and presentation on the legal connotations of justification, see Robert D. Brinsmead, "The Legal and Moral Aspects of Salvation," *Present Truth* 5 (1976): No. 4 (June), pp. 23–30; No. 5 (August), pp. 20–30. Brinsmead observes that Protestants as a whole have lost the Reformational doctrine of justification. Even the conservative Missouri Synod

Lutheran, William F. Beck, has given up the basic teaching of Luther (ibid. 5, No. 4, p. 26). Brinsmead summarizes five results of neglecting the legal aspects of justification: (1) The cross of Christ is emptied of real meaning if the sinner could be saved by moral renewal. (2) God's work in Christ is replaced by a work in man. Man, not God, becomes the center of religion. (3) The objective foundation for salvation is removed and replaced by subjectivism. (4) Sanctification is no longer based on justification, and therefore it is neither legal nor moral. (5) Such a repudiation of the legal aspects of redemption betrays the Protestant cause and loses the gifts of the Reformation. See also G. C. Berkouwer, *Studies in Dogmatics: Faith and Justification* (Grand Rapids: Eerdmans, 1954), esp. pp. 14–17, 54f., 89–100. However, I do not understand Berkouwer's remark which seems to be directed against Elert: ". . . It is quite untrue to say that the tendency toward a forensic or juridical justification during the period leading up to the Formula of Concord was an about-face from Luther's more ethical teaching" (p. 55). Such a description does not fit *Morphologie des Luthertums*, Vol. I, p. 88, Berkouwer's reference, and it is contrary to Elert's position as such.

⁴ Lauri Haikola provided some valuable insights in his address at the 1960 Luther Congress in Münster, "Melanchthons und Luthers Lehre von der Rechtfertigung," *Luther and Melanchthon in the History and Theology of the Reformation*, ed. Vilmos Vajta (Philadelphia: Muhlenberg, 1961), pp. 89–103. However, in his constant attacks on forensic justification he is really attacking the later Luther as well as his intended target, Melanchthon. He faults Melanchthon for having undergirded his view of forensic justification with a doctrine of the Law (pp. 90–93) which really was not so legalistic as Haikola thinks but actually went back to Paul and was also shared by Luther. Throughout his paper Haikola shows his allegiance to the theses of Holl and Hirsch with their indebtedness to Kant and Ritschl. It is unfortunate that Haikola says that one must accept the criticisms of Melanchthon by Holl and Hirsch (p. 100, n. 45), neither one of which had made thorough studies of that reformer in the primary sources. In fact, in the statement of Hirsch which Haikola regards as of great importance, Hirsch, after two pages of abusive language against Melanchthon in which he cites not a single reference from the sources, admits in his own note 82: "I am aware that in my judgment of the relationship of Melanchthon to Luther I have basically only followed the conclusions of previous research . . ." Emanuel Hirsch, *Die Theologie des Andreas Osiander und ihre geschichtlichen Voraussetzungen* (Göttingen: Vandenhoeck & Ruprecht, 1919), p. 229, n. 82. Haikola makes a statement of comparison which is partly right and partly wrong (pp. 97–8): "Eine lex aeterna als ein Gesetz, das eine ewige und objective Ordnung darstellt . . . kennt Luther nicht" makes of Luther an antinomian and is a false statement; but the material in the ellipse is correct: ". . . aus der man materielle Normen für jedes gerechte Handeln Gottes und des Menschen

ablesen könnte, kennt Luther nicht." But neither does Melanchthon teach such a distortion. The next sentence is a misunderstanding of Melanchthon: "Gottes Anspruch auf den Menschen kann nie erschöpfend durch menschliche Regeln umschrieben werden, wie das nach Melanchthon möglich ist."

⁵ Luther at times expressed his agreement and admiration for Melanchthon in rather extravagant words. In his masterpiece, *De servo arbitrio* (1525), Luther told Erasmus that Melanchthon's *Loci communes* were so outstanding that they were worthy of being canonized (WA 18:601 = Packer, pp. 62f.). Luther himself edited some of Melanchthon's works and had them published without their author's knowledge or consent. Luther approved the *Instructions for the Visitors of Saxony* (SA I:216ff.) and wrote the foreword (WA 26:195), so that prominent scholars still cite it as Luther's work although it was really written by Melanchthon. It is generally known that Luther heartily endorsed the *Augsburg Confession*. See esp. J. M. Reu, *The Augsburg Confession: A Collection of Sources with an Historical Introduction*, 1930, pp. 112f., *123, *314ff., *319f., *345f. Cf. Br 5:498f. Luther also declared himself in agreement with the *Apology* (cf. WA 50:470). See also WA 40/III:315, 339, 345 (". . . de merito Christi . . ."), 346, 348. Cf. Br 5:221.

⁶ For a recent, incisive study of hamartiology, see Robert D. Brinsmead, "Man as Sinner," *Verdict: A Journal of Theology* I, 3 (September 1978): 5–14.

⁷ WA 39/II:207, 24.

⁸ See the comments on sin in Luther's treatise against Latomus (1521). For example: "God does not save fictitious but genuine sinners; he teaches to mortify not fictitious but genuine sin" (WA 8:107, 35). "Therefore sin is truly sin, but because the gift and grace are in me, they are not imputed. This is not on account of my innocence, as though my person were not guilty, but because the gift and grace reign in me" (WA 8:121, 5). "The sophists are concerned with minimizing this sin which God so greatly magnifies, for He wills that it be posited against His Son and that all men be pressed and driven to Christ by this exceedingly harsh judgment, so that trembling, despairing, and panting, they will find refuge under His wings. But those people who deny this sin make men sleepy and careless towards the gift they have received. Thereby the grace of Christ is made cheap and the mercy of God is made a trifle . . . Therefore, beware of those most pestilential people and learn that the works of God are great, wonderful, and glorious. Then you will know that you cannot magnify this sin greatly enough" (WA 8:114, 36).

⁹ WA 40/I:87, 22; AE 26:35.

¹⁰ SA I:24.

¹¹ Otto Ritschl, "Die Entwicklung der Rechtfertigungslehre Melanchthons bis zum Jahre 1527," *Theologische Studien und Kritiken* 85 (1912): 518–40. After Otto Clemen had demolished his thesis, he retracted it in "Zu Melanchthons Thesen von 1519," ibid. 86 (1913): 163.

[12] For a fuller treatment of Erasmus' contribution toward the "grammar of justification," see my article, "The Influence of Erasmus upon Melanchthon, Luther, and the Formula of Concord in the Doctrine of Justification," ChH 43 (June 1974): 183–200.

[13] Werner Elert, *Der christliche Glaube*, 3rd ed. (Hamburg: Furche, 1956), p. 459.

[14] Werner Elert, "Deutschrechtliche Züge in Luther's Rechfertigungslehre," ZsTh 12 (1934–35): 23–4.

[15] Ibid., pp. 25–6.

[16] *Elert, Der christliche Glaube*, p. 470.

[17] Ibid., p. 472.

NUREMBERG...

13

Forensic Justification in Melanchthon

Melanchthon's Reformational theology falls into three main periods. The first period extends through the framing of the *Augsburg Confession* and its *Apology* (1531). The second period begins with the *Lectures on Romans* of 1532. The outbreak of the Osiandrian controversy (1550) opens a final phase covering the last ten years of Melanchthon's life and ending with his death in 1560.[1] These periods correspond to events which led him to adjust his teachings to new problems. Although it is implicit much earlier, the markedly forensic nature of justification is not brought out until the second period. This unexpected fact should be a warning against repeating outworn shibboleths about Melanchthon and Luther on justification!

Melanchthon: 1518–1529

We have already covered some of the most salient points in Melanchthon's youthful as well as mature doctrine of justification. The demands of the Law frighten the sinner; the comforting promise of forgiveness in the Gospel raises him up again. All is done through the merits of Christ, whose righteousness is imputed to the believing sinner. All is given classical summary in the *Loci* of 1521:

> We are therefore justified when, having been put to death by the Law, we are brought to life again by the word of grace, which is promised in Christ, that is, the Gospel pardoning sin; and we hold to him by faith, not doubting that the righteousness of Christ is our righteousness, that the satisfaction of Christ is our expiation, and that the

resurrection of Christ is become ours. In brief, that we do not doubt that our sins are forgiven us, and that God is favorably disposed toward us or thinks well of us. Therefore, no works of ours, however good they are or may seem, are righteousness, but righteousness is faith alone in the mercy and grace of God in Jesus Christ.[2]

Melanchthon held this position for the rest of his life. During the next decade his formulations followed the same pattern. Later events did not lead him to retract but to develop and to clarify further. What is noteworthy in this formulation from the early *Loci*, however, is the absence of any explicit reference to a forensic action on the part of God. An important transition had already begun during the writing of the *Loci communes* of 1521. Led by the excesses of the radical reformation during Luther's absence from Wittenberg, Melanchthon began to limit freedom and to place more emphasis upon the ordering effect of the Law. This change became even more apparent in the 1522 revision of the *Loci*.[3] Likewise, Melanchthon began to alter his position on justification and the monergism of God. In his earlier works predestination had been an important factor. But after the traumatic experiences at Wittenberg in 1521 and 1522, Melanchthon placed more and more stress on human responsibility and activity, and the operation of God became increasingly specialized in scope. By 1525, when Luther wrote his great treatise *On the Bondage of the Will* with its defense of God's freedom and man's bondage, Melanchthon found himself in sympathy with Erasmus, Luther's antagonist. Luther's assertions that predestination was not to be probed because it belonged to the inscrutability of the *Deus absconditus* must have been painful for Melanchthon. In any case, predestination continued to recede in Melanchthon's system. In the *Confessio Augustana* of 1530 it was not even mentioned, and in his later writings it virtually disappeared.

Melanchthon's *Scholia on Colossians* of 1527 marked an important step in his development.[4] First published in recent times in the new *Studienausgabe*, edited by Stupperich,[5] Melanchthon states that the central point of this Epistle is the meaning of the Gospel. This can be determined only when Christian righteousness is distinguished from that of men or even from that of the Decalogue of Moses.[6] The world expects to be justified by human righteousness or by the Law, but Paul makes clear how wrong this is. "Paul teaches us that justification does not depend upon any merits of our own, but that it is through faith, if we believe that our sins are forgiven us freely for the sake of Christ. . . ." If justification depended upon our making satisfaction for our sins in any way, we could never have any certainty of salvation, for we could never know whether we had contributed enough. Indeed, our conscience would tell us that our best efforts were inadequate: ". . . *Quia enim lex semper nos condemnat . . .*" (because the Law always condemns us). Justification must therefore be freely given, as Paul teaches. If we believe that our sins are freely forgiven us for Christ's sake, we are justified. This, however, is followed at once by newness of life. "Nor can faith exist without keeping the teachings of God. . . . For faith without repentance is nothing but a meaningless dream." Where faith is real, forgiveness is followed by the work of the Holy Spirit so that ". . . the new being brings a new life, new deeds."[7]

Melanchthon's concern that free justification be followed by appropriate living was expressed in his influential *Instructions to the Visitors of the Clergy in the Electorate of Saxony* (1528), which has often been wrongly ascribed to Luther. On the very first page Melanchthon discusses the libertinism that had become a problem.

> But there are many who speak only of the forgiveness of sin, but who say little or nothing about repentance. If there is nevertheless no forgiveness of sins without repentance, so also forgiveness of sins cannot be understood without repentance. Therefore if forgiveness of sins is preached without repentance, it follows that the people imagine they have already received the forgiveness of sins, and thereby they become cocksure and fearless, which is then greater error and sin than all the error that preceded our time.[8]

Thereupon Melanchthon admonishes that the Ten Commandments be diligently preached so that the people might learn to fear God and be moved to genuine repentance.[9]

> Next it is useful that one preach concerning faith. This should be done in such a way that he who has remorse and suffers on account of his sins will believe that his sins are forgiven him, not on account of

any merit of ours, but for the sake of Christ. The conscience that is remorseful and distressed comes to peace, comfort, and joy, when it hears that its sins are forgiven for Christ's sake. At that point there is faith, which makes us righteous before God. One must diligently admonish the people that such faith cannot exist without earnest and sincere remorse and terror before God. . . .[10]

Justification was grounded upon the doctrine of satisfaction contributed by Christ.

Satisfaction for our sins is not our work, for Christ alone has performed satisfaction for our sins. This part of repentance belongs to the forgiveness of sins and to faith, in order that we may know and believe that our sins are forgiven us for the sake of Christ.[11]

This is important, for it is not sufficient to know that sins are forgiven. One must also believe that they are forgiven for the sake of Christ.

. . . Although we have deserved nothing but damnation, nevertheless God forgives us without any merit of ours, for the sake of Christ. This is merit, for one receives forgiveness of sins through faith if one believes that Christ has performed full satisfaction for us, as John writes in the First Epistle, Chapter 2: 'He is the propitiation for our sins, and not for ours only, but also for the whole world.[12]

Justification in the Apology

The most important of all Protestant Confessions was the *Augsburg Confession* of 1530.[13] Its author was Melanchthon, not Luther, for Luther stood under the ban of the emperor and could not appear at Augsburg. Article IV, which dealt with justification, was disarmingly brief. After stating that justification did not rest upon human accomplishment in any way, it affirmed that ". . . we receive forgiveness of sins and become righteous before God out of grace, for the sake of Christ, and through faith, if we believe that Christ has suffered for us, and that for his sake our sins are forgiven us, and everlasting life is freely given us. This faith God holds before himself and reckons unto righteousness. . . ." This article was vigorously attacked by the theologians of the Roman Catholic party in their reply, known as the *Confutation*.[14] Melanchthon answered their charges and defended the *Augsburg Confession* in his *Apologia Confessionis Augustanae* (1531).

In the *Apology* Melanchthon took note of the fact that the Roman Catholic opponents had found many objections to the doctrine of justification in the *Augsburg Confession*. He accordingly prepared an elaborate reply in which his doctrine of justification by 1531 is expounded in considerable detail. Melanchthon does not forget that what he is writing is not merely a private theology but a document to present the position of all the Lutherans. His emphasis on *solo fide* is noticeable, for this concept otherwise recedes behind the *sola gratia* in his other writings. After discussing the distinction between Law and Gospel, Melanchthon turns to the question, "What is Faith?"[15] He outlines the three component parts of a truly evangelical doctrine of justification. They are the promise, the *solo gratia*, and the merits of Christ.[16] Melanchthon carefully guards against a misunderstanding of what he means by justifying faith. "The adversaries imagine that faith is a knowledge of historical facts and therefore they teach that it can exist with mortal sin," he observes. He corrects this:

> That faith which justifies is not a mere knowledge of historical facts, but it accepts as true the promise of God in which the remission of sins and justification are given freely, for the sake of Christ.[17]

Melanchthon has more to say about the relationship between justification and satisfaction offered by Christ.

> . . . Therefore we are not able to free ourselves from sin and to be justified through the Law, but the promise of the remission of sins and justification is bestowed for the sake of Christ, who was given for us, that he might offer satisfaction for the sins of the world, and become the Mediator or Propitiator.[18]

What Melanchthon says here must be taken in the total context of Articles IV and V of the *Augsburg Confession*. In Article V he wrote: "That we may come to such saving faith, God has instituted the office of the ministry, teaching the Gospel and administering the Sacraments. . . ." This is important to Melanchthon's basic thought that justification is forensic. If God is not to be apprehended through good works, then He is found in His Word.

> But it is not possible for this to be done with God. God cannot be apprehended except in the Word. Therefore justification takes place through the Word, as Paul said: 'The Gospel is the power of God unto salvation for everyone who believes.' Or again, 'Faith comes from hearing.' Or, the argument can be taken up from the point of view that faith justifies because if justification be only through the Word and the Word be apprehended only by faith, it follows that faith justifies.[19]

Thus, the Word of God justifies in a twofold sense: the preaching of the Gospel arouses faith, while the word of pardon itself remits sin. In the context immediately following, Melanchthon shows that with this concept of Word he intends to include also the forensic declaration of righteousness for the sake of Christ (*iustos pronuntiari*).[20]

We have noted that Luther's doctrine of justification could be characterized by the *sola fides*, and Melanchthon's by the *sola gratia*. This is not meant in an exclusive sense. Both concepts appear frequently in either man, but such a distinction can serve as a point of contrast. In his presentation on justification in the *Apology*, Melanchthon frequently mentions the *sola fides*. If we were judging quantitatively, it could not be said that Melanchthon's delineation of justification neglected "faith alone."[21] However, Luther's construction of justification "by faith alone" was based differently. Faith was an action on the part of the sinner in which he capitulated fully before God's judgment of his sinfulness but simultaneously trusted God's mercy and asked for forgiveness. In other words, faith pressed beyond the *Deus absconditus* to the *Deus revelatus* and there found forgiveness. For Luther this was not synergistic because of his view of election and predestination, in which God worked all things. This was not characteristic of Melanchthon. In his theological system free will sometimes seemed to endanger the monergism of divine saving action. Therefore, if we examine justification "by grace alone" in the *Apology*, we shall find that in every instance faith justifies because it apprehends Christ. In other words, in Melanchthon faith justifies in the sense of accepting the forgiveness God has promised through Christ, not in the sense of paying God the honor due Him as in Luther. Melanchthon's entire argument is presented succinctly in this comment on I Corinthians 15:56f.:

> . . . Sin terrifies the consciences; this comes about through the Law, which shows the wrath of God against sin. But we overcome it through Christ. How? By faith, when we are encouraged by trust in the promise of mercy for the sake of Christ. . . . But Christ is not apprehended as mediator except by faith. Therefore by faith alone we get the forgiveness of sins, when we raise up our hearts with confidence in the promise of mercy for the sake of Christ.[22]

This reference is particularly significant not only because Melanchthon handles the *sola fide* in a much more subsidiary manner than Luther, but because it contains the seed of a later divergency. As Elert has shown, Melanchthon's concept of faith as well as of contrition was soon to be ranked with the affections—an important step away from Luther.[23] Furthermore, Melanchthon was soon to develop his controversial trilogy of three causes in "conversion": the Holy Spirit, the Word, and the consenting will of man.[24] And this would be accompanied in turn by a renewed emphasis on the forensic character of justification.

Is forensic justification taught in the *Apology* itself? This was strongly argued in a now almost-forgotten controversy beginning in 1884.[25] It started with an essay by Friedrich Loofs, later to become one of the major historians of dogma but then only a young instructor at the University of Leipzig. Loofs claimed that, contrary to past supposition, Melanchthon's *Apology* contained two teachings on justification that were not completely reconciled. According to Loofs' interpretation of Melanchthon, justification consisted both of forgiveness of sins and moral renewal (*regeneratio*). Loofs' contemporaries were pardonably shocked by this unexpected revelation. They had assumed Melanchthon taught only a forensic justification. Their amazement was increased when Loofs' opponent, Eichhorn, contended that forensic justification was not even taught in the *Apology*.[26] Furthermore, Loofs found that Melanchthon's doctrine of justification in the *Apology* was analytic. He contrasted it with the *Formula of Concord*, which he found had misinterpreted and corrupted the earlier doctrine of the reformers.[27] Loofs' assertions were based upon §72 of the *Apology*:

> ... We do not think of faith in this manner, but this is what we defend, namely that properly and truly by faith itself we are reputed, just for the sake of Christ, or, we are accepted by God. And because 'to be justified' signifies 'to be effected righteous out of unrighteous' or 'to be regenerated', it signified 'to be pronounced or reputed righteous'. For indeed Scripture speaks in either way. Therefore we want to show this first, that faith alone effects the righteous out of the unrighteous ones, that is, that faith receives the remission of sins.

It appeared that Loofs was right. To be justified meant to be effected righteous or just. Here was the effective doctrine of justification in full clarity. Or was it? Loofs put the following sentences into Melanchthon's mouth:

> For to be justified denotes out of unrighteous men, righteous men to effect or to let be born (become righteous, become converted or reborn); to be justified denotes for men to be pronounced or to be reputed righteous (being righteous, or considered righteous by God). By the one as well as by the other understanding of *justificari*, the correctness of this sentence is demonstrated: by faith alone we are justified.[28]

Loofs has Melanchthon say that justification consists (1) in being made righteous through regeneration and (2) in being declared righteous on the basis of actual righteousness. This appears to be an "analytic" understanding of justification.

Loofs was actually not the first scholar to tackle the problem of the seemingly double concept of justification in the *Apology*. The writers of the *Formula of Concord* (1577) had already grappled with the problem. They found that the word *regeneratio* had a twofold sense in the *Apology* and elsewhere. According to the first usage, it referred to justification as rebirth; according to the second, it referred to sanctification or the new life of righteousness that the Holy Ghost worked in those who had previously been justified through faith.[29] The *Formula of Concord* allows either usage but warns against using the term "regeneration" in a way that makes it appear that justification is based upon any works, merit, or worthiness, ". . . whether preceding, accompanying, or following justification. . . ." And it points out that the most important thing is that justification be shown to be based instead upon the righteousness of Christ.[30]

Carl Stange found an answer to the allegedly double view of justification in the *Apology*. He agreed with the statement of Eichhorn that there was no difference between *iustum effici* (to make righteous) and *iustum reputari* (to declare righteous), although Eichhorn had also said the opposite.[31] Nevertheless, Stange basically disagreed with both Eichhorn and Loofs. In attempting to explain *Apology* IV:§§75ff., Eichhorn regarded §72 as the key to §§75–116, and Loofs took it as the key to §75–121. Thus, for Eichhorn §72 was introductory to the subsequent section, "That We Receive Forgiveness of Sins Solely by Faith in Christ." And for Loofs it was to lead into the part, "On Love and the Fulfilling of the Law," which dealt with good works. But Stange correctly showed that §72, with the statement about justification effecting and declaring righteous, was not the key to the subsequent discussion but that §117 explained §72 and the intervening parts. Stange pointed out that in effect Melanchthon had written the following in §117: "Up until now we have shown in considerable detail . . . , [first] that we receive the remission of sins by faith alone for the sake of Christ [cf. §§75–85] and [second] that we are justified by faith alone [cf. §§86–116], that is, we are made or regenerated from unrighteous men [cf. §§75–85] into righteous men [cf. §§86–116]." Thus, Stange showed that Melanchthon had used both Scriptural concepts of justification in the same sense—that is, that justification is by faith alone, through Christ, and that all works are excluded.[32]

Stange buttresses his finding with an impressive study drawn from an obscure parallel source—the Roman Catholic polemic by Berthold of Chiemsee, *Tewtsche Theologey* (1528).[33] Berthold had written:

> In this dangerous time, an old heresy, which had long lay hidden in hell, has been stirred up again, in which men are taught that grace and justification are received by faith alone, without the Sacraments or good works.[34]

Stange then draws word-by-word parallels between Berthold and Melanchthon in which the "opponent" in the *Apology* appears to be Berthold, and Melanchthon's arguments answer his objections. In conclusion, Stange finds an explanation for the much-disputed sentence: ". . . And because to be justified signifies out of unrighteous to be effected righteous or to be regenerated, it signifies also to be pronounced or reputed righteous . . ." Berthold had said that "Faith can be called the beginning of justification, but it does not make completely righteous."[35] Melanchthon answered that not only does faith mean that we are reputed righteous, but it means that we are reputed righteous because we are made righteous—that is, justification by faith alone is complete without any works of the Law.[36]

Let us attempt to summarize the debate over *Apology* IV. Loofs and Eichhorn were mistaken when they thought that Melanchthon temporarily laid aside his insistence upon forensic justification and taught in the *Apology* a justification based somehow upon the moral renewal of the individual. A solution to the problem by Melanchthon's pupil, David Chytraeus, appeared in the *Formula of Concord*.[37] Chytraeus pointed out that regeneration might be understood as either justification or sanctification and said that it meant the former in *Apology* IV. This was a worthwhile observation, but it did not completely solve the problem. Stange has recently shown that Melanchthon's statement was actually a reply to the charge that forensic justification led to ethical quietism and that there is no disparity in being pronounced righteous and in actually being righteous. In other words, since justification is essentially the forgiveness of sins, and since the forgiven sinner has been freed from guilt, he is really just and righteous. Although the believer is still a sinner, he is simultaneously a saint. He is a sinner in regard to his incomplete sanctification, but he is a saint in regard to God's word of justification based on the righteousness of Christ.

Melanchthon, Brenz, and Luther

In any case, even a presentation on justification as lucid as that in the *Apology* IV could still be misconstrued. The discussions of Loofs, Eichhorn, and Stange showed that in the *Apology* Melanchthon had not made the case against the "analytic" view of justification and for the forensic understanding unmistakably clear. Recognition of this lack of clarity, however, did not have to wait until the nineteenth century or even until the framing of the *Formula of Concord* in the 1570's. In the very year that Melanchthon wrote the *Apology* he engaged in a discussion with Johannes Brenz, whom he had known since his student days at Heidelberg (1512). Brenz had been a follower of Luther since 1518 and had introduced the reformation in Württemberg.

What was at stake in the discussion between Brenz and Melanchthon in 1531? Briefly, we could say that Brenz expressed justification in terms which made it appear "analytic." The end result was that both Melanchthon and Luther began to accentuate the forensic character of justification more than they had previously. Brenz' original letter to Melanchthon is not available, but Melanchthon indicates its nature.[38] Brenz had written a long letter to Melanchthon in which he discussed justification. However, he understood justification according to Augustine. This is not strange when one remembers that Brenz was a follower of Luther before Luther had completed the transition to fully Reformational theology. Melanchthon agreed with Augustine in saying that reason does not justify. But when Augustine said that we are justified through the fulfilling of the Law which the Holy Spirit works within us,[39] he was wrong. Melanchthon wrote to Brenz:

> Thus you also think. Men are justified by faith, because by faith we receive the Holy Spirit, so that thereafter we are righteous through the fulfilling of the Law, which the Holy Spirit effects. This idea posits faith in our fulfilling, in our purity or perfection, so that this renovation must needs follow faith.

Brenz made faith the foundation upon which an "analytic" righteousness was constructed. He thereby based justification on the Law rather than on the Gospel.[40] Melanchthon asked Brenz to explain justification by faith, not on the ground that it fulfilled the Law, but because faith was the means by which Christ was apprehended. "It is true that faith justifies," wrote Melanchthon, "but not because it is the new work of the Holy Spirit within us, but because it grasps Christ, for whose sake we are accepted, and not on account of the gift of the Holy Spirit in us." Melanchthon advises Brenz to rid himself of such undue Augustinian influences and to study the *Apology* IV more carefully.

Where did Luther stand in this discussion? Did he, like Brenz, tend toward an "analytic" justification, avoiding the forensic tendencies of Melanchthon? To the contrary. Luther stood side by side with Melanchthon, as his postscript to Melanchthon's letter shows. Luther wrote:

> I also, my dear Brenz, who understand the matter better, try not to think of any quality in my heart such as faith or love, as it is called, but in their place I set Christ and say: 'This is my righteousness.' He is that formal quality, as they put it, my righteousness, by whom I am freed from the Law and works . . . Thus he says: 'I am the Way, the Truth, and the Life.' He does not say, 'I give you the way, the truth, and the life,' as if it was if he were outside me and worked it within me. But these things should be, remain, and live not through me but in me.[41]

It should not surprise us that Luther thus declares himself on the side of Melanchthon unless we are unduly influenced by certain historians who downgrade Melanchthon and only cite the Young Luther. Not only did Luther endorse the *Augsburg Confession* and its *Apology*. He himself spoke in the same manner. In the *De loco iustificatione* (1530) we read:

> If therefore we are justified on works that follow faith, then we are not justified by faith for the sake of Christ but for the sake of ourselves, as we perform good works after faith. This is to deny Christ. Christ is not apprehended by works but by faith of the heart. Therefore we must be justified by faith alone, without respect to any works, before, or after.[42]

How did the controversy with Brenz end? Brenz accepted Melanchthon's argument,[43] undoubtedly prompted more by Luther's affirmation[44] than by Melanchthon's argument alone. In any case, when Melanchthon defended the doctrine of justification against Andreas Osiander after Luther's death, to Melanchthon's chagrin Brenz remained strangely silent. Whether he was completely convinced or not, Brenz chose to acquiesce to Luther and Melanchthon.

Melanchthon's Doctrine after 1532

Following the writing of the *Apology* and the controversy with Brenz, Melanchthon expressed the difficulty he had encountered in writing on justification and his desire to make his position unmistakably clear.[45] As a result, he brought out the forensic quality of justification more positively than before and made a sharper case against effective or "analytic" justification by stressing the distinction between justification and sanctification. Christ remained central in his system. Satisfaction wrought by Christ was made the sinner's own by divine imputation received through faith. The new life of holiness or sanctification was the inevitable result of justification, from which, however, it was carefully distinguished.[46]

In his *Commentary on Romans* of 1540 Melanchthon wrote the significant heading: "The Sum of Doctrine Delivered in the Writings of the Prophets and Apostles Concerning Justification before God." This expressed his conviction that the center of all Scripture was justification.[47] Commenting on Paul's words in Romans 3:21, he wrote: "But now without the Law the righteousness of God has appeared, that is, the imputation of righteousness is given for the sake of Christ, not for the sake of the Law."[48] Commenting on the words of John 1:17, he wrote: "The Law was given through Moses, but grace and truth were made through Jesus Christ, that is, Christ gives us grace, which means the free remission of sins, and effects in us the true knowledge of God, true love, true trust, and true worship."[49] Melanchthon noted the emphasis Paul places on the word *gratis* (freely) and pointed out: "He excludes our merits, and he offers the merits of Christ."[50] This is none other than the proper distinction between Law and Gospel. The Law can only kill. "But the gospel does away with a condition based on our worthiness or merits, and testifies that God for the sake of the merits of Christ is graciously reconciled to us, not because of any merit in us, but because here is faith, that is, confidence resting in the mercy in Christ."[51]

Melanchthon saw a twofold character in justification: forgiveness of sins and the imparting of righteousness. "It is needful that justification be understood as remission of sins and divine acceptance, that is, the imputation of righteousness." Forgiveness rested upon the merits of Christ, while ". . . righteousness is given us by faith, signifying imputation of righteousness or acceptance."[52] From this it is clear that Melanchthon was not thinking of two steps in justification but of one and the same divine act, for in the preceeding two citations[53] acceptance is related to imputation in one case and to forgiveness in the other.[54] Therefore, justification by grace alone (*sola gratia*) means forgiveness for the sake of Christ (*propter Christum*) as it is apprehended by faith alone (*sola fide*). Grace alone, Christ alone, and faith alone—these are the three golden cords running through the doctrine of justification of the Mature Melanchthon.[55] It remained for dogmaticians of the seventeenth century to divide the article of justification into the so-called "Order of Salvation." under which forgiveness of sins and imputation of righteousness became successive steps. These tendencies, of course, were already latent in Melanchthon after 1532, but the division into steps had not yet taken place. It is legitimate to distinguish the various saving acts of God for the sake of clarity. But if these divine acts are separated, their integrity may be impaired. We shall let others decide whether the Orthodox theologians erred in this.

We have seen that Melanchthon's special contribution was the forensic character of justification. It remains for us to note his development of this aspect. Concerning Romans 4:5, he wrote in the *Commentary on Romans* (1532): "Paul develops his argument from the word 'imputing' and reasons clearly that our virtues are not worthy that God should approve them or pronounce them righteous, but that we are pronounced righteous through mercy, by divine imputation."[56] In the *Loci communes* of 1535 he asserts, "The Hebrew word for justify is a forensic word," and then draws an example from Roman history: "The Roman people justified Scipio when he was accused by the tribune; that is, they absolved him or pronounced him righteous."[57] Quoting Romans 3:3, Melanchthon said: ". . . Abraham was pronounced righteous because he believed, that is, because he took his stand that he had a propitious God, not on account of his own worthiness, but on account of mercy promised by God."[58] The whole point was that forensic justification overcame the accusations of the Law. ". . . The Law accuses and condemns sin, marks the transgressor, and brings terror and death to the mind."[59] It is precisely this condemnation of the Law that forces the sinner to God, who alone can still its condemnation with the forensic acquittal. Here Melanchthon's revision of the *Augsburg Confession* is significant. ". . . The forgiveness of sins is given us graciously for the sake of Christ, and justification is through faith, by which we should believe and confess that these are given us for the sake of Christ, who made satisfaction for us and rendered the Father propitious."[60]

The Osiandrian Controversy (1550ff.)

The name Osiander was borne by at least five important and highly respected men. Of these, Andreas Osiander the Elder was involved in the controversy over justification.[61] He was born at Gunzenhausen in Franconia in 1498. It appears that in his youth he was deeply influenced by Johann Reuchlin, the Hebrew scholar and great-uncle of Melanchthon, who was prominent in humanist circles. In 1520 he was ordained a priest at the Augustinian monastery at Nuremberg, where he taught Hebrew. Two years later he became a preacher at the great St. Lawrence Church, where he introduced the Reformation in following years. In considering Osiander, it is important to remember that he was not primarily a pupil of Luther and that important aspects of his teaching were not necessarily intentional deviations from Luther. They were impressions from his independent study of Scripture, his acquaintance with Reuchlin and Pico della Mirandola, or his preoccupation with the Kabbalah, the Talmud, alchemy, and astrology, as Hirsch has shown.[62] It appears that Osiander did not meet Luther personally until 1529. By this time his position had already developed.

Although unknown to the Saxon theologians before 1550, the principal lines of Osiander's theology appeared in public declarations as early as 1524. This is seen in the *First Nuremberg Evangelical Counsel* (1524) and *The Twelve Nuremberg Articles* (1525), prepared by him. They are found in Schmidt and Schornbaum's collection of *Die fränkischen Bekenntnisse*.[63] Osiander's doctrine of justification was completely "analytic." Either God made the believer righteous in the act of justification itself, or God was an ignorant or unjust judge. In his Christology Osiander made an overly-sharp distinction between the divine and human natures of Christ, somewhat like the modern Lundensians. According to Osiander, the divine nature, not the human nature, procured our salvation. In contrast to Lundensian theology, atonement and justification were separated. ". . . That Christ suffered for me is easy enough to believe, but that he shall dwell within me, if I only believe his Word, this I can scarcely grasp."[64] Justification depended upon the indwelling righteousness of Christ, and the means of grace played an important role. In speaking of the Lord's Supper, Osiander wrote: "For as truly as the bread and wine are changed into the human body and blood and no longer separated from Christ, so surely will Christ dwell in us, when we believe his Word, for he himself is the Word."[65] Through Baptism the believer is buried with Christ, and Baptism brings forth the needed work for an analytic justification.[66] In commenting on Romans 1:17, Osiander placed great emphasis on the preached Gospel: ". . . A Christian preacher must show what the Gospel is and how it serves unto righteousness, for fruit in human works. That is, faith, hope, and love."[67] For Osiander the Ascension of Christ was the basis for the indwelling of Christ and therefore an important part of his teaching.

> Inasmuch as righteousness consists in that Christ goes to the Father, therefore we must be in him and he in us, if we shall come to the Father. This however cannot be made visible or palpable. Therefore he also speaks: 'Ye shall see me no more.' The Sacrament of the Altar is the certain sign and proof for the believer of this unity. It is therefore necessary that a diligent preacher show what this Sacrament is, and what it works within us.[68]

Osiander's teaching as a whole has two praiseworthy characteristics. (1) Christology was the central concept of Osiander's doctrine of justification and did not play merely a subsidiary role in the sense in which Melanchthon has often been accused. (2) Osiander developed his doctrine of justification from a dynamic concept of the means of grace—that is, the preaching of the Word and the Sacraments. In both these respects Osiander stood closer to Luther than to Melanchthon. Nevertheless, in the controversy that broke out after Luther's death it became apparent that Osiander's teaching was not able to preserve what Luther had tried to teach about justification. In spite of some weaknesses, however, Melanchthon's doctrine proved responsible for the retention of Luther's doctrine. Because he repudiated the forensic position, Osiander was unable to keep his own teaching from the danger of works-righteousness and from a mysticism in which the dynamic contrast of the divine-human encounter would be lost.

The controversy with Osiander began when he was forced to leave Nuremberg in the Interim (1548). Melanchthon and his associates had made unfortunate concessions to the demands of the Roman Catholic emperor, who attempted to suppress the Protestant cause, while Osiander was one of those who bravely opposed this. Becoming a professor at the University of Koenigsberg in 1549, Osiander delivered his *Disputation on Justification* on October 24, 1550. In it he openly attacked justification by imputation[69] and was therefore suspected of rejecting Luther. He replied very properly that he followed Luther wherever Scripture was on Luther's side and that otherwise he refused to be called a heretic.[70] He was not so complimentary to Melanchthon, identifying him with Judas Iscariot.[71] The controversy was carried to disgraceful lengths, with sermons preached against Osiander and even a chorale sung by the congregation warning against "Osi's" poison.[72]

We are chiefly concerned, however, with the controversy as it affected Melanchthon. Herrlinger has observed[73] that this controversy led Melanchthon to rethink and clarify his own position. Melanchthon thus defined Christ's role more clearly. He no longer spoke merely of imputation of righteousness for Christ's sake but asserted the imputation of Christ's righteousness.[74] Osiander felt that justification could not be postulated until fellowship with Christ had actually taken place. But as Melanchthon correctly noted, this could bring a relapse into medieval teaching and the uncertainty of Roman Catholic empiricism unless it were properly understood.

Melanchthon's reply to Osiander appeared in print in January 1552. Against Osiander's charge that Melanchthon had forsaken Luther's teaching for the sake of Aristotelianism he replied: "I affirm that my intention has never been other in my writings, especially in regards to the important article of justification, than to teach the position held by the honorable Doctor Martin Luther."[75] Commenting on Romans 5:15, he wrote:

> Here St. Paul speaks of two things. The first is grace, that is, the gracious forgiveness of our sins and acceptance of our person before God;

and the second is the gift, that is, the presence of God in us, by which we are renewed, and feel comfort and the beginning of everlasting life. And both of these we have through the merit of Christ. . . .[76]

Here Melanchthon appears to have met Osiander halfway, accepting Osiander's criticism but showing how the presence of God and renewal must be placed within the context of forensic justification. Next he touches a weakness in Osiander's Christology without, however, naming his opponent. He wrote that faith directed itself toward

. . . the whole Lord Christ, God and man, just as this same Lord Christ is God and man, and Mediator and Redeemer, according to both his natures. For although it was only the human nature that received the wounds and suffering, nevertheless the entire Christ was Mediator and Redeemer. For this suffering could not have been payment if the Redeemer had not at the same time been also God.[77]

Like later critics of Melanchthon, Osiander found too little connection between justification and sanctification in his system. Melanchthon countered:

All the churches will bear us witness that we confess clearly and have always taught that a change must take place, and that certainly God the Father, Son, and Holy Ghost work comfort and godly life in us through conversion, so that they also are in us and dwell within, wherever the Gospel is received in faith. . . .[78]

Melanchthon was concerned with Osiander's charge that he had found no place for the indwelling of God. Melanchthon asserted that they were in accord at this point[79] but clarified this against possible misunderstanding. (1) The righteousness for which the believer waits is not forgiveness of his sins but rather that God may be all in all within him. (2) Although God dwells within His saints, ". . . nevertheless much impurity, sinfulness, and lust remains in us all . . ." (3) Therefore, believers should not be made to think that their justification consists in the indwelling of God or in moral perfection ("analytic" view) but should be comforted with the assurance of God's mercy. Again Melanchthon takes positive elements from Osiander and relates them to the forensic view.

> This is placed before us for our comfort, for also after our regeneration, again and again we must receive forgiveness of our sins and grace, for the sake of our Mediator, Jesus Christ, through the merit of his obedience, by which he became the offering for us. . . .[80]

Although Melanchthon conceded that the indwelling of God was important, he felt that due attention must be given to the concept of ransom or expiation so central in the New Testament, especially in Romans 3. "In order to understand the honor of Christ, one must know both his merit and his working. He brings salvation through his merit and also through the communication of himself."[81] Melanchthon quotes several Scripture passages (I John 1:7; Heb. 10:10; Isa. 53:5) that refer to Christ's work as satisfaction. Then he comes to the point:

> This all must be understood that we receive forgiveness of sins and become acceptable to God through the merit of Christ when with a true faith we accept the Lord Christ and believe that God forgives our sins and is gracious to us for the sake of this Mediator; and it is at the same time true that this God dwells within us, as we through this comfort are saved from the deepest anxiety.[82]

Like many moderns, Osiander made the objection that forensic justification would lead to false security. Melanchthon countered: "One must teach what is right, give God his honor and punish sins, and then give true comfort to awakened hearts, even though not all hearers are the same."[83] The fact that some misused it did not authorize Christ's preachers to stop preaching the forgiveness of sins. Just as Osiander had stressed the importance of preaching, so now preaching must rest in Scripture, the heart of which is the free forgiveness of sins.

Thus, the discussion with Osiander had a salutary effect upon Melanchthon. He more clearly presented the relationship to God as it was marked by the indwelling of Christ, while at the same time he clearly indicated the need for preserving the forensic insight. Nevertheless, it is significant that when Melanchthon prepared the final edition of his *Loci communes* (1559), he changed only one non-essential word in the article of justification presented in 1543 before the Osiandrian controversy. The chief source must therefore remain Melanchthon's reply to Osiander, which we have just reviewed. But now let us return to Luther.

Notes

[1] Cf. Albert Herrlinger, *Die Theologie Melanchthons in ihrer geschichtlichen Entwicklung und im Zusammenhange mit der Lehrgeschichte und Culturbewegung der Reformation* (Gotha: Perthes, 1879), pp. 11–12.

[2] SA II/1:88.

[3] Cf. Paul Schwarzenau, *Der Wandel im theologischen Ansatz bei Melanchthon von 1525–1535* (Gütersloh: Bertelsmann, 1956), pp. 13–14.

[4] Luther thought very highly of Melanchthon's *Scholia on Colossians*. When Justus Jonas translated them into German and published them in 1529, Luther wrote a very commendatory preface. He referred to it as ". . . Master Philipp Melanchthon's instruction and lessons in which, both concisely as well as clearly and richly, is contained what Christian teaching and life comprise . . ." Luther then proceeded to a characterization of Melanchthon and himself: "I was born to fight with fanatics and devils and to go to battle. Therefore my books are stormy and war-like. I must clear away stumps and branches, and cut down thorns and brambles, and fill in the mud-holes; I am the common woodsman, who must blaze the trail and make preparations. But then Master Philipp comes, cleanly and quietly; he builds and plants, and watches it and waters it with joy, according to the gifts that God has given him so richly. Oh what a blessed time, insofar as our accursed thanklessness permits us to recognize it! What a treasure this had been for the world, if one could have had such a book twenty years ago!" (WA 30/II:68f).

[5] SA IV:210–303.

[6] Ibid., p. 211.

[7] Ibid., p. 212.

[8] SA I:221.

[9] Ibid., p. 222.

[10] Ibid., p. 223.

[11] Ibid., p. 246.

[12] Ibid., p. 247.

[13] The best work in English on the *Augsburg Confession* is Johann Michael Reu, *The Augsburg Confession: A Collection of Sources with an Historical Introduction*

(Chicago: Wartburg, 1930). The latest work is Wilhelm Maurer, *Historischer Kommentar zur Confessio Augustana*, Vol. I (Gütersloh: Gerd Mohn, 1976), Vol. II pending. Maurer's book represents a lifetime of painstaking research and is a very important contribution to the literature.

[14] The first form of the *Confutatio* is offered in a convenient translation in Reu, Part II, pp. 326ff. This English text is based on Johannes Ficker, *Die Konfutation des Augsburgischen Bekenntnisses*, 1891. The final form of the *Confutatio* (Reu, Part II, pp. 348ff.) is given in Latin in CR 27:82ff. and in the Walch collection of Luther's Works, Vol. 16, pp. 1219ff. This volume from the Walch edition contains many interesting sources regarding the *Apologia*. Since these are in German translation, however, and since the Walch edition does not always have the preferred text, these sources must be used with discernment.

[15] Apol IV:§48. I am citing the definitive edition used for all scientific purposes, BekS (see Abbreviations). The numbers refer to the various paragraphs (§§) of the *Apology* and may readily be found thereby in any of the standard editions. The latest English version is *The Book of Concord: The Confessions of the Evangelical Lutheran Church*, tr. and ed. Theodore G. Tappert in collaboration with Jaroslav Pelikan, Robert H. Fischer, and Arthur C. Piepkorn (Philadelphia: Fortress, 1959).

[16] Apol IV:§53.

[17] §48.

[18] §40.

[19] §67.

[20] §72.

[21] Examples of the *sola fide* in the *Apology* IV are numerous. Cf. §§72, 77, 78, 80, 84, 86, 112, 116, and many more, where *sola fide* is explicitly mentioned, besides additional examples where it is implicit.

[22] Apol IV:§§79–80.

[23] Werner Elert, *Morphologie*, Vol. I, p. 88 (=*Structure*, p. 100). Elert shows how Melanchthon's problem was his attempt to show the rationality of justification, while Luther was content to let the paradox of forgiveness remain illogical. "For this Christ breaks through rational coherence at the decisive point; in place of the logical equivalence of morality, reward or punishment, he places the forgiveness of sins" (pp. 86f. = p. 98).

[24] CR 21:376. Cf. chap. 11, sec. "Justification by Faith in Melanchthon" and accompanying footnote 40.

[25] For literature on this controversy, see the following: Friedrich Loofs, "Die Bedeutung der Rechtfertigungslehre der Apologie für die Symbolik der lutherischen Kirchen," *Theologische Studien und Kritiken* 57 (1884): 613–88. A. Eichhorn, "Die Rechtfertigungslehre der Apologie," ibid. 60 (1887): 415–91. Carl Stange, "Zur Rechtfertigungslehre in der Apologie" NKZ 1899; reprinted in *Studien zur Theologie Luthers*, 1928, pp. 453–95 (additions in reprint). Cf. also Werner Elert, *Morphologie*, Vol. I, pp. 85f. (=*Structure*, p. 97),

and Friedrich Brunstäd, *Theologie der lutherischen Bekenntnisschriften*, 1951, pp. 74f. The original controversy between Loofs and Eichhorn was carried out in the best tradition of the German *Auseinandersetzung* (conversational but scientific analysis) with an amazing objectivity, so that Loofs could write candidly some years later: "Eichhorn's treatment, with right, corrected mine on not a few points. . . ." See Loofs, *Leitfaden zum Studium der Dogmengeschichte*, 1906, 4th ed., p. 825, f.n. 15. Incidentally, Loofs here updated the discussion by some twenty years. For the reader who does not have access to the periodical in which the first essays appeared, the *Dogmengeschichte* treatment will offer a partial substitute.

[26] Eichhorn, p. 479.

[27] Loofs, p. 619.

[28] "Denn *justificari significat ex injustis justos effici seu regenerari* (Gerecht-Werden, bekehret oder neu geboren werden), significat et justos pronuntiari seu reputari (Gerechtsein, gerecht geschätzt werden vor Gott); und sowohl bei jenem, wie bei diesem Verständnis des *justificari* lässt sich die Richtigkeit des Satzes erweisen: *sola fide justificamur*" (Loofs, *Dogmengeschichte*, pp. 825–27). This sentence, with its mixture of German and Latin cases, is almost impossible to translate into English, so I have given the original of Loofs.

[29] SD III:§§18–19.

[30] Ep III:4.

[31] Eichhorn, pp. 477, 474.

[32] Stange, pp. 465–67.

[33] Ibid., pp. 469–70.

[34] Ibid., p. 471.

[35] Ibid., p. 473.

[36] That we are thereby understanding Melanchthon right is established in his letter to Brenz, where he gives the same meaning for Apol. IV:§72. Thus, Melanchthon wrote to Brenz: "You must turn your eyes away from such renovation and from the Law unto the promise and Christ, and you will know that for the sake of Christ we are righteous, that is, accepted before God; and thereby we find peace for our conscience, and not on account of such renovation. Therefore we become righteous by faith alone; not because faith is the ground, as you write, but because it apprehends Christ . . . This I tried to show in the Apology, but there on account of the adversaries and their twisting things around I could not speak freely as I now speak to you, even though I meant it exactly as I have now said it to you. Wherefore will the conscience find peace and certain hope, if it has to consider, in order to be justified, whether such newness of works within is really perfect! What else is this than to derive justification from the Law, rather than freely from the Promise?" (CR 2:501–2).

[37] SD III:80–82.

[38] CR 2:501.

[39] This is of course practically the same thing that the Young Luther had taught fifteen years earlier. Cf. Luther on *opera legis seu fidei*.

[40] CR 2:502.

[41] Ibid., p. 503; Br VI:100; Br XIII:195.

[42] WA 30/II:659. Here in Luther is an almost word-for-word parallel to Melanchthon and to the *Formula of Concord*. I repeat especially the last sentence in Latin: "Ergo necesse est sola fides nos iustificari *sine, ante absque operibus . . .*" Cf. Melanchthon in the *Apology*: "Sola fide in Christum, non per dilectionem, non propter dilectionem aut opera consequimur remissionem peccatorum, etsi dilectio sequitur fidem" (§77). From the *Loci communes* (1521): "et quaqua verteris, *sive ad opera praecedentia iustificationem sive ad ea, quae sequuntur iustificationem*, nullus nostro merito locus est" (SA II/1:108). *Formula of Concord*: "Credimus igitur, docemus et confitemur hoc ipsum nostram esse coram Deo iustitiam, quod Dominus nobis peccata remittit ex mera gratia *absque ullo respectu praecedentium, praesentium aut consequentium nostrorum operum*, dignitatis aut meriti. Ille enim donat atque imputat nobis iustitiam obedientiae Christi; propter eam iustitiam a Deo in gratiam recipimur et iusti reputamur" (Ep. III:4, italics mine).

[43] CR 2:510.

[44] Br VI:134.

[45] CR 2:504.

[46] The most important sources are the *Commentary on Romans* (1532) and the second edition of the *Loci communes* (1535). Other works include the *Variata*, an important work if not an acceptable form of the *Augsburg Confession*, and the revision of the *Commentary on Romans*, both of 1540.

[47] CR 15:499.

[48] Ibid., p. 498.

[49] Ibid.

[50] Ibid., p. 503.

[51] Ibid., p. 504.

[52] Ibid., p. 511.

[53] Ibid.

[54] It is significant that A. Herrlinger's book, *Die Theologie Melanchthons*, 1879, which has never been replaced by a similar study, continues to command the respect of Melanchthon scholars and remains a standard work. But it seems to me that Herrlinger is stretching the point when he writes (pp. 15–16) that Melanchthon's doctrine is twofold—remission of sins and pronouncing righteous. The latter is only the forensic aspect of the former, which is the personal aspect of justification. It seems to me that these are not two but one act seen under two points of view.

[55] From the *Loci* (2nd ed.): ". . . Consequimur iustificationem, i.e. remissionem peccatorum et reconciliationem non propter dignitatem nostrae poenitentiae, sed fide propter Christum gratis" (CR 21:427).

[56] Herrlinger, p. 14. Cf. CR 15:599.

[57] CR 21:421.

[58] Ibid., p. 425.

[59] Ibid., p. 426.

[60] SA VI:15.

[61] The most recent major work treating Osiander is W. F. Schmidt and Karl Schornbaum, *Die fränkischen Bekenntnisse*, 1930, esp. pp. 71ff. For further source material, see J. M. Reu, *Quellen zur Geschichte des kirchlichen Unterrichts in der evangelischen Kirche Deutschlands zwischen 1530 und 1600*, Vol. I/1. The best monograph on Andreas Osiander is that by Emmanuel Hirsch, *Die Theologie des Andreas Osiander und ihre geschichtlichen Voraussetzungen*, 1919, which is marred only by Hirsch's analytic trend coupled with an excessively polemical attitude toward Melanchthon, unfortunately without sufficient independent study of the sources for Melanchthon. Hirsch, of course, was a pupil of Holl. An older study that deserves mention is that by W. Möller, *Andreas Osiander: Leben und ausgewählte Schriften*, 1870. Cf. Herrlinger, pp. 38ff. For a good recent summary with literature, see G. Hoffmann in the *Evangelisches Kirchenlexikon*, Vol. II, s.v. "Osiander." See also *Andreas Osiander d. Ä.: Gesamtausgabe*, ed. Gerhard Müller and Gottfried Seebaß (Gütersloh: Gerd Mohn, 1975ff.), a new edition of Osiander's works which is expected to consist of about eight volumes when complete.

[62] Hirsch, p. 4.

[63] Schmidt and Schornbaum, op. cit. (abbr.: Fr. Bek.)

[64] Fr. Bek., p. 429.

[65] Ibid.

[66] Ibid., p. 456.

[67] Ibid., p. 455.

[68] Ibid., p. 456.

[69] Hirsch, p. 173.

[70] Ibid., p. 174.

[71] Ibid., p. 178.

[72] Ibid., p. 291.

[73] Herrlinger, p. 51.

[74] CR 15:1200.

[75] CR 7:893.

[76] Ibid., pp. 893–94.

[77] Ibid., p. 894.

[78] Ibid., pp. 894f.

[79] Ibid., p. 895.

[80] Ibid., p. 896.

[81] Ibid.

[82] Ibid., p. 897.

[83] Ibid., p. 898.

14

Forensic Justification in Luther

In Luther research there is a growing recognition of three important points relative to forensic justification. First, it is increasingly seen that the study of Luther cannot be restricted to any single period in his life, especially his earliest period, if decisions are to be made regarding his permanent contribution to the Reformation. Second, scholars concede that while imputation played a part in the theology of the Young Luther,[1] this is not the place to look for his forensic teaching. Nevertheless, the forensic view did eventually appear. Third, it is seen that Luther's doctrine contained more than one insight. However large or small the role it played, the forensic view of justification in Luther must be acknowledged. One cannot merely play single aspects of Luther against Melanchthon or even the *Formula of Concord*. Having said this, let us turn to Luther's doctrine of imputation.

Luther on Imputation

Several contemporary writers have tried to show that Luther repudiated the concept of imputed righteousness. They have appealed to a sermon delivered by Luther on the Festival of the Circumcision in 1522. Luther strongly criticizes "certain professors in the modern universities" who teach that forgiveness and justification lie solely under divine imputation.[2] Whom does he mean? Is he thinking of his colleagues at Wittenberg such as Melanchthon? Twentieth-century opponents of forensic justification like to interpret it this way. But was it really Luther's custom to attack Melanchthon in the pulpit? Hardly. When we follow his sermon further, we find that he inveighs against a view in which justification consists negatively in the non-imputation of sin seen as an arbitrary action of God in the freedom of His absolute will. This reminds one of the Occamism against which Luther struggled before he came to the evangelical doctrine of justification. We may therefore assume that Luther does not mean his contemporaries at Wittenberg. Instead, he is speaking against the "modernists"—the Nominalist schoolmen of the late Middle Ages such as the followers of Occam or Biel.[3] It therefore appears that Luther is not attacking the view that the merits of Christ are imputed to the believer—a view not fully developed till later.

When we study the context further, we find that in his sermon Luther is speaking of works being imputed. They were works such as ". . . *beten, fasten, meshalten, studiren, predigen* . . ." (prayers, fastings, masses, studies, preaching) instead of Christ.[4] Hence, this does not prove that Luther opposed imputed righteousness in evangelical theology. He states:

> There are found among the new teachers those who say that the forgiveness of sins and justification by grace lie completely in divine imputation; in other words, that all depends on the reckoning of God, and that it is enough, whether God reckons sin or does not reckon it, that a man is justified or not justified from his sin solely on that account . . . If this were true, then the whole New Testament would be nothing and all in vain. Then Christ would have worked foolishly and vainly when he suffered for sin. Then also God would have carried on purely a shadow-fight or party-tricks without any need thereof. For surely without the need of Christ's suffering he could have forgiven and not imputed sin, or faith other than that in Christ might have justified and brought salvation. Such are they who confide in a type of gracious divine mercy by which they think that their sins are not taken into account. Against this abominable, frightful interpretation, this error, the holy apostle used to bind justifying faith upon Jesus Christ.[5]

God could not simply wink at sin. Christ had to pay satisfaction to God for our sins. In the *Small Catechism* Luther writes: "[Christ] has redeemed, purchased, and won me . . . not with gold or silver but with his holy, precious blood and his innocent suffering and death. . . ."[6]

Commenting on the words of the Lord's Supper, "Given for you, shed for you," he writes in 1521 in his treatise, *On the Misuse of the Mass*:

> The majesty [of God] is much higher than that it might have been propitiated by all the human blood in the world or all the merits of the angels. The body of Christ is given, his blood is shed, and thereby God is reconciled. For it is for you that it is given and shed, as he said: 'For you.' This was that he might turn away God's wrath, which we had deserved by our sins. And when the wrath is gone, thereby the sin is forgiven. Therefore he says, it shall be given and shed for the forgiveness of sin. If the body had not been given nor the blood shed, then the wrath of God would remain over us and we would retain our sins.[7]

Accordingly, any teaching on imputation must be based squarely upon the saving work of Christ. Forensic justification must not become a mere abstraction divorced from the atonement of Christ and from the faith and life of the believer. But Luther does not reject justification as such through the imputed righteousness of Christ.[8]

Without using the word "imputation," Luther said the same thing in his letter to the preachers of Lübeck on January 12, 1530. In this letter Luther expressed his satisfaction with the progress the Reformation had made in Lübeck. However, he warned that changing outward ceremonies was not the important thing. That should be left until later. The teaching of justification by grace should have chief place in their program. Luther wrote:

> In the first place you should handle and implant the head of our doctrine, which is the teaching concerning justification, namely, the alien righteousness of Christ, given freely through faith, which reaches through grace to those who in their conscience have first been terrified and afflicted by the Law, so that they sigh out for redemption.[9]

Here we see Luther incorporating several features found in Melanchthon's doctrine. The stress on the alien righteousness of Christ together with the end result of bringing comfort to terrified consciences could have been stated by Melanchthon as well as by Luther. This short statement contains the three elements also found in Melanchthon: *sola gratia, propter Christum*, and *sola fide*.

Justification in the *Commentary on Galatians*

"Righteousness," active or passive, is different in the theology of the Young Luther than in the *Commentary on Galatians* of 1531ff. In his early years Luther had thought of active righteousness as a righteousness done by man and linked with works of the Law, while passive righteousness was worked by God through Christ. As late as 1519 it was linked with infused grace and seen as a continuous process which would not be perfected until after this life.[10] But by 1531 great changes had taken place in Luther's thought. The Reformational understanding of terms like "faith" (trust) and "grace" (favor of God) had been firmly established, while "righteousness" had become a new concept.

In the first pages of the *Commentary* the axiomatic position on justification is given by the Mature Luther. After describing various kinds of righteousness such as civil, philosophical, household, and moral righteousness, Luther shows that these, important in themselves, are nothing more than explications of the Decalogue, which Moses had taught. They correspond to the righteousness that is of the Law, which has its place in the world but which can never save. Indeed, true righteousness in the sight of God is hidden to the world. (*Haecque est justitia in mysterio abscondita quam mundus non intelligit. . . .*) What then is true righteousness that justifies? The righteousness that excels is that which God imputes unto us for Christ's sake without works. It is not civil or ceremonial righteousness, nor righteousness of the divine law, nor wrested from our works, but it is plainly different—that is, it is passive righteousness. In this matter we work nothing and give back nothing to God, but we receive and we are at the power of another working in us—that is, God. Hence, it is fitting to call this righteousness, which is of faith, Christian or passive righteousness.[11] This "righteousness that excels" (*excellentissima iustitia*) differs from Luther's concept of passive righteousness in 1513 at a decisive point. Then, the contrast was between works of the Law and works of faith (*opera legis seu fidei*), with only the latter allowable for justification.[12] Now, righteousness was taught as completely aside from any works whatsoever within man (*nobis absque operibus*). Righteousness was imputed solely *per Christum*—for the sake of Christ. What Luther meant by this is clear to anyone familiar with what he wrote about the atonement. ". . . He has redeemed, bought and freed me from sin, death, and the power of the devil, not with silver and gold, but with his holy and precious blood, and with his innocent sufferings and death . . . ," Luther confesses in the *Small Catechism*. Aside from its Christological character, Luther wanted to hear nothing about an arbitrary imputation. What then was imputed? The redemption wrought by Christ's innocent sufferings and death and paid for by His blood.[13]

When we see this, we shall avoid Holl's interpretation, based upon Luther's early lectures. Holl and his followers thought it enough merely to assert that this righteousness within the believer was God-worked and not the accomplishment of man. If we listen to the later Luther, this is not going far enough. One statement in the Galatians *Commentary* might appear to support the view gleaned from the Young Luther. Luther says: "In this matter we work nothing and give back nothing to God but we receive and we are at the power of another working in us, that is, of God (*recipimus et patimur alium operantem in nobis, se Deum*)." Wrested from their context, the words of the last clause might appear to support an "analytic" justification. But such an interpretation is not only refuted by the first clause of the sentence (*nihil operamur aut reddimus Deo*), but even more by the observation that this righteousness, imputed for the sake of Christ, is hidden from the world. Luther here will not bend to the desires of his modern-day interpreters to conflict with Melanchthon by providing a place for works of faith in a moralistic justification. Luther nowhere denies that justification is effective in producing sanctification, but he will not accept the statement often placed in his mouth that this resultant sanctification is already a component part of justification. With Melanchthon and the *Formula of Concord*, Luther holds that justification is spoken *per Christum* and not in view of any works that go before, that accompany, or that follow. Grace is free, and grace is not an enabling factor that produces good works in the sense of Augustine, but grace is the benevolent of God unto salvation—*agape*. Grace is the love of God which rejoices at the sinner's faith in the crucified Saviour and imputes that faith unto righteousness because the believer thereby apprehends Christ.

Luther knows how foolish this sounds to human reason. Human reason asks for visible works. Human reason sees righteousness as the fulfilling of the divine law. In contrast, "The highest art and wisdom of the Christians is to overlook the law, and to ignore works and all active righteousness. . . ."[14] The reason is that the believer is justified not by an earthly, temporal, and active righteousness, but by a heavenly, eternal, and passive righteousness which we can never obtain except ". . . through the free imputation and unspeakable gift of God. . . ."[15] Justification is not grounded in works that the believers do but in works that are donated to them: ". . . Not works which we do, but which we apprehend by faith, through which we rise above all laws and works."[16] It is this justification which creates the new man,[17] not the new man who creates justification. This new man is not under the Law or active righteousness but is under the Gospel and Christian or passive righteousness.[18]

Other Examples of Imputation

Luther's familiar paradox, *simul justus et peccator*, which had the content of an "analytic" justification twenty years previously, now received a new meaning. Then the believer was sinful in reality but perfect in the hope of future perfection. Now the believer is sinful in the eyes of the world (active righteousness), but through divine justification and in the eyes of God he is really justified and without sin here and now (passive righteousness), so that he does not have an evil conscience but knows that he is fully and unconditionally justified in the sight of God. Luther expressed this in his sermon on the parable of the publican and the Pharisee. After the publican was declared just by Christ, Luther adds: ". . . And now no one could judge him anymore, none could say: 'That man is a sinner. . . .'"[19] Luther asks, "Who could see such righteousness under the filth? He could already be glorified!"[20] Luther makes a similar point in his marginal notes on the *Apology* in speaking of the fallen woman who anointed Jesus in the house of the Pharisee. Commenting on the often-twisted verse, "Her sins, which are many, are forgiven; for she loved much" (Luke 7:47), Luther writes: "Therefore, to remit stands before to love."[21] Then he speaks of how the Pharisee had proclaimed his righteousness before the world (*coram mundo*) instead of confessing his guilt or faith before God (*coram Deo*). "But she showed her faith before the world. Therefore before the world she is a righteous woman, and no more a sinner."[22]

In his great work against Erasmus, *De servo arbitrio* (1525), Luther wrote: "The righteousness of faith . . . does not consist in any works, but in the favorableness of God, and in God's imputation through grace."[23] In defending forensic justification, Luther reminds Erasmus that the word *reputare* occurs in Romans 4 a total of ten times. Showing how Erasmus' view of freedom had attacked the article of justification at its heart, Luther continued: "Paul here compares working and not working, nor does he leave any middle point between these two. He denies that performing work is reputed as righteousness, but he affirms that not working is indeed reputed to be righteousness, provided that one believes."[24] The case against "analytic" justification could hardly be made more definite. Here in the rejection of Erasmus' synergism was contained the repudiation of Luther's position a decade earlier. In the *Rhapsodia . . . de loco iustificationis* (1530) Luther asserted: ". . . Faith and unbelief are clearly seen to precede works. If they go before, then faith justifies prior to works. Unbelief damns prior to works. And works are the signs of faith and the fruits of righteousness, just as works of unbelief are signs and fruit of unrighteousness."[25]

In his exposition of Psalm 130 (1533) Luther gives further support for imputation or forensic justification. According to the Rörer text, Luther comments on verse 1: "It is the nature of this doctrine that it is not comprehended by any laws or deeds, but we come to heaven when we are pronounced just, not by any righteousness from would but by forgiveness alone."[26] In the redaction by Veit Dietrich we read: ". . . We embrace heaven when we believe that by imputation we become just before God, through Christ . . ." Commenting on verse 3, Luther warns not to put any confidence in one's own righteousness but instead to have faith in Christ and the benefits of His sacrificial death. "Our own death, even if we accept it patiently, and all our other obedience, is reputed to us as sin, if we neglect the merit of Christ and think to raise up these other things before the Judgment of God."[27] Over and over in these lectures, Luther castigates every thought of being justified by any cause whatsoever within the believer. Any form of active righteousness is rejected in favor of the alien righteousness of Christ imputed to the believer through faith. The original Rörer text reads: "He holds us for righteous on account of faith in Christ, and not on account of works."[28]

Also in the Rörer text Luther comments on the words of Psalm 130:4, "But there is forgiveness with thee . . ." He says: "With thee is righteousness and mercy. Otherwise can no one become good but from thee. And that righteousness is the propitiation by which I am able to stand before God [*coram Deo*]."[29] In the published version, prepared by Dietrich, Luther is quoted thus: "I commend therefore this definition of Christian righteousness from David: To mark iniquity is to condemn, and contrariwise, not to mark iniquity is to justify or to pronounce just (*iustificare seu iustum pronunciare*)."[30] It is therefore not surprising when Luther is quoted: ". . . We are just by imputation (*sumus iusti imputatione*)."[31] If we accept the Dietrich version, we here find a completely forensic justification in Luther from the year 1533. In the original transcript by Rörer the forensic view is not so explicit.[32]

Already in 1531 Melanchthon noted that the debates of Luther contained some of his best presentations on justification.[33] This can be readily understood. Since Luther was never able to fulfill his promise of writing a complete monograph on justification,[34] his teaching must be largely reconstructed from other works in which he spoke of justification only incidentally. But in the debates not only did Luther's razor-sharp logic come to the fore in meeting counter-arguments, but he seized the opportunity for obviating misconstructions of what he taught. Perhaps the most important of these debates was the disputation of January 14, 1536. Here a statement was made which took issue with the decidedly Melanchthonian position:

> To justify does not signify to accept or to pronounce just, but it signifies to infuse new qualities, because Peter said: 'Their hearts are purified by faith.' [Acts 15, 9] To purify the heart means nothing else than to infuse the new qualities.[35]

In reply Luther said that Peter was accommodating himself to the terminology of the Jews.

> Peter wanted to say that God purified the Gentiles, whom you of the Jews judged as unclean or impious, but God justified them. The word 'purifying' is in Acts the word for 'imputing.' To purify the heart is to impute purification to the heart. God purified the Gentiles, that

is, he reputed them purified, because they had faith, although in reality they were still sinners . . . Thus the Gentiles, and we as well, are pronounced just, although in reality we are sinners like those unkosher animals. He begins to purge in reality. But first he purifies imputatively, and then he gives the Holy Spirit, through whom we are purged more substantially. Faith purifies through the forgiveness of sins, while the Holy Spirit purifies effectively.[36]

Here we note that Luther, like Melanchthon, is making the distinction between justification and sanctification. Justification is imputative and by faith. While subsequent purification does not belong to justification itself, it is the further working of the Spirit—that is, sanctification. Thus, Luther showed his acceptance of Melanchthon in principle. While he did not deny the value of subsequent sanctification, he showed its integral connection with justification. This is characteristic of Luther and must not be overlooked. If at times the new life was not discussed fully enough by Melanchthon, Luther was very careful to show that justification, however forensic, did not remain alone but that the good works of faith inevitably appeared.

In his book, *The Reinterpretation of Luther* (1948), Edgar N. Carlson has presented a helpful guide to Swedish Lutheran theology. Nevertheless, at least one statement can hardly go unchallenged. He questions the entire forensic statement of justification on the ground that it is difficult to ". . . make clear the relation between the forensic imputation of righteousness and the regeneration of the one to whom this righteousness is imputed."[37] Carlson writes on the following pages:

Justification is not, therefore, either the antecedent or the consequent of regeneration; it is identical with it. Justification-regeneration-sanctification are descriptions, from different points of view, of the same dynamic, ongoing, redemptive encounter of God, in Christ, with man.[38]

This suspends the distinction between justification and sanctification for fear of separating justification from sanctification. The inevitable result of this course would be a return to justification based upon regeneration or sanctification—that is, to an "analytic" or pre-Reformational view. In the preceding chapters we have seen ample proof that Melanchthon and Luther thought differently. They found that the forensic aspect of justification could not be relinquished. It was necessary for three reasons: (1) to give full glory to God and Christ, (2) so that the presence or lack of presence of good works would not throw justification into question, and (3) because only in forensic justification was the voice of the Law overcome, and therefore only forensic justification could free ethics from the Law and give an adequate basis for ethics in the Gospel.[39]

Notes

[1] The word "imputation" can be found in the early Luther. Cf. Vogelsang, *Die Anfänge von Luthers Christologie . . .* , 1929, pp. 84ff. But in the same manner as Karl Holl, Vogelsang tries to see in the early doctrine of Luther a view that is basically the same as his later doctrine (p. 84). Perhaps the reverse is done in the very respectable work of a Swedish scholar, Axel Gyllenkrok, *Rechtfertigung und Heiligung in der frühen evangelischen Theologie Luthers* (Uppsala, 1952). Gyllenkrok avoids the mistakes of Holl and his followers. He finds a doctrine of justification in the Young Luther that is rather harmonious with that of the later Luther. The only problem is that he seeks to find this in Luther's early writings when actually it was only in its initial stages. It appears that Vogelsang wants to impose the Young Luther upon the Mature Luther, while Gyllenkrok finds the Mature Luther in the Young Luther.

[2] WA 10/I/1:468.

[3] Cf. R. Seeberg, *Dogmengeschichte*, Vol. III, pp. 765f. See also Seeberg's article, RE 14:274.

[4] WA 10/I/1:472.

[5] Ibid., pp. 468–69.

[6] II, 4.

[7] WA 8:519, 7.

[8] Among other instances where Luther upheld imputation, see his great disputations upon justification, and especially that of January 14, 1536 (?). "We must truly give thanks to God because his imputation is greater than our impurity and sin . . . This imputation is not a non-entity, but it is greater than the whole world and all the holy angels" (WA 39/I:97f.). "First, he truly purifies by imputation, and afterwards he gives the Holy Ghost, through whom we are also essentially cleansed" (p. 99, 25).

[9] Br V:221.

[10] WA 2:146.

[11] WA 40/I:41.

[12] See chap. 3, sec. "Luther's Doctrine as a Confounding of Law and Gospel."

[13] Cf. the words, ". . . sünd betzallt . . . [paid for sins]" (WA 10/I/2:40, 27).

[14] WA 40/I:43.

[15] ". . . nisi per gratuitam imputationem et per inerrabile donum Dei illam . . ." (ibid.). Cf. the phrase, ". . . iustitia terrena et coelestis . . ." (ibid., p. 46).

[16] Ibid., p. 46.

[17] *Novus homo* (ibid., p. 45).

[18] Ibid.

[19] WA 15:675, 20.

[20] WA 17/I:404.

[21] WA 30/II:489.

[22] Ibid., p. 491.

[23] WA 18:772.

[24] Ibid.

[25] WA 30/II:663, 3.

[26] WA 40/III:339, 7.

[27] Ibid., p. 346.

[28] Ibid., p. 351, 2.

[29] Ibid., p. 349, 2.

[30] Ibid., p. 349, 32.

[31] Ibid., p. 350, 20.

[32] This passage is a good example of the problem one confronts in Dietrich's renditions. It is possible that Luther actually stated what Dietrich prints, but it is just as plausible to think that he was hearing Luther with Melanchthonian ears and supplying an unauthorized addition. A noteworthy example where we know that Dietrich made an unfortunate change is the addition to the lecture on Psalm 51:5. Luther had asserted that the first cause of justification is the merit of Christ or mercy, and then Dietrich added "the acknowledgement of sin" as a "second cause" or as a *sine qua non* (WA 40/III:358, 35–359, 15). Melanchthon was horrified at this unauthorized and clumsy alteration (p. 189) and expressed his distress in a letter to Dietrich, who was now at Nürnberg (CR 3:593f.). Although Luther seems not to have noticed the incident, at one time a similar situation led to a serious argument between Luther and Dietrich, with the latter saying he would not edit any more works of Luther.

[33] Thus also Robert Stupperich in "Die Rechtfertigungslehre bei Luther und Melanchthon 1530–1536," *Luther and Melanchthon*, ed. Vilmos Vajta, 1961, p. 84.

[34] Br V:560.

[35] WA 39/I:98.

[36] WA 39/I:99, 11.

[37] Edgar N. Carlson, *The Reinterpretation of Luther*, p. 212.

[38] Ibid. pp. 213–14.

[39] The fallacy that forensic justification is legalistic is hard for many people to overcome. John Henry Newman liked to attack the Lutheran position, which he perhaps really did not understand. See his *Lectures on the Doctrine of Justification*, pp. 35f., 36f., et passim. He especially decried the separation of justification and sanctification (p. 41). In consequence, he destroyed the Gospel by changing it into an emasculated Law: ". . . Gospel righteousness is obedience to the Law of God . . ." (p. 44); ". . . the Law written on the heart, or spiritual renovation, is that which justifies us" (p. 45); ". . . That Law . . . implanted [in our hearts] is our justification" (p. 46). In Newman the Law is no longer Pauline because it does not accuse, and the Gospel is not Pauline because it is not the unfathomable mercy of God. One's justification must be accomplished by one's own efforts, and therefore one can never have the comforting assurance that he has been accepted by God. This was the heart of the Lutheran doctrine of justification.

15
A Comparison of
Luther and Melanchthon

A Dialogue on Justification between Them

Melanchthon did not always find it easy to live and work under the shadow of the famous reformer. Luther had a strong personality and especially in later years tended to be domineering and polemical. More than once Melanchthon sighed about his "bondage."[1] Melanchthon also had his flaws. He was not always forthright and tended to conceal matters from Luther to avoid possible controversies. Perhaps a major source of misunderstanding was the controversial personalities of other Wittenberg associates such as Amsdorf and Cordatus. While Melanchthon was on a journey in southern Germany during the late summer and fall of 1536, Nikolaus von Amsdorf[2] and Conrad Cordatus[3] accused him and his pupil, Caspar Cruciger, of corrupting Luther's doctrine of justification by teaching that good works are necessary for salvation.[4] At the time of his return, November 1, Melanchthon wrote a letter to Luther and other members of the Wittenberg faculty in which he skillfully defended himself from these charges.[5] But this was not all. The assertion had been made that the consensus between Melanchthon and Luther no longer existed in regard to the all-important doctrine of justification. The accused preceptor therefore arranged a meeting with Luther in the home of Bugenhagen, their pastor, in which he endeavored to resolve the problem. Luther had apparently allowed himself to be swayed by the accusations. Now the reformer must show just where the alleged differences lay! Furthermore, Melanchthon had Luther put their dialogue in writing. We are therefore able to listen to their conversation and see for ourselves how the two men saw their similarities and differences in the doctrine of justification.[6]

In the following dialogue we shall follow the recently-discovered copy of Luther's holograph of 1536,[7] giving in square brackets the additions from Melanehthon's edition of 1552 during the Osiandrian controversy[8] and other variations from the Aurifaber text in the *Table Talk*.[9] The reader will note that Melanchthon enters the discussion several times as the devil's advocate, injecting arguments with which he himself does not actually agree in order to sharpen the discussion and spur Luther toward a more precise formulation.

> **MELANCHTHON:** It seems that Augustine . . . taught that we are just by faith, which is a renewal. If that is correct, we are just not by faith alone but by all sorts of gifts and virtues [given us by God]. . . . Now please say, which of the two do you think is right? Is a man just by that renewal, as in Augustine, or, is it rather by free imputation of something outside us, by faith, understood as trust that is led by the Word?

> **LUTHER:** So I think and am thoroughly persuaded and certain, that this is the true position of the Gospels and Apostles [that we are just solely by free imputation in the presence of God].

> **MELANCHTHON [versus Luther]:** 2. Is a man just by mercy alone?

> 3. It seems that one is not just solely by such mercy, because our righteousness is necessary, that is, a conscience that is good in regard to works.

> 4. Or would you concede that a man is declared just, for the most part by faith and for a lesser part by works? But if faith denotes trust (and we are assuming that this faith remains certain), it is understood that the demand of the Law is no longer required. Instead faith supplies those things which are owed to the Law.

> 5. You concede that there is a two-part righteousness and that both parts are necessary before God, namely, that which is of faith and that which is of a good conscience, whereby

faith supplies that which is due the Law. This is nothing else than to say that a man is not justified by faith alone. Surely you do not think that the usage of Augustine concerning the beginning of regeneration is justified.

6. Augustine did not think that a man is saved freely, but that he is saved on account of moral goodness that is given to him. How do you feel about this notion of Augustine?

7. The whole understanding of Augustine concerning merits is completely different from ours; it abolishes no merit except that of the ungodly.

LUTHER: I hold that a man becomes, is, and remains just, or the person is just, simply from mercy alone. This is truly perfected righteousness which stands against wrath, death, sin, etc., and swallows up all things. And he simply restores the man holy and innocent, considering that there is no sin in him, because the free reckoning [imputation] of God ordains that there is no sin. Thus John says: 'Whoever is born of God does not sin.'[10]

In this dialogue we note several interesting points. In his opening statement Melanchthon is trying to get Luther to disavow the position of Augustine, understood as justification based upon an inner renewal. Luther accepts the view of a free imputation without explicitly rejecting Augustine. Furthermore, Melanchthon cannot get Luther to use the word "imputation"—a circumstance which lends credibility to the authenticity of our text. In Luther's reply to the opening statement the first remark is by Luther, and the clause within brackets is an addition by Melanchthon in his 1552 version.[11] In his second statement Melanchthon first asks, "Is a man just by mercy alone?"—a position supposed to be that of Luther—and then immediately cites the position of Augustine against Luther (Nos. 3, 4, 5). After this he again identifies himself with what is presumably Luther's position (Nos. 6, 7). In his reply Luther states the mature Reformational doctrine in no uncertain terms: A man becomes, is, and remains just out of divine mercy and not out of works. There is no sin in him because of the free reckoning (Latin text) or imputation (German version, *zurechnet*) of righteousness by God. Luther makes it clear that the works which follow justification are not a part of justification.[12] The original question which had sparked the dialogue had been the attack upon Melanchthon and his pupil by Cordatus in which he had inferred that both men taught that good works were necessary for salvation. In this dialogue Luther had closed the gap. He had insisted that works are not a part of justification but had clearly taught that saving faith is never without good works. When Melanchthon suggested that he reject Augustine as teaching that faith replaced works only before justification,[13] Luther did not agree but instead reinterpreted the church Father:

> . . . This expression of Augustine sufficiently shows that he agreed with us, when he said: 'I am disturbed, but I am not thrown into confusion, because I am mindful of the wounds of the Lord.' This indeed clearly states that faith prevails over the beginning, middle, end, and forever.[14]

Luther was here saying that the sound position was that faith replaced works at the beginning, middle, and end of justification, yes, forever, and that Augustine had also taught this. Cordatus had charged Cruciger with teaching that if the tree of faith did not produce good works, then the faith itself was not a saving faith.[15] Luther gently rejected Cordatus' allegations[16] and corrected Cruciger[17] while stating his solidarity with Melanchthon—an undercurrent Greschat overlooked.[18] For the outcome of the whole dialogue was that, over against Cordatus, Luther affirmed that good works, while not "necessary," were always present with saving faith. He rejected Cruciger's exaggeration and solidly affirmed that faith is never without good works. Since Melanchthon had been accused of basing justification partly on good works, Luther here had really supported Melanchthon while clarifying the whole problem in language which was his own.

Pauline or Johannine?

It is commonly assumed that Luther basically followed the theology of Paul. This assumption has been questioned by several recent scholars.[19] One thing is certain: Luther's theology is not so narrow that it can all be forced into the mold of Paulinism. In that sense the characterization "Pauline" is much more applicable to Melanchthon, especially regarding justification. We have seen that forensic justification was Melanchthon's peculiar contribution to the Reformation. And forensic justification is manifestly Pauline. Although Luther adopted many important insights of forensic justification, its relationship to the person and work of Christ, or through faith, as a relationship concept, is more characteristic of his position. But these thoughts are more characteristic of John than of Paul. The prominence of the mystical union with Christ (John 6 and 15) certainly shows the presence of Johannine thinking. Think how prominent John's insight on faith was in Luther's theology: "This is the victory that overcometh the world, even our faith" (I John 5:4). Furthermore, if we examine the bulk of Luther's writings or his citing of Scripture, we find little support for the common idea that Luther was chiefly a follower of Paul. The importance of the four Gospels for Luther is shown in the prime emphasis he placed upon the historical Christ. However, a Gospel from the hand of Paul is unknown.[20]

James Atkinson (University of Hull, England) also observes that Luther not only preferred John over the synoptic Gospels, but that Luther preferred the Gospel according to John even over the Epistle to the Romans. For Luther the Synoptics described Christ's works, while John emphasized Christ's words. Luther wrote:

> If I had to dispense with either the works or the preaching of Christ, I could get along without the works better than his preaching. For the works do not help me, but his words give life, as he himself said. Since John writes little about the works of Christ, but much about his preaching, and again the other three evangelists describe many of his works, but few of his words, therefore the Gospel according to John is the one precious and chief Gospel, and is to be preferred much, very much to the other three, and to be held above them. Therefore also the Epistles of Paul and Peter go much beyond the three Gospels according to Matthew, Mark, and Luke.[21]

In a sermon of 1530 Luther spoke of the doctrine of grace without works. He said: "You will not find this preaching in Gregory, Augustine, Jerome, or much less in the books of the pope. The preaching of the Gospel is found only in Sacred Scripture." Here one might expect a reference to Paul, but Luther proceeds as follows: "For that, turn to John, who fills this office for us. For they believe in nothing. So I also once preached as a monk: 'If you will give a bushel of grain, a hen, or a scapular, I will pray for you.'"[22] In his *Table Talk* he commented: "Every word of John is worth a gulden, for it weighs a hundred pounds."[23]

Atkinson points out a number of areas where the Johannine element in Luther came to the fore. It was prominent not only in the doctrine of the Trinity, Christology, the Incarnation, the Atonement, the Spirit, the Church, the Sacraments, history and eschatology, but also in justification. Atkinson reminds us:

> This seems more than any other to be the *locus classicus* of Pauline theology. Nevertheless it has long been known that in his writings on this doctrine, Luther completely and sufficiently presents a purely Johannine conception. Here for example belongs the term 'being born again', the dualism of flesh and spirit, the oneness of Christ and God, etc. . . . The doctrine of justification by faith would not be diverted into a psychological subjectivism (as now and then happened, and as the temptation always exists), if Luther's understanding of the incarnation had been kept sufficiently in view, according to which justification by faith actually means justification by Christ. This Luther learned in Genesis and the Psalms, in the books of Samuel and Jonah, and from Paul and John; but what he recognized was the theology of the Gospels and not an exaggeration of Paul.[24]

Atkinson then shows how in reforming the understanding of the Church, Baptism, and the Sacrament of the Altar, Luther resorted to Johannine terminology and concepts.[25] Atkinson shows how the doctrine of justification is inseparable from the Means of Grace, through which the Holy Spirit works to accomplish justification. The influence of John should therefore not be underestimated.

Thus, seeing the Johannine element in Luther, it becomes clear that calling his teaching Pauline is one-sided. Those Luther scholars who emphatically deny that Luther taught forensic justification ought to abandon their contention that Luther's discovery was a rediscovery of Paul, since the latest New Testament studies, including those of Rudolf Bultmann, show that Paul's teaching was decidedly forensic.[26] On the other hand, if this volume has served no other purpose, perhaps it will have helped show how Melanchthon was the great teacher and defender of forensic justification to the point of one-sidedness. Melanchthon was therefore the representative *par excellence* of Paul in the Reformation. Christology was neither totally absent in Melanchthon's theology, as some writers have tried to maintain, nor as thoroughly developed as in Luther. Perhaps this was a weakness which Johannine Christology supplied. But Christology was Luther's strong point. Without discountenancing the forensic element in Luther's doctrine, one might say that Melanchthon was the representative of Paul, and Luther the advocate of John.

Justification and Sanctification

The relationship between justification and sanctification,[27] one of the most important subjects in dogmatics, is closely bound with the relationship between Law and Gospel. Where the latter are confused the Gospel invariably becomes a new law (*nova lex*), and the free and gracious gifts of God are corrupted into requirements from God. It is customary to reserve justification for the act of God in which He declares the sinner just and sanctification for the new life of obedience in the believer, at least wherever the terminology of Melanchthon and the Lutheran Confession is followed. This will be the case wherever justification is seen as forensic, imputative, or synthetic. But where justification is explained as the application of "analytic" righteousness of the believer, that which would otherwise be called sanctification becomes a part of justification. Where this is done a great danger arises that justification will be based upon human good works, the individual's certainty of salvation will be thrown into question, and the entire system will be jeopardized. The individual is thrown back into a situation like that of Luther before his evangelical discovery.

Why do so many scholars who are well-acquainted with Luther tend to overlook the distinction between justification and sanctification? That distinction in itself is of course somewhat Melanchthonian in terminology. It is not foreign to the theology of the Mature Luther but is not nearly so congenial to the position of the Young Luther. Since many scholars prefer to limit their knowledge to the first decade of Luther's activity, they pay the price in a serious restriction of their perception of Luther. Tins is one reason why the historian as well as the systematician must seek to understand the various stages in Luther's development, must learn what was of greatest value in each stage and how each related to his total career, and must especially recognize that much which Luther said at the beginning of his development is a historical curiosity. It is unfortunate when writers seek to construct the thought-system of a man upon curious sayings developed before he reached his definite position. In any case, the relationship between justification and sanctification can hardly be solved by an exclusive recourse to Luther's early works.

We noted earlier that justification and sanctification ought to be distinguished but should not be separated. Luther knew of no justification without accompanying sanctification. Speaking of a saving faith, he said: "By that faith, it is necessary for works to be done . . . But by faith we are justified previous to such works."[28] In other words, justification was an act that depended solely upon the mercy of God. It did not in any way hinge on the new life of holiness, but the new life of holiness would inevitably appear unless the believer again turned away from God in unbelief. In his great *Commentary on Galatians* Luther repeatedly said that all works, whether before or after grace, did not in any way constitute the righteousness upon which the justifying word of pardon was based.[29] Luther vigorously protested the medieval idea that faith could not justify unless it contained hope and love in the sense of good works.[30] Nevertheless, he stressed: "It is impossible for faith to be ineffective."[31] Furthermore, he saw good works as confirmation of the genuineness of faith: "Love is the testimony of faith and makes us to have confidence, and with certainty to stand in the mercy of God. For we are commanded [II Peter 1:10] to make firm our calling by doing good works. When the good works follow, then it is clear that we have true faith. When no works are there, then faith is completely gone, just as fruit is the test of the tree."[32] On another occasion Luther said:

> Those who have been regenerated therefore know that they have been justified, that is, accepted to eternal life, not by fulfilling the Law, but that they please God by having faith in the Son, and that afterwards they please him with obedience and avoiding that which they should not do. This doctrine emphasizes sin and grace.[33]

Luther's distinction between justification and sanctification was stressed just as much by Melanchthon. In *Apology* IV Melanchthon repeatedly said that the Law cannot mark the beginning of the new obedience, for the Law always accuses us.[34] The only basis for good works must be the Gospel, not the Law.

> Therefore after we have been justified by faith and reborn, we begin to fear and love God, to pray and expect help from him, to give thanks and to preach, and to obey him in afflictions. We begin also to love our neighbors, because our hearts have spiritual and holy motivations.[35]

To obviate possible misunderstanding he continued: "These things cannot possibly be done, except after we have been justified by faith and as regenerated ones have received the Holy Spirit."[36] The adversaries quoted James 1:18 as though it taught justification by works. Melanchthon pointed out that this was not what James said. Rather, James was speaking of those who had already been justified by faith, and he said that they performed good works. ". . . to be justified does not mean here to effect a just man out of an impious, but in the forensic usage, to pronounce just."[37] Melanchthon clarified this further:

> The doers of the Law are they who have been justified, that is, pronounced just, who believe in God from the heart, and therefore subsequently produce good fruits, which are pleasing to God on account of faith, and for that reason they are the fulfillment of the Law.[38]

The distinction between justification and its fruit, sanctification, could hardly be made more clearly. This reminds one of Luther's development in the three reform treatises of 1520. Faith cannot exist without the observance of God's commands.[39] Through the Holy Spirit, Christ now sanctifies those who have been justified.[40]

In the introduction to his *Commentary on Romans* (1540) Melanchthon gives some of his most brilliant formulations on justification and sanctification.[41] Here he speaks of the gift of the Spirit, which consists of ". . . fear, love of God, love of the truth, chastity, patience, and righteousness toward one's neighbor, as later I will speak concerning works." These virtues he carefully distinguishes

from such a ". . . gift of the Holy Spirit and beginning of eternal
life . . ." as is given in justification. Justification is seen as remission
of sins, divine acceptance, and the imputation of righteousness
(*remissionem peccatorum et acceptationem divinam seu imputationem iusticiae*).[42] Good works are subsequent to justification and not
constitutive. They do not merit the forgiveness of sins or eternal life
in any way. ". . . They cannot even satisfy the Law, nor is Christ's
merit by necessity transferred into our works . . . ," for the promise
would thereby be made uncertain. Nevertheless, that faith which is
the principle of justification denotes the start of eternal life just as
it is the beginning of the new obedience.[43] This is why repentance
and good works are really necessary.[44] Without such exercise faith
would not grow but would wither and die.[45]

In speaking of justification and sanctification, we have used
the term "sanctification" in referring to the new obedience that follows in the life of the believer as the consequence of justification.
When so understood, it is of course essential that justification and
sanctification be kept apart just like Law and Gospel. However, we
must not overlook the fact that sanctification is used in other ways.
In the *Small Catechism* Luther heads the third article of the Creed
". . . Concerning Sanctification" and then proceeds to describe sanctification as the work of the Holy Spirit in creating faith and bringing
the believer to salvation both in the church on earth and in heaven
forever. Under this usage sanctification includes justification and is
entirely the work of God. It is formulated in such a way that all synergism is excluded. Luther says:

> I believe that I cannot by my own reason or strength believe in Jesus
> Christ my Lord or come to him, but that the Holy Ghost has called
> me by the Gospel, enlightened me with his gifts, and sanctified and
> preserved me in the true faith . . .

In other words, Luther says the same thing with opposite terminology! We always need to be careful when using terms drawn from
modern dogmatics in describing thinkers from the past, as in the
present case. Explicitly, the distinction of justification and sanctification is hardly mentioned by either Luther or Melanchthon.
Implicitly, however, it is their chief concern. In Luther's case the

solution of the problem lay in the theocentric origin of faith. In the later Melanchthon, where synergism threatened his doctrine of faith, the forensic concept was needed more urgently. But in both men the concern was to show that justification is due to divine grace alone, irrespective of any good works. It was that which Paul described: "Therefore we conclude that a man is justified by faith without the deeds of the law" (Rom. 3:28).

Simul Justus et Peccator

Thinkers have been intrigued for years by Luther's notable paradox that the believer is simultaneously just and sinful. There has been an unfortunate tendency to jump to premature conclusions regarding its meaning. Actually, this paradox changed content under Luther's advance from his early to his mature doctrine of justification. In his earlier thinking the believer was sinful in the present but was declared righteous on the basis of future perfection which God foresaw in His prescience and worked in His predestination. This was in harmony with Luther's earlier "analytic" view of justification. Later he retained the paradox but meant instead that the believer was a sinner in the eyes of the world but was a just person in the sight of God and under God's forensic declaration for the sake of Christ and His righteousness.

Characteristically, Melanchthon did not employ this paradox of Luther to any noticeable extent. Melanchthon, of course, fully agreed with Luther's later understanding of it. But I have never encountered a statement in which Melanchthon explicitly quoted Luther's famous paradox. Melanchthon disliked startling statements, as noted in his attitude toward Luther's sometimes grotesque formulations of the Real Presence in the Lord's Supper. But Melanchthon said substantially the same in the *Confessio Saxonica* (1551): "Although renovation is simultaneously begun, nevertheless we do not teach that a person is just in this life on account of such new qualities, but on account of what the Mediator has suffered for him."[46] Luther's paradox appears even more in Melanchthon's reply to Osiander (1552): "But in this present life, although God dwells within those who are holy, nevertheless our other nature is still full of impurity and sinful weaknesses and lusts. . . ."[47]

This insight of the reformers was tragically confused in ensuing years. If some seventeenth-century dogmaticians not only tended to distinguish justification and sanctification but also to separate them, the eighteenth-century pietists went to the opposite extreme. They thought one was a sinner and then a just person (in a before-and-after arrangement) rather than as simultaneously sinful and just through forensic justification. The new life of obedience was thereby emphasized to the point of perfectionism, to the utter ruin of justification. Of course, pietists have never liked the concept of forensic justification. But whenever they forgot that the believer is simultaneously sinful and righteous, they strayed from an evangelical understanding of justification. Thus, they abandoned the theology of Luther and Melanchthon.

It is possible to make a comparison of Luther and Melanchthon on justification in which their respective positions seem hopelessly at odds. This was done by many followers of Albrecht Ritschl. It is also possible to make Luther and Melanchthon appear to speak unisonously. This has been done by some obscurantist defenders of the Lutheran Confessions. The truth lies somewhere between. Both men employed their own terminology. At times they used a given word in an opposite sense. Nevertheless, underlying their work, and despite undeniable divergencies, a unity was present which both men affirmed was really there. Typical of the unconcerned manner in which they sensed their essential agreement are the *Theses on Justification* for the debate of Johann Marbach (1543). These theses were formulated by Melanchthon and then defended by Luther. Here, of course, Luther and Melanchthon speak together. They declare:

> Those whose hearts have been terrified, however, know the promise of the Gospel concerning the remission of sins, or reconciliation, or justification, that namely which is free for the sake of Christ the Mediator, and that forgiveness of sins is not on account of any virtues of our own, but by faith, that is, trust in the mercy promised for the sake of Christ. . . . It is an impious error to teach that we are not able to know whether we are in grace, and such doubt is properly sin, for it is engendered by the Law . . . Solely for the sake of Christ we have forgiveness of sins and we are just, that is, accepted by God unto eternal life, not on account of any worthiness of our virtues, while nevertheless the Holy Spirit gives the many virtues which always exist together with faith. . . .[48]

Notes

1 CR 3:594; 6:880.

2 Br VII:540.

3 Ibid., pp. 568-70.

4 Ibid., pp. 541-45.

5 Ibid., pp. 580-81.

6 The principal sources for studying the discussion are in TR VI: 148-53; Br XIV:191-96; WA 39/I:82-133. To these see the introductory articles, and to the latter the supplement in WA 39/II:426f. On the preceding Cordatus controversy, see KK II:444-48. On the controversy over justification and this discussion, see Greschat, *Melanchthon neben Luther*, pp. 230-42, and Robert Stupperich, "Die Rechtfertigungslehre bei Luther und Melanchthon 1530-1536," in *Luther und Melanchthon*, papers of the Second International Congress for Luther Research, ed. Vilmos Vajta (Philadelphia: Muhlenberg, 1961), pp. 84-8. The earlier hypothesis, according to which this discussion had been held in preparation for the arrival of English and French visitors in connection with the "Wittenberg Concord" of 1536, has been refuted by Hans Volz (Br XII:189) and others.

7 Br XII:191-94.

8 Ibid.

9 TR VI:148-53.

10 Br XII:191.

11 Martin Greschat overlooked the fact that the statement on imputation was an addition of Melanchthon. See the critical text of Br XII: 191, 10 and note "c." Greschat's work of course antedated the appearance of Br XII, published in 1967.

12 ". . . The virtues and works are just because Paul is just. Thus the work pleases or displeases because of the person" (Br XII:192, 45). This is Luther's familiar position that first the tree must become good, and then it will bear good fruit. The fruit does not make the tree good, but the tree makes the fruit good.

13 Br XII:193, 88.

14 Ibid., p. 193, 97.

15 Br VII:541.

16 "Not as if they worked or accomplished salvation, but because, being accomplished by faith, they are present or obvious, just as I necessarily will be near to salvation" (Br XII:193, 97). Cf. Luther in the *Disputation on Justification* (1536): "Works are necessary to salvation but they do not cause salvation, because faith alone gives life" (WA 39/I:96, 6).

17 Cordatus seems to have Cruciger assert the necessity of works by saying that a tree that is without fruit, even in winter, really is not a tree (Br VII:541). These words of Luther were against this distortion, rather than

against Melanchthon, when he said that the "legal" phrase, a good tree *ought to bear* good fruit, should be replaced by saying that a good tree *bears* good fruit (Br XII:194, 120). Accordingly, Greschat misses the mark when he thinks this remark was directed against Melanchthon (see next footnote). Nor is the legalism the concept of forensic justification, which is actually that teaching on justification which frees from legalism. But the "legal" way of speaking is that of putting what is in the indicative into the imperative mood—the way of admonitory preaching.

[18] "Beyond a doubt, this closing position of the reformer contained a criticism of certain statements of Melanchthon," Greschat asserts in his discussion of justification and works in the dialogue (op. cit., p. 240). Greschat then proceeds to attribute to Luther his own construction of "die Vorherrschaft des Wortgeschehens" (op. cit., p. 240). It is an unfortunate flaw in Geschat's book that he constantly imposes modern terms, at times derived from dialectical theology, upon Luther and then finds Melanchthon different from this reconstructed Luther. Instead, the researcher must strive to weigh the reformers according to their own terms as much as possible.

[19] Cf. the lecture by the British scholar, James Atkinson, "Luthers Einschätzung des Johannesevangeliums," *Lutherforschung heute*, 1958, pp. 49ff, reprinted in *Zeitschrift für systematische Theologie*. Carl Stange, *Der johanneische Typus der Heilslehre Luthers*, 1949, esp. pp. 49ff. Hans Pohlmann, *Hat Luther Paulus entdeckt?* 1959.

[20] In writing the preceding lines, I am amazed at the great similarity between my presentation and that of James Atkinson, op. cit., pp. 49–51. I have arrived at my conclusions independently, and Atkinson has constructed his case on a different basis, but we both come to basically the same results. In the following discussion I shall refer again to Atkinson.

[21] WA Bibel VI:2ff.

[22] WA 32:245.

[23] TR I:339.

[24] Op. cit., p. 54.

[25] Ibid., p. 55.

[26] See Rudolf Bultmann, *The Theology of the New Testament*, §§28–37. Gottlob Schrenk in Gerhard Kittel, *Theologisches Wörterbuch zum Neuen Testament*, Vol. II, p. 219. See also the commentaries on Romans and Galatians by Paul Althaus.

[27] Attention is called to the fine monograph by Adolf Köberle, *The Quest for Holiness*, 1929 (2nd American ed., 1938, tr. John C. Mattes), esp. pp. 245ff. I am here advisedly employing the modern usage of sanctification, as I will explain it in regard to Luther's usage later.

[28] WA 30/II:669.

[29] WA 40/I:225, 236, 239–40.

[30] WA 39/II:188.
[31] Ibid., p. 247.
[32] Ibid., p. 248.
[33] Ibid., p. 207.
[34] Apol IV:§§38, 128, 285.
[35] §125.
[36] §126.
[37] §252.
[38] §252.
[39] SA IV:212, 23.
[40] Ibid., p. 244, 17.
[41] CR 15:495–546.
[42] Ibid., p. 511.
[43] Ibid., p. 530.
[44] Ibid., p. 531.
[45] Ibid., p. 533.
[46] SA VI:100, 4.
[47] Ibid., p. 456, 26.
[48] WA 39/II:206–7.

LUTHER   MELANCHTHON

16
Summary

We are at the end of our investigation of Luther and Melanchthon's search for justification—a search which ended in the recovery of the Biblical doctrine with a clarity and a concentration it had not known since the days of the apostle Paul. We have seen the importance of Biblical humanism for the Protestant Reformation. It was the archreformer, Martin Luther, in whom the apex was reached in expounding the proper distinction of Law and Gospel, the person and work of Christ, and the doctrine of justification. But he did not reach the summit unaided. His early works eloquently testify to that since he himself later repudiated them. It would be idle to speculate whether Luther could have come to that apex without the aid of the Biblical humanists. Such humanists as Lefèvre d' Étaples, Johann Reuchlin, Desiderius Erasmus, and Philipp Melanchthon equipped him with the linguistic tools by which he unlocked the riches of the Sacred Scriptures. Above all, it was Melanchthon who helped Luther in his recovery of the Gospel. Together, the two men again brought to light Paul's doctrine of forensic justification and proclaimed it with a clarity and vigor that had been rare since the Apostolic Age.

Despite Melanchthon's scholarly leadership and Luther's emphasis upon the created order and natural things, it is ironic that many scholars of the Reformation attempt to study the reformers in a kind of docetic spiritualization. The world in which Luther lived and the associates among whom he moved are disregarded all too lightly. In its American setting even the church named for him has been associated with intellectual obscurantism and hostility toward secular learning. The writer has himself had sad personal experiences in helping Lutheran churchmen to see the implications of their cultural heritage for the American scene today. Those churchmen have often responded with a misunderstanding which borders on Gnosticism. This betrays not only a lack of familiarity with a universal education, but with the theology of their church as well.

It has been said that a university was the cradle of the Reformation. Rightly understood, this is correct. Together, human-ists and reformers came to a new understanding of the Christian faith which was to move worlds. Many modern theologians, however, have wanted the Reformation without Biblical humanism. It did not happen that way in Luther's day, and we suspect it will not happen that way today. The message of justification was not addressed to narrow circles but was proclaimed to the whole world. In its procla-mation today are needed the intellectual skills of Melanchthon and the fervent proclamation of Luther. The church today must learn from an authentic Christian humanism to know the world, and she must learn from the reformers how the needs of the world can be supplied. That alliance between humanist and reformer which once proved so salutary needs to be renewed today. Modern man is beginning to recognize his guilt and culpability. The spiritual bank-ruptcy of our age has become painfully evident. Once again the need for justification before God is felt. In retracing the steps of those humanists and reformers, we have uncovered the trail by which men of our time may seek and find.

Funeral for the Rev. Dr. Lowell C. Green

Psalm 118:17/John 11:25

St. Paul Lutheran Church, Bucyrus, Ohio
Friday in Trinity VI, 1 August 2014

> "I shall not die, but live, and declare the works of the Lord" (Psalm 118:17) and "I am the resurrection, and the life: he that believeth in me, though he were dead, yet shall he live" (John 11:25).

Dear family and friends of Dr. Lowell C. Green: Grace, mercy, and peace be yours from God the Father and the Lord Jesus Christ!

I read recently that Disney World had been declared to be a "death free zone." According to the report, employees were instructed never to record a death as actually taking place on the premises. Of course there are no "death free zones" anywhere to be found in this world where sin has entered the picture, for where there is sin there is death. Lowell C. Green was a sinner and so he too has died. The man that we cherished as husband, father, grandfather, brother, friend, and teacher has experienced the fate that is there for every descendant of Adam, one that also awaits you. These last few years, death often seemed close at hand for Lowell. So his passing from this life last Thursday was not an unexpected surprise. The frailty brought about by age and illness caused many of us to marvel that he hung on as long as he did. But finally no amount of resilience can endure the Word of the Lord which says "Return, o children of man" sweeping us away like grass which fades and withers as we heard in Psalm 90.

Yet in the face of Lowell's death and our own forthcoming deaths, we are bold to say with Psalmist: "I shall not die, but live, and declare the works of the Lord." We can make that confession with the Old Testament poet only because of what Jesus said in to Martha in the cemetery at Bethany: "I am the resurrection, and the life: he that believeth in me, though he were dead, yet shall he live." We are here today because we believe that Jesus' words are true for Lowell and for all who cling to the Savior in faith.

Now there is much that can be said of Lowell Green. He was a husband, father, grandfather, brother to his family. He was a pastor and a teacher of the church. His scholarship was precise and exacting and many in my generation recall with gratitude the fruit that we received from his disciplined study of Luther and Lutheran theology. The life that he lived was remarkable in many ways. I think of his time as a student at Erlangen where he drank deeply from his teachers Werner Elert and Paul Althaus and then returned to pass on what he had learned from them in classrooms and conferences in this country and Canada.

Lowell could be a demanding man with high expectations—and that might be something of an understatement. But let it not be forgotten that he demanded and expected much of himself. He knew that to those whom much is given, much will be required. Lowell was on the receiving end of a legacy of Lutheran theology and hymnody and he recognized his responsibility to preserve and extend it the next generation and beyond. That was not an easy task, especially in a day when so many are willfully ignorant or indifferent.

The sainted Martin Franzmann once said that grief is not a rare vegetable in the diet of a confessional theologian. So also with Lowell for he loved the Lutheran Church and was wounded when pastors and church leaders neglected, denied, or squandered the legacy of the Reformation. He was impatient with such human foolishness for he knew that God has elected to save sinners through another foolishness—what the Apostle Paul calls the wisdom of the cross.

Whatever else may be said of Lowell's life, this we are compelled to say: He was a sinner justified by faith for the sake of Christ alone. Lowell was no antiquarian interested in musty tomes simply for academic self-satisfaction. He was a theologian of the cross and his life was spent in the service of that everlasting Gospel. Martin Luther had a deep passion for Psalm 118. In fact he called it his favorite psalm. He used our text from verse 17 as something of a personal motto, inscribing it on the wall of his room in the Castle Coburg in 1530. Luther wrote of this verse in way which also frames Lowell's life and gives us comfort today. Listen to what the Reformer says: "Though I die, I die not. Though I suffer, I suffer not. Though I fall, I am not down. Though I am disgraced, I am not dishonored. This is consolation. Furthermore, the psalmist says of the help: 'I shall live.' Isn't this amazing help? The dying live; the suffering rejoice; the fallen rise; the disgraced are honored. . . . These are all words that no human heart can comprehend. . . . And here you see this comfort and help is eternal life, which is the true, everlasting blessing of God. . . . If sins are forgiven, death is gone. And without fail there must be the comfort and confidence of eternal righteousness and everlasting life" (LW 14:86)

This little piece from his teacher, Dr. Luther attests to the fact that Lowell's life and work were not in vain. Jesus crucified for our sins and raised again for our justification was his confidence in life and in death. The church which Lowell loved has a future. Lowell though dead has a future. You have a future because Christ Jesus has a future. He was put to death for your sins and raised from the dead never to die again He gives life to you. Your future is His future. Baptized into his death you share in His resurrection.

Lowell was a theologian whose life was given to "recounting the deeds of the Lord." He did that as a father to his children in family devotions. He did that as a pastor to the congregations he served in Texas, Illinois, South Dakota, Minnesota, and New York. He did that as a teacher of the church so students were molded by his rigorous thought and through them as well as though Lowell's writings, he will continue to recount the deeds of the Lord!

But there is much more than living on through one's loved ones or through the monument of one's scholarship. The Lord who shed His blood to redeem Lowell lives and because He lives, Lowell lives in Him. Jesus says "Let not your heart be troubled: ye believe in God, believe also in me. In my Father's house are many mansions: if it were not so, I would have told you. I go to prepare a place for you. And if I go and prepare a place for you, I will come again, and receive you unto myself; that where I am, there ye may be also." (John 14:1–3).

The Lord has now fulfilled that promise for Lowell and so we can be at peace. His sins are forgiven. He has eternal life through the merits of Christ alone.

We now lay Lowell's body worn out and spent from a life time of living into the grave to await the resurrection even as we rejoice that he is even now with the Lord who is the God not of the dead but of the living. "I shall not die, but live, and declare the works of the Lord." Thanks be to God through our Lord Jesus Christ who gives us the victory! Amen.

—Prof. John T. Pless

Index of Names

Page numbers in italics refer to names in notes and references.